The Origins of European Individualism

The Making of Europe
Series Editor: Jacques Le Goff

The *Making of Europe* series is the result of a unique collaboration between five European publishers – Beck in Germany, Blackwell in Great Britain and the United States, Critica in Spain, Laterza in Italy and le Seuil in France. Each book will be published in all five languages. The scope of the series is broad, encompassing the history of ideas as well as their interaction with the history of societies, nations, and states to produce informative, readable, and provocative treatments of central themes in the history of the European peoples and their cultures.

The Origins of
European Individualism

Aaron Gurevich

*Translated from the Russian
by
Katharine Judelson*

BLACKWELL
Oxford UK & Cambridge USA

Copyright © Aaron Gurevich 1995

English translation copyright © Blackwell Publishers Limited, 1995

First published in 1995 by Blackwell Publishers and by four other
publishers: © 1994 Beck, Munich (German); © 1995 Critica,
Barcelona (Spanish); © 1995 Editions du Seuil, Paris (French);
© 1995 Laterza, Rome and Bari (Italian).

Blackwell Publishers Limited
108 Cowley Road
Oxford OX4 1JF

Blackwell Publishers Inc.
238 Main Street
Cambridge, Massachusetts 02142
USA

British Library Cataloguing in Publication Data

A CIP catalogue record for this book is available from
the British Library.

Library of Congress data has been applied for

ISBN 0-631-17963-1

Typeset in 11.5 on 13 pt Sabon by
Neil Curtis Publishing Services

Printed in Great Britain by T. J. Press Ltd, Padstow, Cornwall

This book is printed on acid-free paper.

Contents

Series Editor's Preface

Europe is in the making. This is both a great challenge and one that can be met only by taking the past into account – a Europe without history would be orphaned and unhappy. Yesterday conditions today; today's actions will be felt tomorrow. The memory of the past should not paralyse the present: when based on understanding it can help us to forge new friendships, and guide us towards progress.

Europe is bordered by the Atlantic, Asia and Africa, its history and geography inextricably entwined, and its past comprehensible only within the context of the world at large. The territory retains the name given it by the ancient Greeks, and the roots of its heritage may be traced far into prehistory. It is on this foundation rich and creative, united yet diverse – that Europe's future will be built.

The Making of Europe is the joint initiative of five publishers of different languages and nationalities: Beck in Munich; Blackwell in Oxford; Critica in Barcelona; Laterza in Rome; and le Seuil in Paris. Its aim is to describe the evolution of Europe, presenting the triumphs but not concealing the difficulties. In their efforts to achieve accord and unity the nations of Europe have faced discord, division and conflict. It is no purpose of this series to conceal these problems: those committed to the European enterprise will not succeed if their view of the future is unencumbered by an understanding of the past.

The title of the series is thus an active one: the time is yet to come when a synthetic history of Europe will be possible. The books we shall publish will be the work of leading historians, by no means all European. They will address crucial aspects of European history in every field – political, economic, social, religious and cultural. They will draw on that long historiographical tradition which stretches back to Herodotus, as well as on those conceptions and ideas which have transformed historical enquiry in the recent decades of the twentieth century. They will write readably for a wide public.

Our aim is to consider the key questions confronting those involved in Europe's making, and at the same time to satisfy the curiosity of the world at large: in short, who are the Europeans? where have they come from? whither are they bound?

Jacques Le Goff

1

The Individual is Ineffable

The Individual in the Middle Ages
and the Historian of Today

One of the drawings illustrating the *Garden of Delights* (*Hortus deliciarum*) of Abbess Herrad von Landsberg (late twelfth century), depicts nuns from her convent at Hohenburg and includes a portrait of the author. There are more than sixty portraits in all, but what cannot fail to attract the beholder's attention is the almost exact similarity of all the subjects: not only are their poses and attire identical, but their faces and expressions resemble one another to an astonishing degree. Where it does prove possible to find minor deviations, they are definitely only of secondary importance and in no way can they be seen as reflecting any endeavour on the artist's part to bring out individual features. The Abbess herself is distinct from the other figures only insofar as she is depicted standing and holding a large scroll. The nuns can be distinguished one from another thanks only to the captions revealing their names. They are all 'Brides of Christ' stripped of age or individuality: once having had their hair cut off, they have renounced their individuality which needed to be dissolved in their total obedience to God. Nevertheless, in the eyes of Herrad (or the artist who depicted the nuns), they have not become part of a faceless mass – they are individuals. It is simply that Herrad saw the individuality of each nun not as something manifested in her outward appearance but elsewhere.

This drawing, naturally, provides an extreme case of typification and, in that same twelfth century, other depictions of human figures were created including men and women who were by no means identical. Nevertheless, the custom of emphasizing the General at the expense of the Individual predominated, and that particular era did not know the Portrait as it later came to be understood. Herrad's drawing confronts the historian with the questions: what was Individuality in the Middle Ages? how did the individual view himself or herself, or society view the individual? and what opportunities were available for revealing the Individual?

The question of the individual is a key issue in modern historical writing with its anthropological slant, i.e. with its emphasis on humanity in all its diverse manifestations as historically concrete social beings subject to change in the course of history. Historians have devoted a great deal of time and effort to fruitful study of society from the economic, social and political angles. Yet the human being, the 'atom' of the social structure, is something about which we know little: it has, as it were, been engulfed by structures. Extensive materials have been amassed concerning revelations of men and women through their actions and everyday behaviour: we have at our disposal statements and ideas expressed by many different people in the past. Historians of ideas have uncovered diverse aspects of the picture of the world on which people based their thinking in a particular society and, in this way, they put together hypothetical reconstructions of the sets of values within which that thinking operated. Yet what they were dealing with was mainly collective psychology, the extra-personal aspect of individual consciousness, the general attitudes that are shared by members of large and small social groups, while the unique constellation made up of elements of a world picture in the mind of a given, specific individual escapes our attention in the vast majority of cases.

What we can say, however, with some degree of confidence, is that the question of individuality in history is a two-sided issue. On the one hand it involves investigation regarding the emergence of the human ego, the individual who is moulded within the group but, who at the same time, is aware of what sets him or her apart, that is, the independence of the individual in relation to the group, and can become engrossed in his or her own individual existence. On the other hand, attempts made by historians to investigate the self-determination of the individual and the type of the individual's self-awareness characteristic of a particular society, constitute for all intents and purposes a search for what makes a given culture unique, for what lends the culture under discussion, in its turn, its historic 'individuality'.

The question of human individuality is not merely a focus of interest for the psychologist, philosopher, sociologist or literary historian – it is also an historical question. In the context of the larger issue of the 'Emergence of Europe', the question of the individual assumes particular importance. What turned medieval Europe into the Europe we know today – a world of disparate local civilizations into a space within which the universal historical process unfolds as within a single entity? This must surely, in the final analysis, have been determined by the specific make-up of the individual, who emerged precisely in this region. When we scrutinize the reasons that made it possible for the West to step beyond the confines of traditional society, which in their turn made such a break-through sooner or later inevitable, we point to the development of towns as centres of production and commerce where bourgeois social relations and entrepreneurial initiative were to take root, to the change in religious and ethical principles ('the spirit of Protestantism'), to a special pattern of learning intrinsic only to the West which gave rise to unstoppable progress in science and technology and eventually to the Industrial Revolution. All this is true, yet if we stop for a moment and ponder, then does it not become clear that these achievements in the sphere of material civilization, the emergence of these completely new systems of social relations, and the emergence of these fundamentally new ethical and religious models were in fact none other than diverse manifestations of a specific type of personality which had put behind it the 'clan creature' and set itself free from limitations of social estate, i.e. come into its own as an Individual?

These questions are relevant not merely to the history of past eras. The process of the development of Europe continues today – both in the West, with its trends towards economic and political (and cultural?) integration that have become unusually marked in recent years, and in the eastern half of Europe which, until the last few years, had been forcibly kept out of the 'common European home'. This book is the work of a Russian historian, and I must confess that the subject of the individual and individuality is now coming into its own with unprecedented force in my country. In the past, the totalitarian regime suppressed the individual and individual initiative in all spheres of life, political and material on the one hand, and emotional and cultural on the other. Not merely was the word 'individualism' a term of abuse, but accusations of free expression of human potential, talents or interests could provide grounds for persecution. To save our society from catastrophe, to revitalize it and to create a new intellectual climate, the question of the individual has to assume truly central importance. Russia cannot be drawn into European civilization (and I see no other way out of the present crisis) without adopting certain values fundamental to that civilization.

This is why I have accepted the suggestion made by Jacques Le Goff for me to write this book, despite the fact that I am well aware what tremendous difficulties are involved in the execution of such a task. At this stage I feel able merely to approach discussion of the issues involved and to consider certain aspects of those issues. A comprehensive, properly balanced investigation of this question is a task for the future, and I fear, a rather distant one.

To gain our bearings in relation to this question as to the individual and individuality in the Middle Ages, it is necessary to touch briefly on the relevant historiography. There is a good number of scholarly works in which this question is discussed from different perspectives. I do not intend to consider them all: suffice it to call attention to various approaches and to the succession of these in recent literature.

I should like to start with the book by Colin Morris entitled *The Discovery of the Individual. 1050–1200.*[1] Unlike many other writers who, following Jakob Burckhardt's famous Renaissance formula – 'Discovery of the World and Man', tend to regard the Age of the Renaissance in Italy and, to be more precise, the fifteenth century as the time when individuality took shape, Morris concentrates our attention on an earlier period. For him 'the discovery of individuality' did not involve a sudden cataclysm supposed to have taken place around 1500, but rather a gradual process which extended from the late eleventh through to the mid-twelfth century. He has assembled a wealth of material characterizing the changes in the individual's self-awareness that took place in the scholarly world in the West during that time. Morris traces the origins of that emergence of individual consciousness back to the latter part of Classical Antiquity – to the classical heritage that came up against Christianity and that became part of medieval thought in forms duly reshaped by Christianity.

The idea of intellectual renewal and advance in the West in the twelfth century (the 'twelfth-century Renaissance') had indeed been put forward long before Morris by Charles Homer Haskins and, in academic literature, many aspects of individualism in legal and political life had been discussed previously: the development from 'subject to citizen' (W. Ullmann), the individuality of the writer (P. Dronke, R. Hanning), the individual nature of religious thinkers and ecclesiastical writers in the twelfth and thirteenth centuries, the more prominent psychological sensitivity and 'humanism' (R. W. Southern). Yet Morris, in what is perhaps a more forceful way than other researchers, has underlined that the important fruit of the 'twelfth-century Renaissance' was the emergence of an individual with new psychological leanings, with a more profound vision of the nature of humanity.

Significant social, religious and intellectual changes, to which this cultural advance paved the way, found expression in the fact that more importance came to be attached to personal principles, both in the individual's relationship with God and in relations between individuals. Confession as a means for analysis of the individual's inner world, mysticism, experiments in the sphere of autobiography, attempts to make the transition from Icon to Portrait, reinterpretation of the figure of Christ (in a more 'human' light), love poetry, and the birth of psychological introspection were all landmarks on the path to concentration on the self which, at that stage, became possible for many men of the Church and, in certain cases, for educated laymen. Morris suggests that it was precisely at that period that many of the principles for individual behaviour, that were to become characteristic of Western people right up until Modern Times, assumed recognizable shape.

Perhaps, Morris points out, this continuity stands out more clearly if we compare 1100 with 1900, rather than with 1972 (the year in which he completed his study), for World War I heralded a departure from the tradition of many centuries,[2] but, be that as it may, the period he analyses Morris holds to be the historical turning-point in the cultural development of the West. Although he admits that the content of the concept 'individual' at the period differed from the present-day concept and that the term 'persona' had no semantic equivalent in the vocabulary of the eleventh and twelfth centuries, Morris sees its use as admissible in his study, as indeed is the use of the concepts 'individuality' and 'individualism'.

Morris's work represents something in the way of a milestone in the study of the individual in the Middle Ages. Yet it would be wrong to ignore certain limitations of the approach he uses. He, naturally, focuses attention on the outstanding figures of the 'twelfth-century Renaissance', on the writings and statements of theologians and mystics, troubadours and chroniclers, on the spiritual world of the intellectuals who left behind them written testimony regarding their fundamental principles, aspirations and ideas. It is understandable and, indeed, inevitable that the 'heroes' of his analysis are Abelard and Bernard of Clairvaux, John of Salisbury and Bernard of Ventadour, Guibert of Nogent and Hildebert of Lavardin, Walter of Chatillon and Otloh of St Emmeram.

In this respect, Morris follows in the footsteps of Georg Misch, author of the major work *A History of Autobiography*,[3] which covers an enormous period in time, stretching from the Ancient World to the Modern Age, and treats in particular detail the Middle Ages, not merely in Western Europe but also in Byzantium and the Arab world. Misch naturally concentrates on those areas of writing which can, to a greater or lesser degree, be convincingly classified as autobiographical. Morris, however, does not confine himself to autobiography in his chosen period. He does acknowledge the limited nature of the social range he covers,[4] but accounts for this with reference to the availability of historical sources; the broad strata of society that he was obliged to pass over in silence – burghers, peasants, large sections of the secular aristocracy and lesser knights – did not have the chance to give expression to their views and this was why, he suggests, it is not possible to say anything about them. There is nothing original about this approach to the question: all scholars who have turned to the question of the individual and individuality have regarded it as admissible to restrict themselves to the level of the intellectual élite because, from their point of view (which is often not stated explicitly), only the élite needs to be taken into account.

Even within this closely defined framework, Morris's position is open to criticism. He focused his attention on the process of individualization, on the psychological separating out of the individual from the general, without undertaking any analysis of those groups of which individuals in the period under discussion formed a part. Yet, as has been emphasized by Caroline Walker Bynum, there were groups in the twelfth century taking shape or gaining in strength that were united in their adherence to new ideals, and the individuals who made up these groups did not turn away from them or direct their growing awareness of their individuality against the ideas upheld as a model by the groups to which they belonged.

Bynum confines herself to analysis of ecclesiastical and monastic communities, in which interest in '*Homo interior*' was cultivated. In her opinion, men and women of that period were discovering within themselves their human nature, their 'self' (*seipsum, anima, ego*) as something that was the same for all human beings – an *imago Dei*: this was the kind of individual that was being discovered at the end of the Middle Ages, rather than anything any closer to the modern understanding of that word. It would be wrong to confuse interest in 'the inner landscape of the human being' (the discovery of self) with the 'discovery of the individual'.[5] While stressing the seriousness of intentions in discussion of ethical problems, Abelard and other authors of the twelfth century at the same time attached great importance to imitation of the Life of Christ down to the tiniest of details. It is no coincidence that writers of the time (Gerhoh of Reichersberg, Herrad of Landsberg) felt a deep need to classify, to define various 'estates' and 'vocations' (*ordo, vocatio*). They write of individuals as types or models. Aelred of Rievaulx laments his dead friend who, in his words, was a 'model for my life' (*exemplar vitae meae*) and 'support for my morals' (*compositio morum meorum*). 'Likeness' was a fundamental theological category in the twelfth century, and the self-modification of the individual took place in a context defined by models – Christ, the Apostles, the Patriarchs, the Saints and the Church.[6]

Bynum cites the statement of an itinerant preacher of the twelfth century, Norbert of Xanten, which conveys clearly and graphically the contradictory situation of the individual in the tension field between the poles 'Absolute and Individual':

'Priest, you are not you, because you are God.

You are not yours, because you are Christ's servant and minister.

You are not of yourself, because you are nothing.

What therefore are you, oh, priest? Nothing and all things.'[7]

The human individual was searching for itself and finding itself, without rejecting models but adapting itself to forms already in existence. Yet insofar as the number of social groups had grown and a sort of rivalry had grown up between them (old and new monastic orders), awareness of a multiplicity of social roles became a very topical issue, and the choice of a way of life loomed important. Bynum concludes that it would be wrong to place the isolated individual with his or her inner motivation and emotions in the centre of religious life in the twelfth century, to single out the idea that every individual is unique and therefore seeks a way of expressing individuality: that idea is a contemporary one and alien to the Middle Ages. At the same time, searches for inner motivation went hand in hand with a sense of belonging to a group. No mention was being made at that period of anything like a personal lifestyle. It was not until the following century that the individual and the group began to grow apart.[8]

A perhaps still harsher condemnation of the concept of the 'discovery' of individuality was recently outlined by Jean-Claude Schmitt, who considers such an idea as mere 'fiction'.[9] In his opinion, the history of individuality is far from being a unilinear process. A certain amount of continuity can be discerned, but only traced with difficulty. The history of the concept, writes Schmitt, is for the most part hidden from our gaze. The true point at issue is the question of personality, which has been raised by ethnologists and psychologists[10] and ignored by historians, who substituted their history of individualism for it.

Twenty years have passed since Morris's work came out and it needs to be pointed out that historical knowledge has moved on since the appearance of his landmark of a book. During the 1970s and 1980s, many historians altered their approach to the study of culture and society and therefore to humanity as well. It now appears more questionable than before to maintain that changes in the spiritual orientation of leading figures in the intellectual movement of the late eleventh and twelfth centuries adequately reflect the changes that were at work at the heart of spiritual life in the West. We should not forget that the 'twelfth-century Renaissance' did in fact remain a phenomenon that affected for the most part only the enlightened upper strata of society, and even those only in part. Statements made by intellectuals possessed of esoteric knowledge who promoted written culture, the culture of the Book, can hardly be regarded as representative of society as a whole in which the oral tradition was predominant. The ideas of theologians and poets need to be approached not in isolation but in a more general context shaped by the attitudes of the time, which constituted the universal 'language' of the age.

There is a further point for consideration here. The approach used by Morris, and indeed by many other scholars, is geared to a present-day audience.[11] Those who follow the same path as Morris formulate the question, from which they start out, as follows: at what period in the Middle Ages were the 'lineaments of modern man' to be discerned for the first time?[12] In other words, attention is focused not on the medieval person

as such, as found in its own society and its own age, but
on the prerequisites or precursors of the modern individual. A
similar starting-point is to be found underlying the lectures
delivered by Father M. D. Chenu, the well-known historian of
medieval theology and spirituality, who came forward with
the assertion that the 'awakening of individual consciousness'
took place in the West in the twelfth century, when the
individual became aware of himself as a 'new' man and
'discovered himself' as a subject for contemplation and study.[13]
Chenu holds Abelard to be *le premier homme moderne*, for
whom the human being is an individual possessed of originality
that cannot be eradicated.[14]

Yet is it not time to move away from 'teleologism' of this
kind in historical research and, while still singling out Abelard's
individuality and unique personality, or indeed those of any
other medieval thinker, from among collective attitudes,
nevertheless 'return' them to the spiritual universe to which
they belonged? A more promising approach would seem to be
examination of personality and individuality within the
framework of the social and cultural relations of the period in
which the subjects lived. Our modern era confronts the historian
with certain problems – of that there can be no doubt – but it
is important to resolve these in their capacity as something
linked to a distant past as an integral component of fundamental
processes operating in that chapter of the past, within the
whole system of human relations of the period under
investigation.

What does this involve? What is perhaps most important is
not to separate out the emergence of the individual from the
other social transformations that were taking place in the West
during the Middle Ages: it is essential to scrutinize the self-
awareness of individuals within the context of the social
groups of which they were a part.[15] The 'medieval individual'
is an inadmissibly broad abstraction. The term can acquire
meaningful content only if it is analysed in conjunction with
the place the individual in question occupied in society. It goes
without saying that religion and culture moulded the general
atmosphere that determined the limits within which
individuality (the 'basic personality type' or the 'configuration

of the personality' directed towards the central values of the society under discussion[16]) could manifest itself, yet that individuality assumed tangible shape only within the group.

That is exactly how the question is approached in the collection of profiles entitled *The Medieval World*.[17] The aim of this project, inspired by Jacques Le Goff, was to provide a description of the medieval individual and an interpretation of that figure in the light of the economic and social reality of the period and the attitudes and world of the imagination that went hand in hand with that reality. Constantly moving between the typologies of the Middle Ages and the present day, the ten historians contributing to this volume present various profiles of figures from the period under investigation. They examine medieval people in numerous social roles and guises: as monk, knight, peasant, town-dweller, intellectual, artist, merchant, saint, marginal or woman. This means that the abstraction 'medieval individual' that at first seemed excessively broad, acquires tangible content. Only after the medieval human being has been presented in the most varied of hypostases, complete with a social and intellectual identity and evolving over the eleventh to fifteenth centuries (although the authors are often compelled to make incursions into a still earlier period), is it possible to make so bold as to embark upon generalizations that characterize the 'Medieval Human Being' as such.

These generalizations are offered to the reader in Jacques Le Goff's Introduction. He points out that there have been a good number of periods in history, characterized by a more astute awareness of the universal and eternal existence of a 'human model', than that typical of the Middle Ages in the Christian West. This 'model' was defined with reference to religion, and found its highest expression in theology. This means that it is essential to clarify what a person in medieval anthropology was like. Le Goff notes that the pessimistic view of human nature which predominated in the early part of the Middle Ages, when efforts were being made to achieve greater awareness of Humankind's original sin and its humbling before the Lord, gave way later to a more optimistic view stemming from the idea that each human being was a reflection of the divine image

and that it was capable of continuing creation on Earth and of
saving its own soul.

Le Goff stresses the evolution to be observed in the
interpretation of the individual throughout the Middle Ages
and which, in the final analysis, was shaped by changes in that
individual's social life. At the same time, there also existed
conceptions of the individual that virtually served to define the
phenomenon: '*Homo viator*' – the Wanderer in both the literal
and figurative (spiritual) sense – and the Penitent experiencing
emotional distress. Human earthly existence was seen as the
path which would finally lead humankind to God: in real life
this image of the Wanderer was embodied in the Pilgrim and
the Crusader.[18] The idea of repentance was linked with the
introduction of order into the human being's inner experience
and scrutiny of that experience – self-analysis and confession:
indeed, this idea really does lead us to the very essence of the
question of personality in the Middle Ages.

Changes in personality structure which took place during
the period that is the subject of our study can be traced both
in the transition from anonymity to expression of the individual
in literature and art,[19] and also in the evolution of the image of
the Saint, who becomes more spiritual and acquires more
individuality: it is no longer the gift to perform miracles or a
Saint's social function that takes priority, but his or her life –
the imitation of Christ (*imitatio Christi*).[20] The individual
underwent change in the course of the Middle Ages as a result
of the changing social order; social functions became more
specialized and moral values 'came down to earth' (in the
thirteenth century).[21]

Le Goff singled out certain characteristic traits of people's
psychological make-up in the Middle Ages, signs of their
obsessive natures: the awareness of humankind's propensity
for sin; the distinctive features of their perception of the visible
and invisible that are united as one and inextricably intertwined;
belief in a world beyond the grave, in miracles and in the power
of ordeals; the nature of memory intrinsic to those people who
lived in a world in which oral culture predominated; thought
rooted in symbolism ('medieval man was an ardent de-coder')[22];
an uncanny fascination with numbers, to which symbolic

significance had been attributed long before the thirteenth century, as it had also been to colour and shape; belief in dreams and in visions; a sense of hierarchy, respect for authority and power and, at the same time, an inclination to rebel; rights, liberty and privilege – these were key phenomena in the system of social values of that period.

Scrutiny of the academic literature in this field[23] reveals that there have been two main trends in the relevant research directed towards various aspects of this question, even towards different subjects. They are very closely linked between themselves, yet not identical, because they come from different levels. One trend is focused on the search for **individuality**. In their efforts to single out its traits in the writings of medieval and Renaissance writers,[24] historians and philologists concentrate attention on the texts in which the unique nature and integrity of the individual manifest themselves, together with efforts at concentration on self and self-analysis: these writers were attempting to create autobiographies and confessions, revealing through the latter their own, unique individuality or inner self. Studies of this type are concentrated on values, and researchers using this approach are deliberately or instinctively influenced by the idea of individuality, which has taken root in modern Europe. This means that, in the anthropology of the Middle Ages, they stress those aspects that link it with the Future. One of the questions that preoccupies scholars in this connection is the question of the point in time when medieval men and women emerged as capable of 'discovering' individuality. At the same time, it is not fully appreciated that the historian, who is not confronting living beings (as a psychologist would) but texts and documentary evidence, is hardly entitled to have free recourse to terms and concepts drawn from the field of psychology. It would be more appropriate, therefore, to talk not of 'individuality', but of social, cultural or semiotic 'mechanisms' of individualization, of mental tools (cf. '*outillage mental*' Febvre).[25]

Yet, by doing so, we move on to a different level in our investigation of the question, at which attention is concentrated not on individuality but **personality**. On the one hand, individuality emerges in specific cultural-historical conditions and, in some societies, there is an awareness of individuality and it makes itself known, while, in other societies, a sense of group or clan predominates. Personality, on the other hand, is an inalienable quality of any human being living in society. Within different socio-cultural systems the personality assumes specific characteristics. Personality is what defines the human individual within a specific system of socio-cultural conditions: regardless of the extent to which a personality is unusual, it is inevitably linked to the culture of its times and absorbs the view of the world and value system of the society or social group to which it belongs. Personality could perhaps be defined as the 'half-way house' between culture and society. Those who investigate the question of personality focus attention on mental attitudes or that part of an individual's awareness which sets him or her apart from other individuals or groups.

Human beings can become aware of their individuality only within society. For this reason, while studying the Middle Ages of Western Europe it is important to take both approaches into account. These processes – awareness of one's own worth (the self-affirmation of the individual) and awareness of what sets one apart, namely individuality – are different but inextricably intertwined: they cannot be kept separate and, at a certain stage of European history, the second takes over from the first. Yet to reduce the individual and individuality to one and the same thing would be a major mistake. It would mean that the image of the Individual which had emerged in Europe only towards, or even at the end of, the medieval period would be being applied to the period as a whole, involving criteria that were extrinsic to that particular context.[26]

In view of the above, the historian about to embark upon study of the individual and individuality in the medieval history of the West needs to broaden the field of his or her investigations. One cannot confine oneself merely to an 'anthology' of the ideas of the great figures of the age, because a selective approach of that kind would, a priori, channel one's thoughts to what was isolated, unique and known to be atypical. The ideas, moods and attitudes of the age also make their mark upon the outstanding creative individual. Great people are not loudspeakers serving to do no more than amplify those ideas and moods, however: the latter are given a subjective interpretation and profoundly individual flavour in the consciousness and writings of the colossi of the period. Suffice it to compare the 'visions' of the world beyond the grave that were recorded throughout the whole of the Middle Ages with the *Divine Comedy*. In this way, we can bring out the enormous difference between what a common-or-garden visionary might experience in a trance and then relate ingenuously to a priest, who in his turn would record the account, with the carefully considered creation of the great poet independently constructing a whole cosmos.

It is also important to bear in mind, insofar as we are discussing the Middle Ages, that the statements and ideals of the genius at that period were by no means always guaranteed a broad response from a contemporary audience, because they would be accessible only to a relatively narrow, self-contained circle of the enlightened and educated. Abelard's *Historia calamitatum mearum*, as well as his correspondence with Héloïse, made a name for themselves only in the century after that in which they had been written,[27] and were little known during the writer's lifetime nor immediately after his death. (Perhaps this explains the hypotheses that these works were written at a later date than that which had been ascribed to them well *after* their creation.) It is perfectly possible that the 'feedback' between the individual act of creation and the milieu in which creation took place at that time was fundamentally different from that with which we are familiar today.

Yet, when we speak of the need for historians of the individual and individuality to broaden the scope of their investigations, something quite different is implied. The culture of the Middle Ages developed as a result of the synthesis of the Classical Heritage – embracing detailed knowledge of Graeco-Roman writings and Christianity – with the barbarian heritage that was first and foremost Germanic. The attitudes and behavioural stereotypes of medieval men and women can hardly be adequately expounded if we disregard the barbarian substratum of beliefs and values. Yet, scholars writing about the individual in the Middle Ages usually ignore this aspect of the subject. Through their silence they imply that the question of the individual and individuality is irrelevant in relation to barbarians – a most serious delusion!

The study of Germanic, and in particular Scandinavian, sources points to the opposite. The individual in the society of pagan Europe was very definitely not swallowed up within the group – there was fairly wide scope for self-discovery and self-assertion. I am convinced that the richest sources that have survived in the Scandinavian North should be referred to so that we might obtain a more rounded and balanced picture of the development and transformation of the individual in medieval Europe. There is clearly no justification for confining such studies – as is unfortunately most often the case in the academic world – to no more than two or three countries.[28]

Here it would seem appropriate to refer to the point of view adopted in this connection by Alfons Dopsch that was formulated as early as the first third of this century. This Austrian historian adopted a new approach to a number of questions concerning the social and economic history of Europe at the dawn of the Middle Ages. His theory of the emergence of capitalism within the French state resulted in heated discussion and was subjected to well-deserved criticism, but that is not what we are concerned with here. When explaining his conception of medieval history, Dopsch underlined the role of the individualistic principle in the life of the West in the early Middle Ages. He did not confine his investigations to the economic basis of society but focused attention on a whole range of phenomena which, in his eyes, point to the one-sided nature of the predominant view of the human being in that period as a faceless creature almost totally dissolved in the group, as a type bereft of independence in behaviour and view of the world. While objecting to Karl Lamprecht's characterization of the early Middle Ages as a period in which the 'typical' was what predominated in intellectual life, Dopsch insisted that the beginning of the Middle Ages was marked by 'individualism' (which Lamprecht and numerous other scholars associate with the Renaissance or even the sixteenth and seventeenth centuries). Restrictions laid down upon manifestations of all that was individual in economic life became the order of the day in the latter part of the Middle Ages (the emergence of corporations, economic regulation and monopolization of control over commerce – *Zunftzwang* or 'guild coercion' obliging all craftsmen of a particular trade to join a guild and bide by its charter and the wide-ranging limitation of peasants' rights and so on) but these had been missing at the beginning of the period.[29]

Dopsch draws attention to the individualism inherent in Germanic economic activities and settlements that had been singled out by Roman authors and has been corroborated by archaeological data. Subsequent studies (undertaken mainly in the middle and second half of this century) by archaeologists – in particular, those engaged in settlement-archaeology, palaeobotany, historical cartography, soil science, climatology, radiocarbon dating and aerial photography – leave us in no doubt that communal order in Germany and Scandinavia did not possess the importance attributed to it by the *Markgenossenschaftstheorie* of the nineteenth century (theory of primordial village community). The view of the Germans as nomads with herds is shown to be unfounded: their way of life was indisputably that of settled farmers. Patterns of settlement based on farming predominated and each farmer was in control of a separate holding. Only after concentration of farming populations did group settlements come into being. Tacitus had already pointed out that the Germans organized their villages 'differently from ours' (i.e. differently from the practice accepted among the Romans): 'they will not even have their houses adjoin one another. They dwell apart, dotted about here and there, wherever a spring, plain, or grove takes their fancy' (*Germania*, 16). Archaeologists have succeeded in identifying the traces of these ancient field systems (*oldtidsagre*) separated by boundaries or stone walls.[30]

Many of the suggestions made by Dopsch concerning the economic practices of the Germans have been to a large extent borne out by subsequent research. Aspects of their way of life did indeed bear the stamp of individual initiative, and this is not difficult to deduce from the *Historia Francorum* written by

St Gregory of Tours and in legal treatises dating from the early
Middle Ages, such as *Lex Salica*, and the codes of Scandinavian
laws that were written down much later but which, nevertheless,
reflected approximately the same stage of social development.
What was the picture, though, when it came to the epic
literature of the Germans and Scandinavians? What models of
behaviour have been reflected in the poems of the *Elder Edda*,
in the poetry of the skalds or in the Icelandic sagas? There is no
reason to follow in Dopsch's footsteps here and approximate
these models with the individualism of Renaissance men and
women (Dopsch, for instance, sees little to distinguish Liudprand
von Cremona of the tenth century from the Humanists[31]) or to
compare the 'spirit of capitalism' with the ethics governing the
economy of the Carolingian era. Yet the question remains: was
there a time before the Middle Ages – that period of corporate
identity and types – that could be distinguished on the grounds
of a different self-awareness of an individual who was subject
to fewer inhibitions that might stifle expression of that self-
awareness? Are we justified in compiling a picture of
individualism progressing upwards in a straight line and
steadily increasing the nearer we draw to the modern age?

It is possible that stepping outside the confines of the
Christian world into its pagan fringes (or regions where the
eventual transition from paganism was only to a superficially
assimilated Christianity) might lead us to review the whole
question of the 'discovery of individuality' and approach from
a somewhat different angle the possibilities provided by
Christianity for the unfolding of individualism. As will emerge
later on, the medieval author, who sought to express inner
being either directly or indirectly, was confined within a fairly
rigid framework set in place by religious ethics and literary
rhetoric or conventions regarding subject matter. For this
reason, when we study medieval 'autobiographies' or
'confessions', we are always bedevilled by the sense that we
cannot grasp the individual personality. The medieval
philosophers' formula *'Individuum est ineffabile'* immediately
comes to mind as we study the testimony left behind by the
writers of that period in their descriptions of themselves.

2

The Individual and the
Epic Tradition

The search for individuals in major works of medieval literature is accompanied by many and sometimes insuperable difficulties. Tendencies to subordinate the individual to the general and to understand the particular through reference to type models result in the predominance of clichés that came to be sanctified by dint of time and the influence of authorities with regard to form. For the most part, it was virtually impossible to go beyond these canons and closely defined subject matter to vivid and unique individuals. Latin, which predominated in the literature of Western Europe for many centuries, often also served to blur traces of individuality.

It would therefore be perfectly justifiable in these circumstances to turn first to the rich and colourful ancient literature from Scandinavia. The vision of the world and the presentation of character found there are such that the individual – and by no means only figures occupying a prominent place in society, but also ordinary Icelanders or Norwegians – is widely represented in the writing of the period under discussion and to an exceptional degree! The language in which this literature was created – whether it be the poems of the *Edda*, the poetry of the skalds or sagas – was always the native language of the men and women depicted in the works from these genres.

It would, of course, be wrong to extend the conclusions that we might draw on the basis of an analysis of Scandinavian literature to the whole of medieval Europe. Scandinavia retained many distinctive features in its social and in its spiritual life. Yet it was not cut off from the rest of the world but was an integral part of it. As I hope will be made clear below, the features of the individuals in Scandinavian literature were not all of a strictly northern variety – although these in themselves are of considerable interest – but also reflected principles that applied to the Middle Ages as a whole. The rare riches to be found in this Scandinavian literature provide the medievalist with extremely useful material. For the historian anxious to penetrate the medieval personality, it should be possible to find in these writings certain implications that would be far from alien to other regions of the Europe of that day?

Was Sigurd a Hero?

Let us embark upon this analysis with an examination of what we mean by 'heroic'. It is one of the principal categories to be found in the Scandinavian consciousness. This concept concentrates within itself, in a form larger than life, the idea of the individual complete with its freedoms and constraints. The poems of the *Edda* that have survived in thirteenth-century manuscripts, but which can be traced back to a still earlier period, enable us to acquaint ourselves with a number of aspects of the idea of the 'hero'.

The achievement of great feats is the hero's *raison d'être* and the memory of his mighty deeds is all that lives on in the minds of subsequent generations. Each person living in this world steeped in myths and memories of a legendary past would model his or her own behaviour on cultural archetypes: to an equal extent, behaviour would also be shaped by thought of a future in which his or her name lives on in glory. Time was a two-stranded concept, stretching back to the generations of the past and forward to those of the future. To all intents and purposes, this was the age of the clan, and the hero was a link in the chain of generations. Special importance was attached to the future when each person and each person's deeds would be accorded their true value: this applied not only to the hero but also to humbler figures.

The category of the heroic is very closely linked with attitudes to time because it is in time, or more precisely in the future, that the hero's glory will come into its own. At the same time, the attention of the authors of these ancient poems and their audiences was focused on the death of the hero, for it was an immutable rule that the hero should always perish. His life would be short but, in its brief course, he would succeed in accomplishing something of such momentous stature that his memory would be immortalized. The hero's attitude to death was shaped by his attitude to the future, and death would open up his path to immortal glory. All three categories – heroism, death and time – were vitally important aspects of the ethical code by which the peoples of Northern Europe lived throughout the Middle Ages.

To the above three we need to add a further category, Fate, which serves to embrace and incorporate them all. In Eddic poems, the feats and demise of the hero are viewed not as the results of personal initiative, freely chosen behaviour or a combination of circumstances: an intrinsic component of the figures from the Edda legends is the heroic principle that is followed come what may. The hero is not free when choosing the path along which he accomplishes his feats and meets his eventual downfall: the road through life is 'programmed', as it were, predetermined and sometimes even foretold by some prophet or prophetess able to see into the future and predict the hero's destiny.

One such wise visionary was Grípir, Sigurd's maternal uncle. He told Sigurd what the future had in store for him, predicting his downfall and his feats and finally revealing to him the secret of his death as well. *Grípir's Prophecy (Grípisspá)* is a poem that serves to summarize, as it were, the whole cycle of poems concerning Sigurd. Yet knowledge of the fate which awaits him is revealed not only by Grípir but by Sigurd himself: by the end of the poem, it comes to light that he too knew how he would perish. In the context of a prophecy we discover the hero's attitude to his own destiny: we learn of his path through life, which admits of no deviations from what has been determined in advance, and which the hero accepts as inevitable.

Nevertheless, fate, in the system of ideas peculiar to the Germanic peoples, was not some faceless *fatum* above and beyond this world, nor was it the wheel of blind Fortuna. Although destiny was 'implanted' in the hero like a 'programme', it was also perceived as part of a personal attitude to life: the hero would not only follow its dictates, he would 'create' it, actively bringing it to pass. Thus, the hero's fate is an expression of his very essence, which the hero makes known freely, as it were, assuming it as his own personal responsibility – often to the amazement of those around him who do not understand the significance of his actions. The hero's fate is part of his very being: in fact, his inner being is the embodiment of that fate. Such epithets as 'personal' or 'individual' which, we for want of anything better, are obliged to use, do not adequately convey the ethical situation in which the Eddic hero finds himself. In the 'clan individual', the personal and suprapersonal are indivisible. The hero, as a rule, does not find himself faced by any choice as to how he might act. He subordinates himself to an obligatory pattern of behaviour, but he does not perceive this as something external, forced upon him like an unavoidable onerous obligation, from the performance of which he cannot, alas, deviate. He sees a particular course of action as the only possible one, he can conceive of no other. This is *his* course of behaviour, his very being is internalized fate.

In this way a latent conception of the human personality emerges through the representation of the hero, one that is intrinsic to Germanic-Scandinavian cultures. Yet the phenomenon of the 'heroic' remains highly contradictory and far from clear in modern interpretations of these works of literature. At least two extremes are to be observed.

Some scholars extol Germanic heroism, lending it aspects of the modern perception of the heroic and depicting the nature of the hero in a tragic-romantic light. They refer to 'heroic humanism' in the epic poetry of the Germanic peoples,[1] to the 'faith in man and his freedom' which allegedly permeates the heroic poems, to the 'tragic nature of his freedom', which is a 'law of life' for the hero and which finds expression in his 'free faithfulness to his own ego and his own law' and in his awareness of his own destiny. When the heroic is interpreted in this way, it is presented as one of the essential features of the 'Germanic spirit' that allegedly survived unassailed in the German people of the ancient past and has lived on right up until the age of the Hohenstaufen.[2] Deliberations of this kind do not, however, help us to understand either the essential nature of the 'heroic' as perceived by the Germanic peoples, nor the nature of the individual in the context of their culture. The character and the specific nature of the individual's self-awareness in that distant age are precisely what need to be explained.

Other scholars, on the other hand, are inclined to call into question the very concept of the 'heroic' in relation to the German and Scandinavian peoples. Michail Steblin-Kamenskij has attempted to 'scale down to size' the characters that people the Eddic poems. He calls attention to the differences to be found in interpretations of heroines and heroes as presented in the poems of the *Edda*, rightly pointing out that the image of the heroine is a dual one: in the poems she appears as a woman in a tragic situation, experiencing the loss of husband, brothers and children, mourning over them and seeking revenge for their death, yet at the same time she assumes the role of a supernatural being, endowed with abilities and knowledge that ordinary people do not enjoy. She is reminiscent of a Valkyrie and sometimes even is one. Heroes, on the other hand, are clearly inferior to these women, according to this particular author. Heroes' strength of mind, meanwhile, is only manifested in their contempt of death: when it comes to strength of feeling, they are apparently far from hero-like: Steblin-Kamenskij would have us believe that they are characterized by 'mental impotence'.[3] He dwells in particular on the figure of Sigurd, the most illustrious of the Eddic heroes. A whole cycle of poems has been devoted to this hero: he is glorified (as Siegfried) in the German epic *Nibelungenlied* and there are also Scandinavian and German works in prose which immortalize him.

'What heroic feat did Sigurd actually accomplish?' asks Steblin-Kamenskij. Sigurd is also known as Slayer of Fáfnir but, as the author points out, Sigurd, while carrying out this act, spent only his physical strength, without manifesting any strength of mind. He then crept into a pit in the path of an unsuspecting dragon and pierced it with a sword. This was no honourable fight, merely an ambush! Steblin-Kamenskij sees the motivation for this act of Sigurd as no more than simple gain, the urge to acquire the gold that the dragon was guarding. Not content with that, Sigurd, after slaying Fáfnir, resorts to treachery: anxious not to have to share his booty, he killed his brother Reginn, the blacksmith, who had fashioned Sigurd's mighty sword for him and told him how to kill the dragon.

According to Steblin-Kamenskij, Sigurd's other feats testify still less to his heroic spirit. His wooing of Brynhild for Gunnar, when Sigurd assumed the guise of her betrothed, was based on deception. Yet this deception was later to be exposed and Sigurd, when he boasted of the ring he had obtained from Brynhild, paid for it with his life. As Steblin-Kamenskij sees it, Sigurd did not reveal any strength of feeling with regard to Brynhild, nor with regard to his own wife Gudrún. Nor even at the moment of his death did he manifest any nobility of spirit: his death was sudden and all he had time to do was to cleave his murderer in two, but that after all was a manifestation of physical rather than spiritual strength.

A similar approach is adopted by Steblin-Kamenskij in his approach to other epic heroes – Helgi, Hamdir, Sörli: as they accomplish their war-like feats and make manifest their physical strength, they exhibit no strength of mind. Moreover, their feats are accompanied by actions which are not in keeping with the halo of glory which surrounds them. Indeed, in Steblin-Kamenskij's opinion, the Eddic heroes are not heroes at all. While Otto Höfler extols the heroes of Germanic and Scandinavian epic literature to an excessive degree, idealizing and modernizing them as he does so, Steblin-Kamenskij denies them heroic qualities.

In this situation, the question then naturally arises: why have Scandinavians and other Germanic peoples preserved for centuries the memory of Sigurd/Siegfried and other figures and extolled them in their poems again and again? After all, they knew perfectly well that Sigurd had indeed made his way to Brynhild by deceit, wooing her for Gunnar and pretending to be Gunnar; that Fáfnir had been slain from an ambush, that he had sought to gain possession of the Rheingold and killed his mentor Reginn. It would appear that these circumstances, that lead the modern scholar to ask questions, did not worry the writers and performers of the Eddic poems in the slightest and were in keeping with the expectations and tastes of their audiences. This fact alone gives us plenty of food for thought.

It should be stressed that interpreting the feats of Sigurd is by no means as simple a task as it might at first appear. Let us start with the fact that his desire to gain possession of the gold cannot be reduced to no more than common greed. The gold was, after all, the cause of friction between the *aesir* and the *álfar*, the brothers Reginn and Fáfnir: it possessed magic properties and could bring about 'success' for him who owned it. It would thus appear to embody power and prosperity, and it would be wrong to disregard its symbolic function. Furthermore, Sigurd had been led to attack Fáfnir by his brother and had then killed Reginn after he learnt that Reginn had been planning to kill Fáfnir. The battle with the monster, into which Fáfnir had turned himself while protecting the gold that had fallen to his lot (incidentally, as a result of patricide) was not subject to the rules that would have governed the actions of figures in Icelandic sagas, avenging themselves against those who had offended them. It is well known from folk legends that, in the world of magic and sorcery, ordinary ethical norms are not applicable, and the legends concerning Sigurd are permeated with fairy-tale motifs of this kind. The battle between the hero and a monster is a motif widespread in myth, epic literature and folklore.

Let us compare Steblin's efforts to belittle the importance of the slaying of Fáfnir with the words exchanged between Sigurd and Grípir: Sigurd asks the old man to name for him 'brave exploits / which have on earth / not been seen as yet' while Grípir replies, that Sigurd shall kill 'the fierce snake', and Sigurd exclaims: 'Great will be the joy, / if I achieve / such an exploit / of which you tell' (*Grípisspá*, 10-12).

The assertion that, strictly speaking, Eddic heroes are not heroes at all, stems from the belief that the concept of the 'heroic' in the ancient past and in the Modern Age is one and the same. A hero who accomplishes a martial exploit is – from the modern point of view – a person who possesses first and foremost strength of mind: he does not necessarily have outstanding physical strength, at least such strength is not essential. The heroes of Ancient Scandinavia, on the other hand, stand out for their strength of mind and also for their physical strength: these are seen as united and indivisible and, therefore, no contradiction between the two was recognized. Sigurd's fearlessness enabled him to penetrate Brynhild's abode, and his inexhaustible courage gave him the strength to cut down his killer, even after he had been dealt a fatal blow in his heart by a sword: his loyalty to his blood-brother Gunnar was the reason why Sigurd did not deflower Gunnar's betrothed, with whom he spent three nights.

Spirit and matter were not seen as separate entities in that period and neither were the moral state of the hero and his physical qualities. A dichotomy between these would have been alien to the system of values which then held sway. The hero's outward strength was an external expression of his great spirit. A man was valued for fearlessness and loyalty, just as he was valued for his physical skill and his muscular strength. It is not by chance that reference is made in the poems to Sigurd's 'splendid countenance' and this does not merely imply handsome appearance and fighting strength: Sigurd was the embodiment of perfection in the eyes of the peoples of that age. Naturally the martial exploits accomplished were of supreme importance for the Eddic hero and all other qualities are on a lesser place in the poems. Yet the men and women of those times did not need to wonder whether the hero possessed any other prowess apart from that of the martial variety. Grípir predicts for Sigurd: 'You shall be great, / like no-one else beneath the sun, / you shall be higher / than the other kings, / rich in gold, / poor in flight, / you shall be fair of mien / and wise in words' (*Grípisspá*, 7). The great hero is great in all things – in both his physical and spiritual qualities.

The 'mental impotence' of the heroes in Eddic poetry is none other than an attempt to read into the text content that is alien to it. The status of the hero presupposed certain emotions and, for example, a sense of friendship and loyalty to a blood-brother, for whom Sigurd undertakes the exploits connected with winning the bride, comes clearly to the fore. The true extent of the villainy that has been perpetrated against Sigurd becomes clear when we take into account the fact that Sigurd remained loyal to his friend Gunnar to the very end, while it was Gunnar who finally plotted his death. Even on his deathbed Sigurd consoles Gudrún by reminding her that she has three brothers (the very same people who have brought about his downfall) and he assures her that they will – so he believes – provide her with protection and support.

A similar misconception is the idea that Sigurd is incapable of love for a woman: his feelings for Brynhild are clearly described in *Grípir's Prophecy*. All this is very far removed from 'mental impotence': the hero is capable of a range of feelings, including loyalty to his friends, love for a woman, anger, and a sense of honour.

Steblin-Kamenskij suggests that the exploits of the hero are often at odds with his glory. As if anticipating such a suspicion, Sigurd himself asks Gunnar whether he might become caught up in some kind of villainy. Grípir replies: 'No, in your life / there shall be no disgrace, – / may you know this, Sigurd, / O worthy king; / it shall be glorified forever / among men, / summoning forth a torrent of spears / your name' (*Grípisspá*). Thus, the contradiction that Steblin-Kamenskij suggested as existing between the glory of the hero and his allegedly unheroic behaviour strikes only the modern scholar, who approaches the analysis of the Eddic hero with criteria that are inappropriate to the moral conceptions of the Middle Ages. From the point of view of the people of that age, the hero and his deeds, on the one hand, and his glorious reputation, the verdict that posterity arrives at, on the other, are perfectly compatible. If a figure from an Eddic poem does not appear in a heroic light to a scholar of today, all this means is that ideals have changed. A hero of the *Edda* might just as well be accused of having perpetrated murder, indulged in plunder, commanded that slaves be killed on the occasion of his own burial, set fire to his palace and turned his own cremation into a general hecatomb. These actions by the hero did not in any way contradict his reputation: they met the criteria for valour which were seen as the norm in the society that gave birth to

these heroic poems, and were regarded as natural for the
behaviour of a legendary hero.

To achieve a closer understanding of the heroic principle in
the Eddic poems, it is important not to forget that everything
which happens in them belongs to the distant past and took
place, from the author's point of view, in times immemorial.
In *The Lay of Hamdir* (*Hamdismál*, 2) it is written: 'Not now,
not now, / Nor yesterday, / But long ago / Has that day worn
by, / That ancientest time / The first time to tell of . . .'. The time
in which the Eddic poems are set is absolute epic time. They are
irrevocably majestic, the good old days, the only time when
such imposing figures, of whom the heroic poems tell, existed.
All that happened in those early days is past and complete.
Between the heroic era and the time when the poems were
recited lies, to use Mikhail Bakhtin's expression, 'absolute epic
time'.

For this reason, modern criteria should not be applied to
epic heroes, but neither should those standards which were
applied to the characters of sagas. Sagas tell of men and women
going about their ordinary everyday lives, while Eddic poems
extol heroes that exist in a qualitatively different dimension.
The actions undertaken by a character in a saga can be inspired
by heroic examples, drawn from the *Edda*, but an unbridgeable
gulf is to be observed between the ethics of the age of the sagas
and the ethics of the heroic past.

The Lesson of the High One:
aphorisms and worldly wisdom

The Lesson of the High One (*Hávamál*) is the longest of the
poems in the *Edda* and stands somewhat apart from the rest of
the cycle. While the other poems are peopled by pagan gods or
Ancient Scandinavian heroes, this one contains for the most
part exhortations of worldly wisdom including proverbs and
aphorisms. Yet it does not come over as unified, and instead
represents an apparent compilation of what seem to be
heterogeneous poems. Apart from the first part, which contains
rules of conduct, and *The Lesson for Loddfáfnir* (*Loddfáfnismál*

– which in part has similar content), the poem includes other verses addressed to Odin (about his relations with women, his self-sacrifice, on the strength of which he gained his knowledge of runes), and finally a list of various spells declaimed by Odin. All these things together constitute a collection of heterogeneous poems, which possibly date from different periods in time. Yet what is of interest to us is not the question of the original composition of *The Lesson of the High One*. We have before us the text which was circulated in Ancient Scandinavian society (it is not absolutely clear whether that meant Iceland, where the *Edda* was written down, or Norway, whence came most of the people who colonized Iceland) and that is enough.

In *The Lesson of the High One* provision is made for the behaviour of an individual in the most varied of life-situations. Who is the person to whom this advice and exhortations are directed and whose moral code is embodied in them? Some scholars hold that what we have here is the moral code of the Vikings, who relied exclusively on themselves and their own resources, because in the poem no Christian influence makes itself felt (nor indeed influence of belief in pagan gods). Yet the surviving text of the *Edda* has been dated (with reference to palaeographic data) as from the second half of the thirteenth century, while the campaigns of the Vikings had ceased 200 years earlier. Other scholars are of the opinion that the praise meted out to modest means and the declamation about the vanity of wealth point to the fact that this work embodies the morality of a humble man. The range of his interests and cares does not extend beyond the everyday. In this poem the vanity of wealth is stressed and 'honest poverty' is held up for praise.

> A house of your own is better,
> though it is only a little one.
> Every man is a person of consequence
> at home. Even if you only have two
> goats and a cottage thatched with fibre
> it is better than begging.
> A house of your own is better, though
> it is only a little one. Every man is
> a somebody at home. It is heartbreaking

to have to beg food for yourself for
every meal.

(*Hávamál*, 36,37).

Yet it is not clear to what extent it is permissible to compare
the views of simple peasants with the morality of the nobility
or wealthy in such countries as medieval Norway and, still
more so, medieval Iceland. The small store set by material
prosperity, that is to be encountered on several occasions in
The Lesson of the High One, could be interpreted as mere
moral philosophizing rather than as a reflection of the views of
a particular social stratum. Yet it is difficult not to agree with
Andreas Heusler who points out that, in *The Lesson of the
High One*, the lofty tone and heroic principles that characterize
the finest sagas about Icelanders are missing.[4] What we have
here is probably the everyday morality of the humble person.
The contrast Heusler mentions in this connection is worthy of
comment: sagas sometimes lend a heroic flavour to reality,
directing attention away from the 'prose' of everyday life and
disregarding domestic detail. In *The Lesson of the High One*,
on the other hand, things look rather different: their 'down-to-
earth' character provides the historian with a rare opportunity
to penetrate a plane of reality, which was not subjected to lofty
stylization. Yet, lest we should move with undue haste to link
the existing text with a specific social class, let us look first at
the content of the exhortations that might be relevant to the
subject of our study: what can they tell us that sheds light on
the individual?

What advice is provided in *The Lesson of the High One*? As
we read it, we glean the impression that the person to whom
the various moral precepts are addressed is alone.[5] He is
obliged to sojourn alone in an unfriendly world fraught with
many perils and he has only his own wits and strength to rely
on. Hence the idea, which is to be found throughout virtually
the whole of the poem in one guise or another, to the effect that
the person has to be careful and behave with the utmost
caution. The world is full of chicanery and it is vital always to
be on one's guard – inside the home and out, at gatherings or
feasts, during journeys, in courts of law, even while in the

embrace of a woman. Not for a moment should a man be parted from his weapon, 'for it can never be known with certainty when he will need the use of his spear as he goes forth on his travels' (*Hávamál*, 38). This advice does not in any way contradict what we read in Icelandic sagas, in which concrete life-situations are described in place of exhortations. The hero of sagas must be ready to respond to any insult or infringement of his rights with a blow of his sword or spear. It is possible that later on he will be refused the help of kinsmen or friends, but, at the moment when conflict breaks out between him and another man, everything depends on his own qualities.

The author of *The Lesson of the High One* starts out from the assumption that men do not sit around at home, but go out to visit others. The question of social interaction for people who lived in isolated farmsteads scattered at considerable distances from each other was bound to occupy an important position in the poem. This is why the central figure in this poem is an individual who finds himself in someone else's home, where he might well find himself in danger. The poem begins with the advice: before making your way up the hall you should observe and note all the doorways, for you can never be certain when you will find enemies present (*Hávamál*, 1). Even if there is no such threat it is still imperative to remain on one's guard. A guest needs to be restrained and to be quiet rather than chatter: he should listen carefully to everything around him and keep his eyes wide open (*Hávamál*, 7). If a guest takes part in a conversation it is important that he should earn the praise and the goodwill of those present, listen to their advice, but not take what anyone says on trust. When a man receives guests in his own house, he needs to be welcoming and skilled with his words, but first and foremost keep to the path of reason (*Hávamál*, 103, 132-135).

Worldly wisdom is more precious than any treasures ('In a strange place it will be better than riches, and it is a means of existence to him, who is destitute'. *Hávamál*, 10). With regard to intelligence and wisdom, which are constantly being mentioned in the poem as conditions for the correct and successful behaviour of the individual, it is necessary to point out that they are usually presented in the form of circumspection and cunning, rather than that of extensive knowledge. The author of *The Lesson of the High One* stresses insistently that a mind of moderate size is also acceptable, for after all 'all men are not equally wise, for mankind is not always perfect and every man should be moderately wise, never excessively so', and there is no need at all for a man to philosophize to excess. Indeed 'those people who know a very fair amount have the best time', and 'the heart of a wise man is seldom glad if its owner is a man of very great wisdom: he who does not foresee his fate has a mind most free from care' (*Hávamál*, 53-56).

The 'hero' of the poem is literally obsessed with the fear that other people might take him for stupid: to be restrained and sparing with words are signs of intelligence. It is necessary to endeavour to make other people engage in conversation while, at the same time, revealing as little as possible about one's own thoughts and intentions. It is wrong to trust the smiles of one's interlocutors, for they might conceal contempt at the foolishness of a chatterer, and the foolish man will not find moral support in the places where it is most important, such as in a court of law (*Hávamál*, 24-29). Too much talk might offend someone and, in this way, one can imperceptibly acquire enemies. At feasts it is easy for quarrels to flare up, but it is difficult to put out the flames. Sometimes a man might appear to be a friend but then, on close examination, turns out to be an enemy. Mistrustfulness and hypocrisy are encouraged. While nursing evil intentions against the enemy, it is best to conceal these behind smiles and sweet utterances. 'The tongue is the destroyer of the head; / Under every fur coat / I expect to find a hand lurking' (*Hávamál*, 73). Mistrust towards everyone and everything is the leitmotif of this poem, and the list of persons, beasts, other living creatures and objects arousing suspicion occupies several verses: the list includes 'a bride's bed talk, a king's child, a brother's slayer, a ravening wolf, an independent slave, a broken sword-blade, a twanging bow, a horse exceeding swift, a horse with a broken leg, a coiled snake, ice from one night's frost' and much else besides 'no man should be so trustful as to trust in any of these!' (*Hávamál*, 85-91)

This is why constant self-control is vital. It is particularly dangerous to forget restraint and become drunk in someone else's house to the extent that tongues are loosened. Drinking at a feast is acceptable, but in moderation, for the first commandment for the clever and experienced man should be to try to find out what other people are thinking. In the same way, it is important to observe moderation in eating for, 'when a fool mixes with intelligent people, his gluttony always makes him an object of derision' (*Hávamál*, 20). Best of all is to eat adequately at home before setting forth as a guest and it is as well not to linger under the host's roof for too long. Otherwise it is easy for a friend to turn into an enemy.

The assumption underlying the exhortations in *The Lesson of the High One* is that the individual encountering potential bringers of danger is solitary and obliged to find his own path within the world of men, relying on caution and cunning as he does so. We are confronted by a society in which it is difficult to secure goodwill or support. Admiration requires neither candour nor spontaneity in the expression of emotion but, on the contrary, that a man be ever suspicious and on his guard.

A similar picture is also to be found in the sagas. The characters in them are, as a rule, sparing with their words. They prefer short statements or brief hints to lengthy speeches. Their intentions and moods are more likely to be revealed through their deeds. Scholars characterize the way in which the inner world of a saga hero is depicted as 'symptomatic' – it is possible to judge a character's emotional state on the basis of outward 'symptoms'. In fact, the authors of sagas had nothing in common with the omniscient author of the modern novel nor indeed with their own contemporaries, the creators of knightly epics, who would hold forth about the thoughts and emotions of their characters. The author of a saga conveys to us only what an outside observer might have seen – people's actions. This feature of the method used to depict characters' inner worlds could be taken for a literary device. It would, however, be highly unlikely: much more probable is that it expressed a general principle of life. The individual man within society, as described in the literature of Ancient Scandinavia, cannot but be extremely restrained and prey to inner tension. His caution does not abandon him for a moment. Even when experiencing deep emotion, he does not let this show. While planning to avenge himself against another who has offended him, he does not hurry to put his plan into effect while circumstances are unfavourable. He does not give vent to his feelings in complaints or angry outbursts. Even when tense as a taut string, he maintains outward calm. Reticence is the overriding norm for social behaviour, and this even finds its expression in the poetic style of the saga, which does not allow the author knowledge of the thoughts and feelings of the characters mentioned, who themselves say nothing on the subject.

Now let us return to *The Lesson of the High One*. People cannot survive in isolation within a society where caution and potential hostility are the order of the day. They have to secure someone's support. The author of the poem does not extol the emotions binding friends together: he sees friendship to be more like an alliance based on calculations of mutual interest ('Two together are death to the single man'. *Hávamál*, 73) rather than an expression of disinterested intimacy. Is it not telling that the subject of exchanging gifts is introduced into *The Lesson of the High One* immediately after a reminder to the effect that a man should not for a moment distance himself from his weapon, for no-one knows when he might have need of it while on his travels? (*Hávamál*, 38). Since he lives in this state of continual tension, the individual needs friends. It is easiest of all to attract them and to bind them to oneself through gifts, and it is wrong not to be generous with these, particularly because what has been promised to a friend might fall into the hands of a foe and then 'things often turn out worse than we anticipate' (*Hávamál*, 40).

The subject of exchanging gifts is discussed in great detail in the poem. Such exchanges were an important institution in ancient societies, 'a universal social fact' (M. Mauss). Such exchanges in that society were first and foremost not economic in character but symbolic: they embodied the 'social contract', drawn up between individuals or families, that served to establish relations based on shared interests and presupposing mutual help and loyalty. 'A gift always looks for a recompense' (*Hávamál*, 145) was a principle that the Ancient Scandinavians abided by come what may. Otherwise the man who received a gift without responding in kind would find himself in an intolerable position: he would be at the mercy of the giver.

The situation was rather different when it came to relations between nobleman and commoner. A man-at-arms might pester his commander for gifts. Yet his efforts were not merely an aspiration after wealth, although they might have appeared as such. According to the ideas of the day, the king possessed special capacities for 'good fortune' or 'luck' and could share these with those whom he rewarded. A ring, sword, cloak or other precious object which he bestowed upon his retainer, embodied part of that 'good fortune', and this magic 'fortune' extended to the recipient of the gift and might help him in his endeavours. Thus, the greed manifested by the men of the king's entourage was in its way a symptom of their urge to assert themselves, to acquire 'good fortune'.

So caution was also the order of the day when it came to exchanging gifts. Apparel and weapons given to friends consolidated the alliance and ensured their loyalty, and for this reason it was wrong to be mean. Yet a rich gift was not required in every situation: 'esteem is often bought at a small price: with a half loaf and a tilted bottle I have picked up a companion' (*Hávamál*, 52). Yet to be mean was dangerous: if a gift was not made, the result could be a harmful curse from the offended man.

In the harsh world described in *The Lesson of the High One*, that is fraught with all manner of dangers, it is possible only to rely on close friends or relatives. In the part of the poem entitled 'The Lesson for Loddfáfnir', practical advice for everyday life is proffered once again. Yet the morality expressed here does not seem as selfish as that found in the previous Lesson. The general pragmatic maxims, stripped of all emotion found in *The Lesson of the High One*, are complemented with emotional aspects found in 'The Lesson for Loddfáfnir'. It is in these particular verses of the poem that friendship is extolled. It is important to visit a friend frequently, to abide by friendship and to cast no shadow over it: 'It is a sign of the closest intimacy when a man determines to reveal his whole soul to someone. There is nothing worse than to be fickle. He is no friend who never says anything unpleasant' (*Hávamál*, 124). In this part of the exhortations somewhat more human warmth is to be found. Friendship emerges here as a positive value. Yet here too the author does not forget to underline the practical advantage to be gleaned from ties of friendship.

Among sources of prosperity and happiness named in these lines as well as wealth and health, sons and close relatives are also mentioned (*Hávamál*, 68, 69). Yet wealth is transient and can even be harmful (*Hávamál*, 75). Happiness is to have a son, even if he is born after his father's demise: he shall set up a memorial stone, on which the name of his dead father shall be cut out in runes. Stones of this type bearing inscriptions are scattered all over the Scandinavian countries: they were erected by children and kinsmen of Vikings who had died or been killed.

It is interesting to note that children (to be more precise, sons) are mentioned as people capable of immortalizing the memory of their father, but they are not presented as possessing emotional value in their own right. No mention is made of a father's love. This is because the most important thing of all, according to the author of *The Lesson of the High One*, is not property, nor relatives, nor even life itself – it is the 'acts' of an individual, that can bring him glory or enable him to be well remembered. Their reputation was what the Ancient Scandinavians held most dear. The most well known lines of this poem declare: 'Cattle die, kinsfolk die, even to us ourselves will death come. / But the good fame which a man has won for himself will never die. / Cattle die, kinsfolk die, even to us ourselves will death come. / One thing I know will never die – the reputations we all leave behind at our death' (*Hávamál*, 76, 77).

The judgement mentioned here is the memory a man leaves behind him for future generations. The idea of an individual, the assessment of his actions by those around him, these are what live on from generation to generation. Concern for posthumous glory permeates all Germanic poetry. An echo of the sentiments found in *The Lesson of the High One* is to be found in the Anglo-Saxon poem *Beowulf*: 'As we must all expect to leave / our life on this earth, we must earn some renown, / If we can before death; daring is the thing / for a fighting man to be remembered by. / . . . A man must act so / when he means in a fight to frame himself / a long-lasting glory; it is not life he thinks of.' (*Beowulf*, 1385 ff., 1534 ff.).

To what extent the Ancient Scandinavians were concerned to preserve their reputations, i.e. above all the reputations of their own names, can be deduced from a reading of the *Bosa saga*. The hero of the saga refuses to learn sorcery, and the motivation behind this action is most interesting: he 'does not wish that it should be written in his saga that he accomplished anything thanks to sorcery instead of by relying on his own courage'.[6] The man evaluates his current behaviour looking at it as if from the vantage point of the future, from the position of the author of the saga that he hopes will subsequently be written about him. The Ancient Scandinavians had not yet taken on board the concept of sin: their thoughts were focused on the Earth as they knew it and no-one was inclined to harm his or her own reputation. It was not their inner state, nor any preoccupation with the redemption of their souls but the opinion which society held of them that was their central concern.

The awareness of the solitary individual recorded in *The Lesson of the High One*, an individual who is obliged to rely first and foremost on his own capacities and make his own way in life amidst all manner of dangers, is nevertheless one that takes note of society throughout. 'Public opinion' exerts the strongest of pressures on this individual: he is totally dependent on it emotionally and intellectually: it is via public opinion that he assesses his deeds and, in the final analysis, his very ego. As Heusler was also to note, the author of *The Lesson of the High One* does not penetrate the secret recesses of the human heart, for his attention is focused mainly on what passes before human eyes.[7] This work directs attention not to moral imperatives, but to generally accepted morality that dictates to the individual the script for his behaviour.

When he raises the morality issue, the 'High One' starts out from the contrast between the clever, wise or knowing and fools, but it is presented in a guise all of its own, appropriate to the pagan consciousness. Clever is he, who knows the rules of behaviour and conducts himself in society in accordance with those rules: foolish and unwise is the man who ignores social norms. Success will fall to the lot of the well-informed, wise man. Human beings evaluate their own deeds with reference to generally accepted and universally binding principles laid down unconditionally. The concept of conscience is hardly appropriate here, demanding as it does moral self-control on the part of the individual, who independently formulates moral precepts and evaluates these. In a society where clan traditions hold sway and where personality emerges as 'clan personality', moral issues regarding the individual could not yet have acquired any substantial importance. Hence the famous ethical neutrality of *The Lesson of the High One*, which is particularly conspicuous when we compare it to the Christian exhortations of the Middle Ages.

In *The Lesson of the High One*, what we really have before us is not a subjective appreciation by an individual of his own behaviour as something that does or does not correspond to the highest moral values which were assumed to be well known to the said individual and accepted by him as his own imperatives. What is advocated is the practical expediency of abiding by the rules of the group that are binding for all its members.

The Individual in the Saga

The Lesson of the High One contains precepts that make it clear how the individual should behave in various life situations, often of a far-from-easy nature. The rules implied are revealing, and it is important to be acquainted with them, yet the historian's desire to establish the way people were actually behaving remains unsatisfied. Let us therefore turn now to the narrative prose of the Scandinavians, to their sagas.

The saga is a literary genre and historical source that was unique in the Middle Ages. Scholars concentrating on literary works further inland were, apart from rare exceptions, deprived of the opportunity to examine individuals: the evidence is rare and sparse. Historians studying sagas, on the other hand, were more likely to encounter *un embarras de richesses*, because the material they offer the historian ready to ask the appropriate questions was so extensive and so rich. The Latin used in many categories of works composed in Europe does not convey adequately the patterns of thought peculiar to the people of that time, but the language of the sagas draws us into the inner world of their creators. Sagas come nearer to a depiction of life than any other genre in medieval literature. They bring us real conflicts and situations which existed or could have existed in Scandinavian society. The characters of the sagas are people who, as a rule, had actually lived at some time or other. Sagas are not novels: their authors, as well as their audiences, were convinced that the stories narrated were true to life.

We should not, of course, forget that the sagas were written down in the late twelfth or thirteenth centuries, while most of the people and events described relate to the ninth, tenth or eleventh centuries. Naturally, the sagas present the past in their own way: in part, they 'modernize' it, in part, characters are lent heroic stature and idealized. The historian anxious to piece together some features of the medieval personality will not, however, be unduly worried by this stylization, for he or she is not concerned with facts but with characters, with ethics, with reflections of social behaviour relating to the period when the sagas were written down.

Medieval reality, however, is very different from that which we understand by reality nowadays: it incorporated a good deal from the realm of the fantastic and miraculous. Apart from real people, the sagas also present to us all manner of supernatural creatures, werewolves and the 'living dead'. Among the factors determining the course of events, prophecies and dreams, which come true without fail, play an important part, as do sorcery and a wide range of acts involving magic. All this is presented in the same manner and with a similar degree of conviction as people's ordinary deeds and conversations.

The 'realism' or 'naturalism' of the sagas does not rule out the heroes' need occasionally to join battle with monsters or with magic powers vested in inanimate objects – even including the ability to recite verses they have composed: nor do they prevent a severed head, that has flown away from its body, from continuing to count money in a competent fashion and so on and so forth. Actions of the heroes in sagas, which could be interpreted as acts of free will, can turn out to be the result of sorcery.

The dead caused a good deal of unpleasantness for those living on their estates, leading to all manner of harm, until a suit had been brought against them and legal proceedings had been instigated in the abode of the head of the household: these proceedings were exactly like those that would be instituted to deal with living criminals. Those who had returned from the dead would be accused of breaking into the dwelling and of depriving members of the household of health and life. Witnesses for the prosecution would be appointed and all the necessary formalities would be observed. After a verdict had been reached, ghosts had to leave the estate never to return there in accordance with the court's decision. Once having left the house, the ghosts would hold forth with alliterative phrases dwelling on their reluctance to leave the estate (*Erbyggja saga*).

Stories of real events and people who had once lived were to be found side by side with fictions which also made their way into these narratives: the fiction was not necessarily perceived of as such and it is smoothly woven into the fabric of the sagas. It is unlikely that the author of a saga felt himself to be its all-powerful creator freely moulding his material. He did not invent characters, for they were virtually all people who had once lived: neither did he invent events (these for the most part had actually taken place and memory of them had lived on till the time when the sagas were written down). Neither could such an author feel that he was an independent creator when it came to the form in which the sagas were written down; unlike the skalds, who came to excel in the use of metric verse and delivery of the kennings, the authors of the sagas tried to 'tell their sagas as they happened', i.e. to expound history according to its actual course. The sagas often contain pointers to the fact that they had existed before they were written down, and they also frequently contain allusions to other sagas (sometimes those that did not exist in written form) in which the same characters appear.

Authors of sagas were not inclined to turn their backs on

tradition: there exists a whole group of narratives about Icelanders and an individual author would merely write down one of them. The author of a saga would see his work as part of a wider Saga of the Icelanders, and each author was, as it were, adding something to that Saga or providing clarification through additional detail of a particular part of it. What we have before us today is a truly unified text of Ancient Icelandic prose, from which creations of individual authors can only sometimes be separated out. As a rule, the authors of sagas about Icelanders are unknown. Unlike the writers of skaldic poetry, the creators of sagas did not sense a need to name themselves and to record themselves within their creations. Neither did their contemporaries make a point of doing so.

Medieval authors in general, not just Icelandic ones, were keenly aware of the existence of an acknowledged text. Given that there was no pressure to innovate or to break with tradition, an author's perception of his subject matter was naturally very different from that found in modern times. If we take the modern European conception of authorship as the 'norm', then medieval authorship, in particular as it relates to the sagas, would appear 'inferior' even 'unconscious'. If, on the other hand, we leave modern criteria to one side, then perhaps it would be right to talk of authorship that embraced both individual and collective inspiration and, moreover, the balance between these two varies depending upon the particular genre of medieval literature involved. While a skald is a literary creator manipulating complex and fanciful forms and clearly aware of his authorship, the author of a saga probably belongs to the category of 'collective' creator.

In a saga there is not merely no free invention, but no clear author's stance nor clearly defined values of the author either. In this respect a saga resembles an epic. Evaluation can be gleaned only through allusions to the opinion of an entourage which praises or condemns what is happening. Yet this does not reflect the author's own individual position: the author merely conveys the stance of the collective, just as he might convey other information that has been brought to his knowledge. He cannot say: 'this action is bad' – he resorts to such expressions as 'People thought this action was bad'.

Moreover, in a saga, different opinions on the same subject are not provided. After Njál with his sons have perished in fire, one person rode up to Flosi and his retainers, who were standing by the burnt dwelling, and said: 'You have taken drastic action here'. To this Flosi replied: 'People will call it a drastic action and an evil one too' (*Njáls saga*, 130). Thus, a participant in the slaughter condemns himself starting out from what he assumes will be the assessment of his deed by other people; indeed, his assumption is presented almost as certainty.

Yet, at the same time, the 'ingenuous', 'prosaic' quality of the sagas, the simplicity of the language used, and the everyday nature of the utterances made by their characters are just as much an illusion as the idea that the sagas reproduce ordinary situations from life. Without fail, sagas depict crisis situations, moments of decisive, sometimes fateful importance in people's lives. At the centre of attention is conflict between individuals and families, strife that is usually accompanied by murder and blood feuds.

While drawing on folklore and maintaining close links with epics, sagas at the same time constitute works of high artistic value, with a poetic style and conventions all of their own. It is hardly likely that the work of their authors was 'unconscious', as M. I. Steblin-Kamenskij would have us believe,[8] because it was deliberately focused on material that each time was reworked by its author in his own way, although of course within the limits laid down by the epic tradition. It is evident that the author's work, his shaping and creation of the text, on the one hand, and the author's self-awareness, his conception of his activity and its very nature, of the framework within which he was creating and the implications of his activity, on the other, did not always coincide. The creative activity of the author of a saga did not go hand in hand with the author's increasing awareness of himself in the capacity of creator: it was more likely to make him aware that he was simply recording an already existing text and carrying one stage further the long chain of a group tradition. In the case of the sagas, authorship would appear to us now as a rather diffuse phenomenon. Without doubt, this sheds light on the type of individuality that was possible within the society in which sagas were composed.

The objective nature of the saga finds expression in the way in which the inner world of the characters, their feelings and emotional experiences, unfold. According to some, descriptions of this sort are entirely absent from the sagas, because sagas about Icelanders did not, allegedly, set themselves such a goal at all: the human personality did not yet attract sufficient attention for it to become the subject of literary representation, and what is being described in the sagas are not people as such but events – feuds, hostilities, vengeance.[9] It is difficult, however, to name works of literature in which the human personality was not a focus for depiction. Methods for the artistic probing of personality can cover an extremely wide range – from heroic poems to the psychological novel, from the *Book of Job* to *Faust* – just as types of personality moulded by different cultures can vary enormously. When it is pointed out that the personalities depicted in the sagas are different from the personality as found in contemporary literature, this goes without saying. Yet equally indisputable, in my opinion, is the fact that keen interest in humankind and the inner world is manifest in the sagas.

First of all, the feuds, which are indeed the central preoccupation of the author of the saga, are conflicts between people that stem from their interests and passions: they are 'human' events in which the qualities and characters of those involved find expression. The merits of the heroes of the saga are measured through these feuds, and the human value and essence of the characters are put to the test by them. Feuds are set in motion by human characters and, if the motives underlying them are not always strictly personal or individual, this is not because the individual possessed no value in the eyes of society, but because the individual at that time was not yet clearly defined within the group and was still guided in his or actions and ideas by the principles of the group. Among the motives propelling the individual towards clashes with others, concern for honour and merit, for his own good reputation and that of his family, kinsmen and friends always comes first.

When describing an act of vengeance or armed conflict, once again it is people who are at the forefront of attention. The author concentrates on demonstrating the courage of the hero, his strength and his fighting skill. The endless descriptions of this kind in the sagas are repeatedly based on the idea that it is in battle with his enemies that the hero experiences the climax of his life, its supreme and central moment: that is why any saga about Icelanders is centred round such episodes.

Secondly, it is difficult to accept the suggestion that there are no descriptions of feelings or emotional experiences of the characters in the sagas because, in fact, emotional states are depicted although not in the same way as in medieval literature of continental Europe or as in contemporary literature: they are depicted, not through analysis of the heroes' inner world and psychological states, but 'symptomatically', through actions, people's utterances, indications of changes in facial expression, laughter and so on. Emotional experiences are brought clearly to the fore through such 'symptoms'.

When Bergthóra, wife of Njál, tells her sons that they have been designated as 'Little Dungbeards, and their father as 'Old Beardless', Skarphedin replies: 'Our old mother is enjoying herself' and he smirks 'but the sweat broke out on his forehead, and two red spots flared in his cheeks, which had seldom happened before'. At night Njál heard the sound of a poleaxe being taken down from the wall and saw that there were no shields at the spot where they usually hung (*Njáls saga*, 44). Words to the effect that Njál's sons were beside themselves with anger and burning with thirst for revenge are unnecessary.

The shepherd told Gunnar that his enemy was reviling him and maintains that Gunnar wept when his enemy rode him down. 'We must not be oversensitive,' Gunnar commented to the shepherd: 'but from now on you need only do whatever work you wish.' It is clear that Gunnar took these words to heart. Indeed, he saddles his horse, takes up his shield, sword and spear and dons his helmet. The spear clanged loudly and this noise reached the ears of Gunnar's mother, who said: 'You look angry my son . . .I have never seen you look like this before'. 'Gunnar went outside. With a thrust of his halberd, he vaulted into the saddle and rode away' (*Njáls saga*, 54). Gunnar's agitation and intentions are utterly clear and are borne out in the description of his fight with his enemies which follows later.

The following scene from the *Saga of the Sons of Droplaug* (*Droplaugarsona saga*) provides an example of extreme restraint in the depiction of heroes' profound emotional experiences, and also of the 'symptomatic' method for conveying emotion. After Droplaug's son Helgi has been slain, his younger brother Grímr did not laugh for several years. Finally, he succeeded in killing his main enemy and, after escaping his pursuers, returns home where he is asked for news but merely replies that nothing has happened (heroic restraint that is typical for characters in the sagas!). The next day, when Grímr is playing chess with a guest who has come to visit him, a small boy, his son Jórinn, comes running into the room and upsets the chessmen by mistake: the boy is overcome with fright and farts with fear. Grímr bursts out laughing and then Jórinn comes over to him and asks : 'But what really happened during your journey last night, and what news have you brought?' Grímr answers with a few lines, from which it emerges that he has avenged the death of his brother. The modern reader might not link the reason for Grímr's laughter with the fact that he had not laughed since the death of his brother, but the woman in his house reacts appropriately to Grímr's guffaws that immediately attracted her attention. The game of chess and the child's embarrassment after his unwitting interruption of the game serve as a 'trigger', and Grímr's laughter releases the tension into which he had been locked until he killed his enemy. The artistic effect of this sequence of events was precisely calculated and is right on target.

It is worth mentioning that the greatest degree of restraint is to be found in the sagas at those moments when the emotional experiences of the hero reach their climax. On learning that a close relative or friend has perished, a man will maintain his silence and not give vent to his grief. It is not that he is emotionally shallow nor do saga audiences lack interest in emotional experiences or the individual: on the contrary, the silence and restraint are signs of profound and intensive efforts to grapple with emotions and ideas within. The hero is concentrating on the most important thing of all – the need not to weep over the dead, but to avenge them! For this reason, there are often scenes in sagas in which a wife, old father or young son learns of the death of husband, son or father and then, without tears or lament, takes up a weapon if the culprit is to hand. This restraint, described in sagas when violent emotion might be expected, is rather a depiction via opposites.

In sagas, collisions of character opposites are often depicted: a peace-loving, noble hero comes up against a treacherous enemy – Gísli, a man sensitive to belittling of his family's traditional values, and Thorkell, his kinsman, who attaches no importance to such values. Characters in sagas are naturally different from those found in the realistic literature of the nineteenth and twentieth centuries. Epic characters that tend to be 'monolithic' lack ambivalence or inner contradictions. Yet they are by no means always free of contradictions: Gunnar is a brave man, who admits that he finds it difficult to kill; Bolli, after killing Kjartan, at once bitterly repents of this deed (*Laxdæla saga*, 49). Contradictions in the mind and heart of the epic hero do not, however, paralyse his will. Both Gunnar and Bolli accomplish the deeds that are expected of them in accordance with the ethics of their day: regrets and self-criticism follow from deeds and, therefore, the inner contradictions for a hero are represented as if 'split' in time: first the hero carried out his duty and only then does he let his individual feelings surface.

The epic character does not develop: a character is noble or crafty from start to finish. This is why, as soon as a character is mentioned in a saga, his qualities are outlined; they are as irrefutable as his origin. From childhood, Grettir was wilful and eager to pick quarrels; Egill's difficult character is a mark of his whole family, rather than of him alone; Hallgerdr did not grow bitter as a result of a hard life but had been so ever since the moment of her first appearance in the first chapter of *Njáls saga*, where mention is made of her 'thief's eyes'.

It might have been expected that some kind of inner upheaval could have come over sagas when their heroes adopted a new faith. Yet even this major change is depicted, not as a sign of a protracted psychological process, but as a sudden, miraculous rebirth (of a kind reminiscent of medieval hagiography). At any stage of the narrative, the main characters are consistent and free from contradictions. The souls of characters in sagas do not become the arena for a struggle between the metaphysical powers of Good and Evil, as can be observed in the ecclesiastical literature of the same period.

The qualities of the characters in sagas are revealed in the course of conflicts. The factors giving rise to these conflicts can vary considerably. Sometimes, rights of property have been violated (damage to crops, theft, disputes over inheritance or ownership and so on), or there occur conflicts in love (rivalry between suitors, unhappy marriage, female jealousy), insults or attempts on human life. In short, all or almost all conflicts stem, in the final analysis, from actions that are perceived as offensive by one of the parties concerned, as a blow dealt against his or her self-respect. What gives rise to conflict is not theft of property as such, for instance, but the moral blow bound up with it. The individuals represented in the sagas are extremely sensitive to the slightest nuances of other people's behaviour towards them: even an insignificant action or a careless word can cause offence, and offence demands satisfaction. The epic hero looks at himself through the eyes of those around him, whose approval and respect he needs: their contempt is something he cannot endure. He is constantly seeking to maintain his position in public opinion and, indirectly, his own opinion of himself.

In this sense it is true to say that love, for instance, does not exist as an independent motif in the sagas. It too provides a means for the self-assertion of the hero. This, however, does not belittle the significance of the love element in sagas. Steblin-Kamenskij suggests that 'romantic emotion' did not appear to be something worthy of depiction. Yet, in a work such as *Laxdæla Saga,* the importance of the love element is extremely great. The unhappy love between Gudrún and Kjartan leads to the death of the hero, and the outcome for Gudrún is equally unsatisfactory. Naturally this subject surfaces only in a few specific places in the narrative, but is it not this theme that serves to a large extent to take the plot forward?

On the other hand, love does not appear in the sagas as an all-important motif that determines their subject-matter, nor is it the only factor influencing the actions of the main characters as, for example, in the legend of Tristan and Isolde. Sagas are more objective and provide a more realistic portrayal of characters complete with their motives and actions than the knightly romance. Kjartan loves Gudrún but, in addition, he serves at the royal court, wanders and runs his estate. Unlike Tristan, he does not live in an artificial world of 'pure love' for he is a full-blooded individual. In sagas love is portrayed very differently from the way it is presented in the medieval romance, but this only makes it more convincing. In the *Laxdæla Saga*, there is no description of pining lovers but, nevertheless, enough is said for Gudrún's passion to be clear to the audience.

It would surely be wrong to look upon the epic restraint inherent in the sagas as evidence that 'insufficient attention is being paid to the inner world' of the characters. When a hero accomplishes an exploit and refers to it as 'accidental', we cannot imagine that, in fact, he attributes no importance to it. After the fight with the dead man Kárr, which took place in the burial mound filled with ancient treasure, Grettir comes to the house of Thorfinnr, where the latter asks him what urgent business he has that leads him to behave not as other men. Grettir replies, 'Many a trifle could come to pass at night!': immediately afterwards, he proceeds to bring out all the treasure that has been removed from the burial mound (*Grettis saga*, 18). The boys (who, as it is later to emerge, are sons of Vesteinn, Gísli's friend, killed either by his brother Thorkell or by his son-in-law) kill Thorkell with his own sword and then run off. Someone asks them what the noise is all about and why they are running off. The youngest answers, 'I do not know what they are talking about over there. Yet I think they are arguing about whether only daughters remained after Vesteinn's death or whether he had another son' (*Gísla saga*, 28). Nothing more is said about this but, from the remark quoted above, it is perfectly clear to any Icelander what exploit the boy had accomplished by killing the perpetrator of his father's death.

I stress once more that any narrative concerning emotional experiences is implicit rather than explicit: passions, inner promptings are not analysed or described directly. They have to be inferred from actions, from short comments or from skaldic verses. Such is the poetic style of the saga which would appear to be reflecting certain aspects of the spiritual life of the Scandinavians.

Infringements against property rights often set conflict in motion in the sagas. Bondsmen or free men protect their property from thieves. The most important consideration in these situations is not the loss of property, but the moral slight, which the householder suffers if the robbery or seizure goes unpunished. Loss must be made good and, to achieve that, still greater losses are often incurred. A character in the *Bandamanna saga* is anxious to bribe influential members of the *Thing* to ensure he wins a property lawsuit, and promises them considerable riches. The nobleman, anxious about prestige, proceeds to pay without any hesitation a disproportionately large sum of money for the plot of land (*Eyrbyggja saga*). As is the case with relations based on love, so too property relations in the sagas are not a subject specially selected for inclusion in the narrative, but this does not in any way belittle their importance.

The laconic restraint with which the inner world and emotions of the characters are depicted in the sagas sometimes prevents the contemporary reader from appreciating the whole depth of the tragedies experienced by the heroes. For Gísli, his brother Thorkell's refusal of help is a terrible blow, but Gísli does not express what he is going through in anything like eloquent detail straightaway. Our perception of a saga is essentially different from that of medieval Scandinavians. Our sensitivity to the nuances of words, to the significance of passing over things in silence, to what might seem unimportant responses to signs concealing passions (to things such as a bloody spearhead or the cloak stained with the caked blood of a dead man, or a torn towel in a widow's house), has been blunted by a literature on a very different emotional plane, by a far more expressive tradition for the conveying of human feelings. Indeed, such taciturn restraint, which forces us to assume that there exists some kind of 'subtext', is far from typical for the rest of medieval literature. Suffice it to compare, for example, the conflict between family ties and love for a husband experienced by Thordis in the *Gísla saga* with the depiction of the drama of Margrave Rüdeger in the

Nibelungenlied, where the description of the allegiances of the knight to his mistress and to his friends, that prove incompatible and conflict with each other in Rüdeger's soul, occupies a whole episode in the epic.

Hence the possible impression that the characters suffer from emotional poverty, an impression which is totally false. The characters in the sagas do not beat their breasts or hold forth with long speeches about what they are experiencing, yet they do not ignore the tiniest of insults or allusions and they store in their memories everything that has some bearing upon their sense of self-respect. They might stall when it comes to revenge ('only a slave revenges himself immediately, but coward never', *Grettis saga*) and for that tardiness they will be reproached by women who, in general in the sagas, serve to promote and to protect family honour more assiduously than their husbands and sons. Yet, sooner or later, the pent-up emotion will burst forth for 'he who rides slowly also reaches his goal', according to peace-loving Njál, and then the avenging blow will be duly struck. Characters in sagas hatch plans for revenge against their enemies in silence and implement them despite all the dangers that may stand in their way: they are not held back even by the prospect of their own inevitable death.

The extreme restraint of the characters in sagas, and their reluctance to reveal their emotions and thoughts often give rise to behaviour that might appear inadequate. Grins or laughter occur at what appear to be unsuitable moments. Yet behind these lurk profound emotions and an unswerving determination to act.

Interest in the human personality was, of course, quite different from what we find today. In the sagas, personality is conveyed in an extremely vague way, with blurred outlines as it were. In contrast to the 'atomic' interpretation of personality in a culture that is closer to us and easier to understand, the personality of the individual at that time was not so self-contained and not so sharply set apart from all other people. The individual is, however, quite clearly contrasted with 'outsiders' or strangers, with whom he is not linked by any ties of family, property or friendship. In relation to those people, the individual adopts a cautious stance that can easily shift to one of hostility: if the situation demands it, nothing can stop a man from attacking such people, from committing murder or other violent acts, for it is acceptable to deceive a stranger. Standards of behaviour when among 'outsiders' are expounded clearly and openly in *The Lesson of the High One*. The dividing line between oneself and 'outsiders' is defined in precise terms. In the sagas that dividing line is drawn in blood, blood that is easily shed in the endless skirmishes and feuds.

Relationships between the individual and 'his own kind' – with the members of his own family, with people who are linked to him through marriage or friendship – are on a completely different footing. To this inner circle there also belonged those who took in a child from the hero's family to bring him up, and to some extent dependants who were part of the household. The ties between a man and his 'own kind' were virtually inseverable: kinsmen were obliged to help one another in every possible way, to protect their relatives and to avenge them if they were killed or came to any harm. Within the circle of a man's 'own kind' dividing lines between individual personalities were far from clearly defined. Within that circle, the law of vengeance did not apply for to seek vengeance against a member of a man's 'own kind' was impossible and, for a Germanic hero who had suffered injury or insult, the thought that revenge was out of the question would be intolerable.

Njál and his sons perish in fire because Skarphedin and his brothers violated the rule that no blood might be shed within the circle of a man's 'own kind' by killing Höskuldr, whom Njál had taken into his care. Gísli cannot reconcile himself to the fact that his brother Thorkell refuses to give him the help he so sorely needs.

The contrast drawn between an individual and 'outsiders' is clearer and more sharply defined: a character in a saga is unable to set himself apart in this way from his 'own kind'. On the contrary, he is more likely to dissolve into their group. The individual is merely a link in the chain of generations. It is important to explain why the sagas are so thickly 'spiced' with genealogies. The genealogical lists mean nothing or very little to us but, for the Scandinavian of that period, they would without doubt have been scrutinized with great interest, for a similar genealogy of his own family was something with which he was intimately acquainted. Each name in one of these genealogies would have a story behind it for him, and some of those stories would have made their way into the sagas. As a result the genealogies in the sagas were highly revealing: now, though, it is difficult to reconstitute their meaning. Indication of a man's name, of the names of those who were linked with him through family or attributes served straightaway to characterize the individual in question, for his name would immediately classify him as part of a particular group, introduce him into the life of a particular locality, and serve as a reminder of events in which this man and his group had been involved.

According to the laws of Ancient Scandinavia, disputes over inheritance of land would be won by those who were able to list a particular number of generations of relatives who, in an uninterrupted line of descent, had owned the land in question. When preparing himself for a lawsuit against one Angantyr, Ottarr in *Hyndla's Poem* (*Hyndloljóa*) addresses questions about his ancestors to a female giant: according to the prophetess, his clan is enormous and can be traced back to the ancient heroes and even to the *Aesir* (gods). In this way, Ottarr himself is characterized, because the nature of a particular clan will be reflected in its individual members. 'Tell me who your ancestors are, and I shall know who you are' is how this idea might well be expressed by a character in Germanic sagas. Qualities of ancestors are transmitted to their descendants. It would be difficult to expect merits from those who have no lineage. Yet it would be equally unlikely to expect a villain or nonentity to appear in a noble clan. Sometimes an ancestor is quite simply reborn in one of his descendants. For that reason it was the custom to hand down names of a man's most illustrious ancestors so that, with the name of the dead man, his 'good fortune' might also be passed down to his young namesake.

Thus, we do indeed have before us individuals, and keen interest is constantly shown in them in the sagas. The individuals in the sagas, however, are historically concrete figures and very different from the individual, as found in modern Europe, which we consciously or unconsciously take as our model. The Scandinavian was part of a close-knit group and can be understood only as a member of that group. Consciousness is not of an individualistic variety: the mental categories used are those of a unit, the individual's own group: they look at themselves from outside as it were, through the eyes of society. They are incapable of reaching a different assessment of themselves from that which society metes out. References have frequently been made to the 'individualism' of characters in the sagas. From the above there emerge the tight limits of that 'individualism'.

Individuals continue to look at themselves through others' eyes, even in those situations when they have been placed outside the law, i.e. outside society. Even when in that predicament, they are not inwardly prepared to set themselves apart from the group. For a person to be declared beyond the law is a disaster and, in the sagas, there are cases when the individual who has fallen into disfavour refuses to set off into exile, even at the risk of death. After being placed outside the law, Gunnar had indeed made ready to leave Iceland when he then stops in his tracks and returns home. This scene in the saga is depicted in the following words: 'Just then Gunnar's horse stumbled and he had to leap clear from the saddle. He happened to glance up towards his home and the slopes of Hlidarend. "How lovely the slopes are," he said, "more lovely than they have ever seemed to me before, golden cornfields and new-morn hay. I am going back home, and I will not go away."' (*Njáls saga*, 75). This is not a question of rapture in the face of Nature, which would be quite out of character for the medieval Icelander, but an outward form allowing the hero to express his inability to tear himself away from 'his own kind' and his reluctance to submit to his enemies: contemplation of the beauty of his homeland merely provides the trigger that enables Gunnar to take a decision. Gísli is also outcast from society and not merely on the strength of a decision by the *Thing*, but also as a result of sorcery: it has been decreed by society that it is impossible for him to remain anywhere in Iceland. Yet, for a long time, he clings desperately to his homeland, hiding on the islands and skerries of its outer fringe.

Constituted in this way, the individual cannot exist as a person of value outside the group to which he or she belongs. Yet remaining in his homeland is not enough – to feel he is of value, it is essential for a man to uphold and to consolidate his integrity, his self-respect, in other words, to enjoy the recognition of the group. Yet this recognition need not merely to come from 'his own kind' but to be universal. When a man has suffered a slight, either moral or physical, or when his property has been encroached upon, then his merit and value as an individual are immediately under a shadow. These situations, when an individual's inner sense of well-being has been undermined and he then, with the help of various specific steps, regains that sense of well-being and harmony for himself and his entourage, are the very stuff of sagas.

It could be maintained that the saga is a tale of how balance in life is disrupted. Then an insuperable urge to re-establish that balance arises – above all on an emotional plane – to satisfy the individual's deep psychological need to preserve his integrity and once again to attain the state where he can feel satisfied with himself and his social entourage. For this balance to be re-established, it is imperative first to wreak vengeance and subsequently to achieve reconciliation. An act of vengeance was not seen as some primitive act to satisfy blood-lust, but as a means to restore the avenger and his kin to a full life within society, to free him and them from the unbearable pressure of their sense of hurt and degradation stemming from the loss of a kinsman and the disruption of harmonious relations between the individual and the group.

The hero of a saga, whose interests and well-being have been undermined as the result of a hostile onslaught, is filled with a deep sense of depression. Relief from this is achieved only when he has obtained due compensation, which provides material expression for recognition of the hero's social worth, or after lawful vengeance has been won that re-establishes the hero's honour and value in the eyes of the group and indeed in his own. Vengeance that the hero wreaks successfully and boldly, restores self-respect to the individual concerned. Hávardr, whose son has been killed, lies robbed of his strength on his bed for a whole year: he is suffering not only from sorrow, but also from a sense of profound moral hurt. The failure of two attempts to obtain compensation for the death of his son convinces Hávardr that happiness has deserted him and, altogether, he spends three years in bed. When at last a chance to wreak vengeance presents itself, his kinsmen cannot believe their eyes: the human ruin is transformed into an energetic youth! (*Hávardar saga Isfirdings*).

Gudrún loves Kjartan but is not destined to be united with him: devoured by jealousy, she makes sure that her husband Bolli, Kjartan's friend, kills him. On learning that Kjartan has been slain, Gudrún goes out to meet Bolli as he returns and asks what time of day it is. Bolli replies that it is already past noon. Then Gudrún states: 'We have accomplished great deeds: I succeeded in spinning yarn for twelve ells of cloth and you have slain Kjartan' (*Laxdæla saga*, 49). Those words conceal a complex maze of contradictory emotions, but one thing is immediately clear: acts of vengeance are always referred to, as in this instance, with the phrase 'great deed'.

The fact that the final goal of strife is to re-establish shattered harmony is made clear by the scrupulous care with which the two sides in any conflict calculate and evaluate the loss they have inflicted on each other: the number of dead men, their degree of breeding, the respect they enjoyed, the nature of the wounds inflicted, the size of compensation received. These calculations, carried out as if by a careful auditor, are dictated by the parties' concern to make sure that moral injury is adequately compensated. The calculations are an indication of social prestige. The main issue at stake is not the material wealth that will be transferred from one party to another, from the slayer to the relatives of the person who has been slain. Suffice it to say that, in a number of Germanic codes of laws (*leges barborum*), we come across scales of compensation for a murder, a wounding or other damage, based on the so-called principle of 'active gradation' (*Aktivstufung*). The scale of this compensation grows according to the noble status of the person who has committed the crime, so that the persons of highest rank pay the largest amounts of compensation. The social assessment of the individual is taken into consideration, not only when he receives compensation, but also when he pays it, and for this reason, the nobleman who might insist that he should pay the maximum amount was thereby confirming his noble rank and social influence.

There is another 'figure' in the sagas, which is constantly either melting into the background or looming forward to the forefront of attention, but is always present in the minds of the saga heroes. This figure is Fate. As has been mentioned earlier, Fate for the Germans and Scandinavians was not *fatum* standing above the world and handing out rewards and punishments blindly, with no care for the identity of the recipients. Each person had his or her own fate or destiny, in other words an individual measure of good fortune and luck. It was possible for people to judge to what extent a person was lucky or unlucky from that person's behaviour and even from his appearance. The individual could know what his or her fate was. When Skarphedin is told by a number of individuals, who had not come to any agreement with one another in advance, that, to judge from his appearance and habits, he was unlucky and not blessed by fortune, that happiness would soon desert him and he did not have much longer to live, he knows there is nothing he can do about it. If he rails against those who speak of his 'misfortune', it is only because that will give them grounds for not helping him. On one occasion he admits himself that he is unlucky, when he replies to Gudmundr's gloomy prediction with the words: 'We are both men of ill luck, each in his own way' (*Njáls saga*, 119).

The acts of some individuals reap favourable consequences while those of others, including people of value, turn out unsuccessfully and lead to their downfall. How can this be explained? The sagas provide no clear idea of reasons why an individual should be lucky or unlucky. On the one hand, the individual's character is the source of the deeds he or she carries out, and therefore good fortune or misfortune can be seen to depend upon that individual. On the other, however, even the wisest and most astute of heroes in the sagas suffer defeat on numerous occasions and perish. Then it looks as if a man's fate does not depend on his individual qualities. 'Merit is one thing, and good luck another' (*Grettis saga*, 34). Yet there are unlucky people who bring unhappiness to those with whom they associate. One such is Hœnsa Thórir, hero of the saga which bears his name. Admittedly, he is not just unlucky but also an evil man to boot. There are also lucky people, who bring good fortune to others. A person of this kind was known as a *gæfumadr* – 'he who possesses happiness and good fortune and takes them with him wherever he goes'. Thus, good fortune is represented as something within an individual and also outside and independent of that individual. Yet an important consideration is the following: a person should not rely on personal good fortune; it must be actively experienced: 'We do not know how things look with regard to our good fortune, until we put it to the test'; 'it is not easy to change what has been decreed by Fate' but it is nevertheless necessary to fight on to the end (*Hrólfs saga kraka*).

Njál can serve as an example of a man who suffers misfortune in his clash with Fate despite his outstanding qualities. This wise and careful man seeks to avoid conflict and goes out of his way to resolve it. When he is first introduced into the saga, Njál is described by the author as follows: 'He was so skilled in law that no-one was considered his equal. He was a wise and prescient man. His advice was sound and benevolent.' (*Njáls saga*, 20). Indeed, all this is borne out later on: Njál is more keenly aware than other people of the logic of the events unfolding around him, yet he understands no less clearly that he is not in a position to change that course of events. Thus, his wisdom consists not so much in the prudence that helps him to avoid Evil, as in his grasp of what is inevitable. It is probably for this reason that his efforts are directed not towards dissuading his bellicose sons from taking part in a feud, but towards avoiding any acceleration of events. While approving the acts of vengeance undertaken by his sons and servants without any hesitation, Njál can foresee the tragic outcome of the mounting tide of murders for himself and for his kin. Njál concentrates his efforts on ensuring that the unavoidable vengeance be wrought in conditions as propitious as possible for his family. He reasons that the enemies who mock him and his sons are foolish men: therefore, it is necessary to take action only when those enemies are seen to be at fault. He points out to his sons that that is why they have to cast such a wide net and go on pulling at it for a long time until they drag out a fish.

It might seem as if Njál himself was creating circumstances and bringing his influence to bear on the course of events. Yet, if we take a closer look, then it emerges that all Njál's advice, despite what we might expect, leads in one way or another to disaster. He is powerless to avert Gunnar's downfall, or the slaying of his favourite ward Höskuldr, in whom he had hoped to find a guarantee of pacification: Höskuldr, too, perishes at the hands of Njál's sons.

It may be that, in these cases, it was impossible to anticipate the tragic course of events. Perhaps. Let us turn, though, to the scene in *Njáls saga* which is the key moment in the unfolding of the central conflict and, as I see it, for our understanding of the idea of Fate in the sagas as a whole.

First Episode

After the death of Höskuldr, Njál succeeds despite everything in achieving reconciliation at the *Althing*: an enormous sum of compensation is agreed upon for the slain man, the money is collected and is available to be paid over straightaway to Flosi and his relatives. Njál thought that 'our case has found a happy solution' and merely asked his sons 'not to spoil' what had been achieved. Njál laid out a long silk cloak and a pair of boots on top of the pile of money that was due to be paid to Flosi, who was looking on approvingly. Then, however, he took hold of the silk cloak and asked who had spread it out there. Nobody answered, although Njál was standing close by. Flosi again 'waved the cloak and asked who had given it, and laughed'. This laughter was ominous and promised evil things to come. Again nobody answered and at that moment an argument broke out between Flosi and Njál's son Skarphedin: fatal insults were exchanged and the reconciliation was over. What had been behind all this? Hallr explained it in these words: 'There are men of too much ill luck involved in this'. Njál, who had shortly before been counting on peace, said to his sons: 'I have long had the feeling that this case would go badly for us ... and so it has turned out ... it will end in disaster for everyone'. Similar presentiments had also troubled Snorri godi (*Njáls saga*, 123).

What was it, however, that necessitated the silken cloak and why should Njál, who had spread it out, not have admitted that he was responsible? In relation to the narrative as a whole, this appears illogical and incomprehensible. The general meaning would appear to be the following: the people concerned had not really wished to be reconciled (as is pointed out in another saga: accepting compensation for a murdered man is tantamount to 'holding a son in a purse' i.e. consider him despicable, like money). Yet, for this episode with the silken cloak and Njál's silence in response to Flosi's question, I can provide only one explanation: Fate is intervening and reshuffling all the cards. That which is due to happen cannot be averted. There is no logic to be found in the appearance of the silken cloak or in the silence regarding it, yet the intervention of Fate is always something irrational. This is the 'logic of fate', not the logic of human decisions, which could serve to avert something. Fate intervened here at the decisive moment, after which the deaths of Njál and his family are inevitable.

Second Episode

When the enemies approach Njál's house, Skarphedin suggests to the men that they should go out to meet them and engage in battle in front of the house, but Njál insists that they defend the house from inside, despite the fact that Skarphedin warns him that the enemies might not stop even at burning the house with them inside it. Yet Njál is a wise man, he can see more clearly than his son. How else can his blindness, fatal for himself and all his kin, be explained? They burn to death in the house which the enemies set alight. A possible explanation is that Njál was deliberately going out to meet his Fate, realizing it to be inevitable. On the very eve of the attack on Njál's house, his wife, Bergthora, said to all the members of her household, as she laid food out on the table, that she was feeding them for the last time. Njál himself has a vision of everything around him dripping with blood. Presentiments most evil! Yet nothing is done to avoid the catastrophe that is to befall the house. Once again an irrational decision is taken.

Do not these episodes in the sagas echo certain scenes from the Eddic poems, in which the hero acts in a way that is clearly irrational? It is impossible to conjoin the ethics of that heroic poetry and the ethics of the sagas, yet certain parallels are worth identifying: the hero's sudden, spontaneous decisions, that cannot be explained with reference to logic, lend both poems and sagas a new dimension. The subject of Fate is closely linked with insistence on the heroic principle.

In the two decisive episodes in the story of Njál his family, to which I referred, Fate cannot be averted. 'Non-fate' is a concept central to this saga, comments one of the scholars who made a study of it.[10] Fate forces its way through all human contrivances, wiping out plans and intentions. This is why the wisest and most far sighted of people cannot avert what has been decreed by Fate. King Olaf the Saint points out as much to Grettir, telling him that he is very unlucky and is unable to control his grim fate: 'You are a man condemned to misfortune'. Other characters in the saga also make mention of Grettir's bitter fate and, indeed, Grettir himself does not contradict what they have to say.

Fate, which occupies such an important place in the sagas, is a key concept for the whole of Germanic epic literature. It lends the narratives enormous tension and dynamism. The idea of fate serves to explain the significance of conflicts between people, and makes clear the inevitability of various deeds and what they will lead to. Sometimes it assumes material guise in the form of objects, which bring their owners luck, or rob them of that luck if they are lost. Examples of such objects are the cloak, spear and sword that are given to Glúmr by his grandfather: Glúmr's kinsfolk attached great faith to these objects but, as soon as he lost them, Glúmr also lost his good fortune (*Viga-Glúms saga*).

In the sagas, Fate appears as a link, as the logic behind human actions dictated by moral inevitability: yet this logic of behaviour, which is of a subjective, individual variety, is perceived, and indeed depicted, as something objective and inevitable that does not depend on human will and to which people have to submit. A sense of global determinism is inherent in human consciousness in this epic literature. This, in its turn, finds expression in the idea of Fate.

Closely linked with the theme of Fate are prophecies, visions and dreams anticipating the future. They lend a structural unity to the narrative and shed light on the hidden links between events and how these predetermine each other, and also on the way in which these events were viewed by the people of the ancient past. The unexpected was not appropriate to the saga: the audience knew in advance what fate lay in store for the various characters. Yet, because this anticipation assumes the form of prophecy, it does not reduce tension and interest in the narrative but, on the contrary, intensifies them, for it is important to know exactly how that which has been ordained will come to pass.

The subject of Fate and people's knowledge in advance of what the future holds in store for them predominates in the poems of the *Edda*. The awareness of the Ancient Icelanders was 'stereoscopic': they responded to heroic legends against the background of their own life or the life of their ancestors and, at the same time, they viewed their everyday life from the perspective of the heroic ideals and images taken from Eddic poetry. There was a level of imagination in the consciousness of the Ancient Scandinavians that could be traced back to the heroic *plusquamperfectum*: the images and motifs latent within this exerted an undeniable influence upon their behaviour.

Egill Skallagrimsson: Skald and Werewolf

Egill son of Skalla-grimr (Grim the Bald) was the most famous of the northern skalds. It was not for nothing that a whole long saga was dedicated to him, in which his verses are quoted. Thanks to this we are able to acquaint ourselves with his life, and to understand how the work and the personality of this skald were viewed in the early thirteenth century when the saga was written. Yet Egill's poems are much older than the saga: he lived in the tenth century, between approximately AD 910 and 980. He, like other skalds, composed his poems orally and they were written down over 200 years later. Nevertheless, there is good reason to believe that this verse, at least Egill's

long poems, survived in the oral tradition in what was for the
main part their original state. The intricate forms of skaldic
poetry stood in the way of the kind of transformation which
folklore and epic poetry usually undergo: the syllabics, the
predominance of kennings or condensed metaphors, internal
rhymes and alliteration, and the interweaving of one phrase
with another. Another feature which deserves particular
attention is that, unlike the anonymous epics and sagas whose
authors as a rule were not named, skaldic poems do have
individual named authors. It would never have occurred to the
Icelanders or Norwegians of the Middle Ages to compose a
saga about a particular person, who wrote or recorded sagas,
yet several sagas have survived that tell of illustrious skalds.

The individuality of the skald and his 'rights of authorship'
were acknowledged. Only skaldic art would apparently have
been regarded as art of this kind. It would, however, be wrong
to imagine the skald as a professional poet engrossed in the
composition of poems. On the one hand, many Icelanders –
women and men, adults and children – were able in specific
situations to start speaking in verse. Usually this urge to
present what they had to say in the form of skaldic poetry came
over them at moments of great excitement or when it was
necessary to relay a specially important piece of news. To judge
from the abundant number of fragments of skaldic poetry that
have survived, Icelanders set store by poetry and understood
it well.

On the other hand, the skald, a person who turned particularly
frequently to poetry and mastered this art, was a warrior in the
service of a Norwegian or other northern king who, from time
to time, would compose poems. Thanks to his extolling of his
lord's martial exploits and other deeds, he enjoyed the lord's
favour and would receive rich gifts as reward for his poems.
The songs of praise composed by the skalds were highly
regarded for, not only did they serve to immortalize the king
concerned, but they also lent him the magic strength to extend
his power. No less effective were the skalds' songs of abuse
which could have the most disastrous effect on the reputation
of the man against whom they were directed, even so far as to
undermine his health and prosperity. Concern for reputation,

in the present and in respect of future generations, was inextricably linked with belief in magic and sorcery, which might also stem from skaldic poems.

Yet skaldic verse did not extol only the exploits of leaders: they might be composed for virtually any occasion. Time and time again a skald would tell of his own deeds and emotions in a poem. The range of emotions expressed was wide: hate and love, friendship and betrayal, grief and joy, threats and contempt, triumph and lewd abuse and finally self-glorification and praise of a skald's own ability within the field of poetry – the 'mead of giants' according to myth, that Odin had stolen from them and then given to the skalds as a reward. Moreover, in the poems of the skalds, the direct contact between poet and audience is clearly to be felt. His poems were not lyric messages to an unspecified recipient: the skald turns insistently and sometimes in a commanding tone to his audience and has particular people in mind. The songs of the skald were *ad hoc* poetry.

Therefore, the poetry of the skalds is emphatically and blatantly personal poetry and, in this respect, it is radically different from the epic variety. The skald often proudly refers to his creative gifts. A far from insignificant proportion of skaldic verse is dedicated to the poet's contemplation of his own work: skalds extol their own poetic ability or discuss and criticize poems by other skalds. 'Listen to my poem, O King,' the skald Sigvat exhorts King Olaf son of Harald, 'for I am skilled at composing verse and even if you, ruler of Norway, ever did berate other skalds, you will praise me'. Twenty years later he was again to write: 'Those who understand poetry will find only few weaknesses in the verse of Sigvat and anyone who insists on the contrary is, without doubt, a fool'. To some extent it could be said that skaldic poetry is none other than a poetic commentary on the poet himself.[11]

The most prominent person in skaldic poetry is not some abstract or fictitious lyrical 'I', which need not necessarily be a mask for the poet's true personality,[12] but the actual poet himself, whose verse reverberates with a high degree of his awareness of himself as creator. 'I am called a skald', proudly declares one of the most ancient of the known skalds, Bragi the

Old (first half of the eleventh century); after listing a number of kennings (poetic devices alluding to the origin of poetry from the mead stolen by Odin from the giants), he concludes with the rhetorical question: 'What is a skald if not that?'

In this connection it is necessary to call attention to another important fact: this tendency to accentuate the personal, which was clearly visible in skaldic poetry from its very beginnings, did not increase with the passing of time (as might well have been expected) but, on the contrary, declined as a result of Christian influence that was pushing it into the background. The demand for personal humility impeded the development of preoccupation with the Individual. It was precisely during the twelfth century, the century of the 'discovery of the individual' in Europe (according to one widespread point of view) that the self-revelation of the skald came up against this ideological hurdle.[13]

In *Egills saga* the personality of the skald and a specific appraisal of his work are presented with exhaustive clarity. To start with, it is indicated that Egill came from a family that was not only of noble blood but that also possessed certain distinctive characteristics. Egill's grandfather and father were clearly perceived by the audience of the day to have been werewolves: as dusk began to fall they acquired extraordinary physical strength but, at the same time, came over sleepy and sought to avoid the company of other people. There were good grounds for calling Egill's grandfather Ulfr, Kveld-Ulfr (Evening Ulfr). In battle, fury took hold of him so that he resembled a Berserk,[14] and he acquired supernatural strength. In addition, these mysterious properties continued to manifest themselves after his death. Kveld-Ulfr was overtaken by death on board a ship, on which he was sailing to Iceland with his family and members of his household (like many other noblemen, he left Norway at the time when her king embarked on unifying the country and stripping the nobles of their former independence). Before his demise, Kveld-Ulfr commanded that he should be placed in a coffin and dropped overboard: like a pilot, the coffin showed the travellers where they should land and settle. With reference to his son Skalla-Grimr, Egill's father, the Norwegian king, was known to have said: 'From the appearance

of this bald giant it is clear that he is full of wolves' thoughts':
in a similar vein, another character commented, after observing
Skalla-Grimr and his men: 'In build and appearance they are
more like giants than ordinary men'.

Egill himself had attracted attention since his childhood
because of his unusual height and enormous strength, and also
because of his wild and unbridled disposition. Once, when he
had grown angry during a game, he had killed a playmate. Yet,
at the same time, his skill at composing poetry also made itself
known. It is interesting to note, however, that initially this skill
was closely bound up with his excursions into the world of
magic: while reciting the first poem he had written, Egill carved
runes on to the horn from which he had been drinking beer,
and stained them with his own blood promptly shattering the
horn into smithereens. This close link between poetry and
sorcery was to make itself felt on a number of occasions. While
at odds with the Norwegian King Eirikr and his wife the
sorceress Gunnhildr, Egill fixed a horse's head on to a pole and
pronounced a curse, calling down all manner of calamities on
the royal couple. The sorcery duly took effect and Eirikr was
soon banished from Norway. Yet the magic powers of
Gunnhildr would appear to have been no less effective because,
thanks to her, Egill was to fall into the hands of King Eirikr,
when the latter began to rule in Northumbria (in the north-east
of England). He managed to save his skin only thanks to the
poem, in which he praises his enemy, that he composed in a
single night, and the poem is in fact called *Ransom for a Head*.
Although Egill was accused of killing his close kinsmen, the
king granted him his life, because the song of praise he had
written would, in the words of his friend Arinbjörn, 'endure for
ever'.

Egills saga presents him as a man possessed of remarkable
physical strength and powers of endurance, yet most ugly in
appearance.[15] The phrase 'enormous like a troll' was used of
him just as it had been of his father. He was invincible in battle
and cruel towards his enemies. This courageous warrior would
launch into unequal combat without hesitation and he would
emerge without fail as the victor. He was a greedy man,
tenacious in his efforts to gain wealth. He relied only on his

own strength but always alluded to his rights and to the law which he was allegedly upholding. When sword and spear did not produce the necessary results, he was capable of knocking down his foe and tearing out his throat with his teeth.

Yet this merciless slayer of men and rapacious Viking was also deeply emotional. When he caught sight of a girl whom he wished to win for his own, he lost his peace of mind and could only regain it after composing verse. He poured his feelings into his verse and addressed the girl in code, and, later gained her consent and that of her father. Reference will be made later to the deep grief he experienced after the death of his sons.

In my opinion, it is the final scene of this saga which makes it perfectly clear that Egill was held to be an unusual creature akin to a troll or werewolf. Soon after Egill's death, the Icelanders adopted Christianity and they built a church at the spot where he had spent his old age and died: moreover, from beneath the altar, the skeleton was dug up of a man whose bones were far larger 'than ordinary human bones, and people are confident that these were Egill's because of the stories told by old men'. The priest, 'a man of great intelligence', took up Egill's skull, that was unusually large and heavy, and resolved to test just how thick it was: he tried to cleave it with an axe, but the skull did not even dent or crack: 'from that anybody could guess that the skull would not be easily cracked by small fry while it still had skin and flesh on it'. There is no denying that to take an axe to a dead man's skull is a somewhat strange undertaking for a priest! Here the negative view Christians held of men who smacked of wolves or giants as did Egill, his father and grandfather, comes clearly to the fore.

Skalds, or at any rate those such as Egill, were linked with the world of Utgardr, the outer world of giants and monsters, that stood opposite the human world. It is surely appropriate to recall here that the poetic gift of the skald was, according to Scandinavian myth, derived from the mead of giants, from whom it had been seized by Odin? Egill is regarded as the most remarkable and ingenious of the Icelandic skalds. At the same time, he was viewed as an unusual creature, so out of the ordinary that demonic traits were ascribed to him. The saga telling of Egill has naturally come down to us after undergoing

Christian 'editing', and it is quite possible that certain traits of his character were highlighted as a result.

How much weight should we attach to the description of Egill's behaviour and appearance at the feast provided by the English king Aethelstan in the *Adalsteinns saga*, after the death of Egill's brother who, like Egill, had fought in the service of Aethelstan? (Let us note in passing that the description of the saga's hero is not provided until the fifty-fifth chapter where, as we shall soon see, it has a specific function to perform.)

> Egill had a large face, a wide forehead, bushy brows, a short nose, but the very fat lower part of his face was enormous and the chin and cheek-bones were wide in the extreme. He had a thick neck and powerful shoulders. He stood out among other men on account of his formidable mien and when angry he inspired fear.... While he sat there in Adalsteinn's chamber, one brow was lowered right down as far as his cheekbone, while the other was raised up to the roots of his hair. Egill had dark eyes and brows that met in the middle above them. He did not drink when horns were brought to him, but kept raising and lowering his eyebrows.

After noticing Egill's unfriendly mood, King Adalsteinn rose and held out towards him over the burning hearth a sword on the end of which there hung a costly bracelet. Egill went over to the hearth straightaway and accepted the gift. When he had put on the bracelet, his brows were no longer knit in a frown: laying down his sword and helmet he accepted the drinking horn that had been brought to him and drained it. After that he recited a poem which extolled the king's generosity. Two chests of silver were presented to him in compensation for his brother's untimely death.

These men might appear like big children: as soon as they are given gifts, their moods improve and they forget about losses inflicted upon them. Yet this is only a superficial impression. They are far from being either children or simpletons. Their sense of balance and harmony lost as a result of a kinsman's

death, of infringement of their rights or of material loss is
restored to them when they are granted compensation. Gifts
and compensation presented publicly symbolize the restoration
of their self-respect and their respect from the group of which
they are a part. When Egill is given a bracelet his brows are
released from their formidable frown: once more he is able to
drink and to feast. In addition to all that, his poetic gift once
more comes into its own.

Wherein lies Egill's poetic gift? To what extent is this gift
truly individual? Is it possible through Egill's verse to penetrate
the secrets of his personality? The answer does not come easily.

Skaldic poetry belongs to a culture so different from our
own that an immediate aesthetic response to it is impossible.
The verses of the skalds, saturated with kennings and
conventional poetic names, constitute 'puzzles' that the modern
scholar has to solve not just read. It is difficult to penetrate as
far as the true feelings behind these poems to the immediate
emotional experience of the skalds, and still more so to the
poet's inner world. Regardless of who the individual poet
might have been, the skald would be referred to as a 'tree of
battle' (i.e. warrior), or, even if he was not a hero by any stretch
of the imagination, as a 'cowardly tree of battle': the kennings,
'crusher of riches' or 'bush of riches', could be used to refer to
poor men and so on. A ship would be referred to as a 'horse of
the sea'; a battle as a 'storm of spears'; blood as the 'sea of a
sword', the 'wave of a battle', a 'raven's beer', a 'wolf's drink';
a raven as a 'goose of blood'; gold as 'fire of the sea'; the sea
as the 'house of eels' or the 'path of whales'; a prince as a
'crusher of rings' and a woman as a 'birch bracelet' or a 'lime
bench'. Many of the kennings incorporate mythological images
and characters, and then a man might be referred to as 'Tyr of
the Helmet' or 'Njordr of the Treasure', while a woman might
be designated as 'Gerdr of the Gold' (*Gulls Gerdr*): there was
an enormous number of similar mythological kennings used to
refer to women, and what is interesting to note in this connection
is that these particular kennings never contain any allusion to
a woman's external appearance.

The above examples are relatively simple kennings consisting
of a mere two words. Yet there were others that were more

complex. The designation for gold – 'flame of the hand' – could be used to make up a three-word kenning for a woman 'Freja flame of the hand' or for a man 'Baldr flame of the hand'. A sword might be referred to as 'ripper of Fenrir's jaw' (after he had been bound, Fenrir the world wolf had a sword thrust into his mouth, and it would have to remain there until the 'sunset of the Gods', i.e. until the end of the world). Still more cumbersome kennings can be encountered: a warrior or man might be referred to in one of these poems as a 'flame-thrower in the storm of the moon-witch's horse from the ship-yards'. A seven-part kenning like this needs to be unravelled from its end backwards: a 'horse from the ship-yards' is a ship; a 'moon of a ship' is a shield; a 'witch's shield' is a poleaxe; a 'storm of a poleaxe' is a battle; 'flame of battle' is a sword and a 'sword-thrower' is a man. Long kennings like this consisting of many different words are rare, but skaldic poetry brims over with kennings of varying degrees of complexity and so the question still remains: how can we penetrate beyond conventional symbols of this sort to reach the individual poet?

Yet try we shall. . . . Apart from individual lines that are not interconnected (and whose authorship is dubious), which Egill pronounces on specific occasions, long poems have survived. Turning points in the life of the skald brought them into being. The first of these is *Ransom for a Head* that has already been mentioned. According to the saga, Egill composed that poem in the course of a single night and the next morning recited it to King Eirikr. In view of the great skill with which it has been composed – in it for the first time in the history of the poetry of Ancient Scandinavia rhymes at the end of lines are used – some scholars assume that the poem had been prepared in advance in Iceland and merely adapted at the last moment to be recited in Eirikr's honour. Indeed, *Ransom for a Head*, like many other songs of praise composed by skalds, extols the exploits of the ruler to whom it is addressed, and, so that it might be used on a variety of occasions, its content is non-specific. This feature of *Ransom for a Head* has even been interpreted as a sign of deliberate disguised irony in relation to King Eirikr.

After Egill has avoided reprisals, he returns home and

composes another poem in honour of his friend Arinbjörn, thanks to whom he was able to avoid death while in the domains of King Eirikr. In this poem he praises the loyalty, courage and magnanimity of his friend. Yet here, as in his other poems, Egill does not forget himself, the great skald, who is proud of his poetic gift. The *Song of Arinbjörn* ends with the words: 'I pile the praise-stones. / The poem rises, / My labours is not lost, / Long may my words live'. These words can be interpreted as an expression of pride at the immortal nature of Egill's creative feat, and Georg Misch, who devoted an inspired essay to Egill in his *History of Autobiography*, recalls Horace in this connection.[16] Yet it is possible to interpret these words in another way as well: 'the praise-stones' can relate to Arinbjörn and his posthumous reputation. There is no reason, surely, why this should rule out the poet's proud self-awareness?

The ruthless Viking and the refined court poet, the murderer and the loving father, the man yearning for gifts and wealth and the loyal friend – these are the contradictions that make up Egill, as he is presented in his poems. What we have here is, of course, no ordinary 'autobiography' – something Egill would not have even contemplated – yet nevertheless the outline of his personality, complete with its various aspects that sometimes appear contradictory, does emerge to some extent from his poetry and from the saga that has been devoted to him. Moreover, what appear to us as contradictions in his personality are unlikely to have done so to him.

The work which is Egill's crowning achievement, and which gave the fullest expression to his inner world, is his last major poem, *Lament for My Sons*. When approaching old age, Egill lost his favourite son, his first-born Bodvarr: in the prime of life Bodvarr drowned in the sea during a shipwreck. After laying him to rest in a burial-mound next to his own father, Egill returned to his home at Borg and locked himself in a small chamber, where he used to sleep. Not a single member of the household dared to talk to him, but they could hear how deeply Egill was sighing and how his tunic and hose burst apart because he was so swollen. Egill refused all food and drink and he had no wish to go on living. The family informed his daughter, who lived separately from the rest of the family, and she made haste to reach Borg. Trickery enabled her to gain entry to her father's chamber, for she declared that she wished to die with him. She used her cunning once again to make him drink milk. Next she succeeded in persuading him to go on living so that he might compose a dirge in memory of his dead son, and she promised to carve it in runes on to a tree. Egill succumbed to her persuasiveness and began to compose the poem and the more he composed, the stronger he grew. Soon Egill was restored to health and was merry and cheerful in spirit. Turning back to his poetry restored him as a well-balanced individual.

In this poem Egill recalls all the close kinsmen he has lost – father and mother, brothers and sons. He mentions the fact that his son was a loyal support to him. It is difficult, however, to avoid the impression that the personal emotion of the father towards his son derives from a more general attitude to a man's own kin viewed as a united group. All the losses Egill has suffered made unbridgeable gaps in the solid fence surrounding his home – that was how Egill viewed his family. The poem does not finish on that note, however, and Egill turns to Odin: he had trusted him until Odin had betrayed him and taken away his son. If Egill had had enough strength he would have taken vengeance on the god of the sea for the loss he suffered but, by now, he was old and weak. Egill had no further desire to be seen in public and nothing brought him joy any more, for it was not easy to find a friend in whom a man could really trust. Nevertheless there was one gift from the gods which made up for every calamity – his ability to compose and recite impeccable verse, and precisely this poetic self-awareness gave Egill strength to await his own end without complaints. The second of the two themes touched upon in this poem – the loss of his sons and then the emotions experienced by the skald as a result of that disaster – took precedence over the first to such an extent that it came to constitute its main subject matter. Even for those who agree that respect for tradition and the choice of topic here are most important, it would still be difficult to deny that the poet's attention is focused above all on himself, his poetic gift and his creations.

Sad thoughts called forth by his life that is now drawing to an end fill certain other scattered verses quoted in the last chapters of *Egill's Saga* (incidentally, their attribution to Egill is not accepted by all scholars). The old man is tired of time that passes so sluggishly. In his old age Egill is physically weak and blind: in his verses can be heard a note of complaint at his own powerlessness and at the women of his household who have driven him from the hearth where he would like to warm his feet ('I walk on two widows . . . needing the old flames').[17] In another poem he laments the fact that his weakness makes him stumble even on flat ground.

How can all these signs of faint-heartedness be reconciled with Egill's intention to set off to the *Althing* not long before his death to cast down from the Rock of the Law the silver coins that had been given him in the past by the English king? Egill is comforted by the thought of the tremendous fighting there would be over those treasures! Egill's relatives managed to persuade him to abandon this ridiculous scheme but, immediately afterwards, he lit upon another way of disposing of his silver. After loading the two chests of coins on to horses with the help of slaves, he took them to a distant ravine, after which he returned without the chests and without the slaves. It became clear to all that he had hidden the silver in the ground or in hot springs and killed the slaves, so that no witnesses should remain alive. It appeared that from time to time mysterious powers came over the old man, powers that had not abandoned him throughout his life as a warrior and Viking.

The combination of the saga and Egill's own verses helps us to understand him as an individual and, and at the same time, complicates our understanding of him. The saga and verses help us insofar as inclusion of excerpts from Egill's poems into the series of events that make up his life brings us a more rounded, complete picture of the poet: we see him 'from outside' and 'from inside' at the same time. The combination complicates the situation because the saga and the poems belong to different eras, and it is impossible to be sure that the saga of the Christian thirteenth century did not influence the presentation of Egill's deeds, deeds of a man who had lived in the pagan tenth century. It is, however, important that Egill's poetry should appear in the saga as an integral part of his life, closely linked with his deeds and rendered comprehensible precisely because of this link.

The tone of the poem *Lament for My Sons* is somewhat different, for wholly understandable reasons. Egill is an old man who has already lived out his life: the Viking raids and battles, the feasts, the exchanges of gifts and the respect which he enjoyed at court on the one hand and the dangers which he bravely overcame on the other are all now behind him. The ideal of the Scandinavian hero was to die young and in full possession of his powers, sword in hand: the finest death was death in battle, after which a man would immediately set forth to Valhöll and to Odin, where the feasts and duels would begin once more. No such heroic end was in store for Egill: he lived to a great age and to know extreme weakness. Naturally he could not fail to sense this humiliation, to be aware of his physical weakness and the fact that he was no longer useful to those around him: this feeling of being superfluous became all the more acute after the untimely death of his sons. Consolation for the old man would have been to see his line continue and go from strength to strength, but Egill was to be deprived even of this comfort. Hence the sense of weariness and despair that permeates his last poem.

Perhaps it was precisely these sombre emotions that first gave Egill the idea of going to the *Althing* and provoking a fight between its members, by casting before them his silver? Yet Egill selects a different way of using his wealth: he hides it carefully in an uninhabited part of Iceland. This way of disposing of his treasures, that had been granted him by the English king, was more in keeping with the needs and hopes of pagan Egill. After all, according to Scandinavian beliefs, precious objects received from a ruler (coins, rings, weapons) were the tangible expression of the 'good fortune', 'luck', or 'happiness' that rendered a king 'rich', and his trusty warriors or skalds, on whom he bestowed such gifts, could, through them, enjoy part of their ruler's 'good fortune'. After hiding Adalsteinn's silver and placing it out of reach for any man alive, Egill made sure of his own 'luck' in the world beyond the grave: such a deed was particularly important in his case because he was condemned to a 'death on straw' rather than a death in battle.

So even in his ripe old age Egill remains true to himself, to his Viking ideals and to the values that were intrinsic to his age. After securing for himself glory after death through the poems he had composed, and a place in Valhöll thanks to his treasure, Egill had every reason to be able to wait for his death peacefully.

If we look further ahead now and compare the personality of Egill, son of Grim the Bald, as it emerges from his own poems and from the saga dedicated to him, with descriptions of the personalities of writers from the unmistakably Christian period later on, then we can say that the personality of this skald does not appear fraught with inner contradictions like those characteristic of authors of confessions ('autobiographies') in the twelfth and thirteenth centuries. The individuals in the latter group – priests, philosophers, theologians – confront the Absolute and measure their own imperfections against their Lord's moral requirements, convincing themselves, as they do so, that they cannot escape from their own sinfulness and are thus condemned to inner confusion and spiritual torment. Only if they repent of their pride and of their inability to overcome their earthly passions and impulses, will they be able to stand firm: Christian ethics condemns the individual to inner struggles, from which he or she cannot emerge as the victor. The texts left behind by these authors tell us, not so much about the outer framework of their lives, as about the psychological crises which they experience, crises of the solitary individual struggling to identify with the surrounding social world or with sacred models and prototypes.

There is no such ambivalence about Egill. He is ready to take risks and yet his personality has not been set apart from his clan group clearly enough for him to feel that he has been abandoned in an alien world. Egill acts, but does not ponder: to be more precise, he considers his actions *post factum*. He sets off on a Viking raid or to take part in a lawsuit, commits murders or acts of plunder, and then, after wiping his bloody sword or shaking drops of beer from his beard, he recites a skaldic poem in which he informs his audience of what has been accomplished, interpreting the deed concerned and incorporating it into a chain of inevitable events. It would not occur to him to make some feeble effort to justify or to explain his actions: he sets out to immortalize them. He does not doubt for a moment that they were justified or inevitable. While, for Christian authors, life and its generalized representation in literature are two separate things, for Egill they are one and the same. He is not confronted by a moral dilemma: he acts in accordance with a code of ethics transmitted to him by his clan or group, and he derives profound satisfaction from the fact that he is capable of carrying out the group's requirements in the most effective possible way. This is how he expresses himself as an individual, within the limits laid down by his own culture.

King Sverrir: stereotype or individual?

Sagas about Norwegian kings, which are historical works presented in the traditional format of the sagas, concentrate attention on rulers. Yet it would be a hopeless task to try to glean a picture of any king as an individual from them. The authors of the sagas depicted types, rather than living men, even when they added distinctive characteristics to the stereotyped portraits of certain of the kings. Although the sagas were written down in the twelfth and thirteenth centuries, they tell of Norwegian kings who lived in the eleventh and twelfth centuries. This time-gap did, to some extent, bring to the sagas an epic sense of distance and, in the sagas, most of the kings emerge as ideal heroes and warlords. The shorter the time between the period of the narrative and the composition of the saga, the greater the differentiation in characterization and the fewer clichés that are to be observed. Nevertheless, the only saga about kings which brings us an approximation of an individual is the *Saga of Sverrir* (*Sverris saga*) that tells of a usurper of the Norwegian throne.

Sverrir appeared in the historical arena in the 1170s when the internecine wars which had long gripped Norway were at their height. First of all, Sverrir led a band of *déclassé* poor peasants, known as 'Birchlegs' (*Birkebeiner*) because they had no shoes and wrapped their feet with birchbark: after a grim battle, he succeeded in overcoming King Magnus Erlingsson, the first of the Norwegian kings to have been anointed by the clergy. Sverrir succeeded in gaining the support of part of the peasantry and even in winning over to his side certain of the nobles, but his immediate support came from the *Birkebeiner* who, in the course of the war, achieved higher status after seizing lands and office that had previously belonged to supporters of King Magnus. From the ranks of the *Birkebeiner* there emerged servants of the new monarchy, who were elevated in status during the reign of Sverrir and his descendants. Sverrir died in 1202 without experiencing the end of the internal dissension, for it was only in the fourth decade of the thirteenth century, during the reign of his grandson, Hakon Hakonarson, that Norway's 'age of greatness' (*Storhetstid*) began.

It was also during that same period that most of the sagas about the kings were written. The earliest of these was the *Sverris saga*,[18] and work on this had started when Sverrir was still alive. As mentioned in the prologue of this saga, the first part was based on a work by the Icelandic abbot Karl Jónsson: 'and King Sverrir himself settled what he should write'. Later in the prologue we are told that the narrative had been provided by men who had been witnesses of battles or even taken part in them on Sverrir's side. Thus, it can be seen that the epic distance referred to before that was characteristic of narratives relating to kings of earlier periods was absent in this case. The *Sverris saga* was written in the immediate aftermath of events, which meant that the strong emotions and interests of Sverrir and his entourage. In the early sections of the saga, Sverrir's own voice can be 'heard' giving what to him appeared to be an accurate assessment of past events. Through that assessment we can also glean how he rated himself as man and ruler.

There is no doubt that, thanks to this particular saga, we know more about King Sverrir than about any other Scandinavian monarch of that time. Nevertheless it is difficult to glean a complete picture of him as an individual – there is much that escapes us. The medieval author concentrates on bringing out the general and recurring elements, that could make Sverrir appear as a type and model: the author was not inclined to record unique traits of the man and he was at a loss to know what to do with individual characteristics. The description of Sverrir's character at the end of the saga is no more than a panegyric: it is a string of superlatives, there are no shadows. We are presented with an ideal ruler, a man beyond reproach. He is clever, eloquent, restrained, calm; he has exquisite manners, is moderate in eating and drinking, capable of great bravery and endurance; cautious, astute and fair. The fact that he is secretive is seen as praiseworthy in a ruler. After his death his friends mourned him, and 'even those who had been his enemies declared that no man like Sverrir had appeared in Norway in their time' (Chapter 181). It is interesting to note that the English chronicler, who was hostile to Sverrir and had evidently obtained information about him from leading clerics in Norway (who had excommunicated Sverrir), nevertheless admitted that he had been a man of great good fortune and intelligence, merciful to his enemies and respectful towards churches and monasteries.

The hero of the saga is an outstanding personality. This unknown figure from the Faeroe Islands, who presented himself as the bastard son of a Norwegian king and who was unable to offer any proof other than his own assertions to demonstrate his claims to the throne, nevertheless overcame the protégé of the leading churchmen and nobles, Magnus Erlingsson, married a Swedish princess, and founded a dynasty that ruled Norway for the next 185 years. Everyone had been against him at first, yet Sverrir achieved such astonishing success that his enemies attributed it to the Devil, and Sverrir himself to divine intervention.

Although the *Sverris saga* presents the struggle within Norway mainly from Sverrir's own point of view rather than from that of his enemies, it does not actually contain any direct judgements. Abiding by the ban on the open expression of such judgements that was peculiar to this particular genre, the author(s) uses other devices to make clear his view of the events described and to lend the work the desired tone.

One of the most important tasks for this pretender was to establish his rights to the throne, rights rejected not only by

King Magnus and his entourage, but also by the majority of the
population. Closely bound up with this task was another
objective – that of discrediting his opponents. How was it
possible in the *Sverris saga* to maintain 'epic distance' and
accomplish the other tasks? Earlier it was pointed out how,
despite the apparent 'objectivity' of the narrative, the authors
of sagas had ways of making what should be concealed
obvious. First of all they could use dreams. In the first part of
the *Sverris saga*, written with the direct participation of the
king, a number of his dreams are related. They perform such
a vital function that it is necessary to look at them in more
detail.

According to the saga, Sverrir, in his youth, had known
nothing about the fact that he came from a royal line: his father
was held to be a comb-maker by the name of Unás, while
Sverrir himself had originally intended to take holy orders.
Later, according to Sverrir, his mother admitted during
confession after a pilgrimage to Rome, that his father had in
fact been the deceased king Sigurd Haraldsson, who had
perished in 1155. The Pope, who was informed of this
confession, allegedly gave instructions for Sverrir to be informed
of this secret. Sverrir was, however, unable to come forward
with any proof of his royal descent. In this respect, Sverrir's
dreams are particularly important, because they provide
pointers to divine approval.

First Dream

Sverrir sees something that is interpreted as a prophecy of his
great future. He dreams that he assumed the form of a bird,
whose beak touched the eastern border of Norway and whose
tail reached as far as the northern regions inhabited by Finns
and whose wings covered the whole land. The sage, whom
Sverrir asked to interpret this dream, found it difficult to give
a precise answer, but assumed that Sverrir would enjoy power
(Chapter 2).

Second Dream

According to his own testimony, Sverrir dreamt that he arrived in Norway to be made a bishop, but encountered 'feuding'. King Olaf the Saint, the great unifier of the land, who brought Christianity to its shores, died a martyr's death, and was numbered among the saints soon after his demise, was fighting then against King Magnus and his father, Erling. Sverrir gave his support to Olaf and was well received by the latter. Sverrir was the only man whom Olaf allowed to wash in the same water which he himself used, and he gave Sverrir the name Magnus. Then Olaf's enemies drew near and the king gave orders for his men to arm themselves and go out to fight, assuring them that he would protect them with his shield. He gave Sverrir his sword and standard. When one of the enemy tried to strike down Sverrir, Olaf protected him with his shield and Sverrir held the standard aloft. After that the troops of King Magnus Erlingsson retreated (Chapter 5).

According to that dream, Sverrir's rights to the throne of Norway stem not from his origin, of which no mention is made, but from quite a different source: he was the Chosen One of the 'eternal king' of Norway, Olaf the Saint, who had washed him in the water of his holiness, given him a new name, entrusted him with his sword and standard, and protected him with his own shield. If we recall that the son of King Olaf had been called Magnus, then Sverrir's plan is clear: he is the chosen heir of Olaf the Saint who was waging war against the son of Jarl (chieftain) Erling. Later Sverrir substantiated his opposition to the theocratic claims put forward by the Archbishop through references to the 'laws of Olaf the Saint'. Sverrir rejected the hereditary right to royal power and the claims of his rival Magnus Erlingsson, who had been placed on the throne by the leading churchmen and nobles of the land: instead he insisted on the right of divine selection, for God the Creator, naturally, stood behind Olaf the Saint. Sverrir was king with divine blessing – such was the import of this dream.

Third Dream

Sverrir dreams that he is in Borg, a town in the East of Norway. A rumour circulates to the effect that the son of a king is in the town and that everyone is looking for him. Sverrir knows that he is the man. During a service in church, a white-haired old man with a countenance that 'inspired great awe' comes up to him and reveals a secret to the effect that he, Sverrir, shall become king. The old man is none other than the Prophet Samuel and he had anointed the palms of Sverrir's hands with holy oil, so that they might be holy too and possess strength with which to pursue his enemies and rule the land. According to the saga, after that dream, Sverrir's 'disposition seemed . . . to undergo a great change' (Chapter 10).

All these dreams are concentrated in the first part of the saga, that was written down with the participation of the hero. While the dream with Olaf the Saint incorporates Sverrir into the history of Norway as a lawful and rightful descendant and heir of King Olaf, his anointing with holy oil by the biblical prophet gives Sverrir a place in sacred history. Sverrir's dreams are designed to shed light on his divine mission and make his rights appear beyond dispute. The saga includes other miraculous and prophetic dreams that came to Sverrir but there is no need to dwell on these in such detail.

In the text of the saga these dreams make an important contribution towards substantiating Sverrir's claims to the throne through references to God's will and to the fact that he has been chosen by God. While still in the Faeroes Sverrir was given a religious education and was known to be a man of vivid imagination and an inventive turn of mind. Sverrir's dreams were directed first and foremost at his entourage but, at the same, time he was anxious to appear fully armed before his most dangerous ideological opponents, namely the clergy. The priests would see in the story of the dream, in which the prophet Samuel figures, a parallel with King David who had been anointed as king by Samuel and who then overcame Saul, just as Sverrir proceeded to overcome Magnus Erlingsson. Both rulers – David and Sverrir – had been elevated by God from humble beginnings.[19] Sverrir introduces a comparison of

Saul and Magnus Erlingsson into a speech he delivers after the death of that king (Chapter 99).

The idea of Sverrir being chosen by God is presented in the saga for the most part as the main substantiation for his lawful right to the throne, but not exclusively in that light. It can be assumed that the author wants to convince his readers that Sverrir had been sanctified. Hints to this effect are to be found on several occasions in the saga. Both during his lifetime and after his death, Sverrir is depicted as God's chosen servant. Yet he is very definitely presented as God's chosen servant for Norway and, in the saga, every effort is made to underline the link between Sverrir and King Olaf the Saint who was a symbol of royal power and of independence for Norway. Sverrir acquired for himself the name Magnus, son of Olaf and he issued coins bearing the inscription 'Rex Sverus Magnus': he authenticated state documents in the name 'Sverrir Magnus king', i.e. 'Sverrir the Great' and his seal bore the name 'King Sverrir-Magnus'. In this way Sverrir is seen to have been resolved to appropriate a name which had already been used by a number of Norwegian kings, whereas the name Sverrir was plebeian and was never given to members of the aristocracy. His struggle to establish his power over the land was also a struggle to ensure that neither the papacy nor any neighbouring country should encroach upon Norway's sovereignty.

In other sagas about Norwegian kings, the author's stance does not make itself felt so pointedly and deliberately. Even in *Sverris saga*, though, this stance is mostly expressed indirectly. The courage and other virtues of Sverrir's enemies are not concealed from the reader, and the pretender himself acknowledges their merits in his speeches on more than one occasion. In these speeches Sverrir does not always refrain from mocking their negative qualities, but his sarcasm is veiled and cautious, while men from the camp of Erling and Magnus address coarse invective and curses at Sverrir and his *Birkebeiner*. The fact that Sverrir's enemies call him a usurper, murderer, heretic, tool in the hands of a sorceress or simply the Devil and a priest in the service of the Devil discredits the aristocrats concerned rather than Sverrir himself.

Sverrir's words testify to the fact that he was a clever and shrewd politician, who freely and skilfully selected the means for achieving his far-reaching aims. His speeches were probably composed when the saga was being written down and, insofar as *Sverris saga* was initially written with his participation or at least with that of his entourage, they deserve our attention: the speeches are not simply literary accessories, they reflect Sverrir's intentions. In the first place they are designed to spur on the fighting men in his service. When referring to the great hardship which he and his supporters had to endure in the course of the war against their enemies, Sverrir promises them rewards and booty if they prove victorious. Many of Sverrir's comrades-in-arms were indeed rewarded and elevated in rank. The former 'Birchlegs' retained the name associated with their former status but none of its other attributes.

Sverrir's speeches vary in their tone. Sometimes he comes over as extremely serious, but he does sometimes resort to jest, sarcasm and irony. In a speech delivered over the bodies of his slain enemies he declares: 'For, indeed, it is known to many that Archbishop Eysteinn and many other learned men have constantly said concerning all who die fighting for King Magnus and defending his land that their sons will enter paradise before their blood is cold upon the ground. We may here rejoice at the sanctity of many men who have become saints . . .' (Chapter 38) From this it is clear that, because of their subtlety and refinement, Sverrir's humour and sarcasm contrast sharply with the speeches we know from other sagas. The impression emerges that, unlike other Norwegians of the period, Sverrir (or the author of his saga) was capable of approaching a particular person or phenomenon from diverse points of view.[20]

Another category of speeches made by Sverrir includes those aimed at justifying the cause for which he is fighting and describing new situations resulting from his victories. In a speech to the men of Bergen and to peasants that he delivers after the funeral of Magnus Erlingsson, Sverrir mocks his enemies, who had thought he had allied himself to the Devil, and at the same time warns all those who hate him and wish him dead to be careful (Chapter 99). Sverrir is keenly aware that the era of his rule is a uniquely important moment in the history of Norway. Before him, power had been in the hands of the Archbishop, the Jarl and the King – his three main opponents, whom he has overcome. Sverrir goes on to point out that now 'times are greatly changed, as you may see, and have taken a marvellous turn, when one man stands in place of three – of King, of Earl, of Archbishop' (Chapter 38). Sverrir is aware of himself as a man standing at the very centre of historic events, a man who has changed the course of those events, and of his lofty destiny he has no doubt.

Sverrir was the first of the Norwegian rulers who had the idea of creating a saga about himself. There is little doubt that the logic of the struggle waged by this usurper of power led him to place himself in the forefront of the events described, yet he still had to substantiate his exclusive importance. Sverrir was not the 'herald of the New Age' and he did not 'shape his time' as historians of the nineteenth and twentieth centuries used to assert.[21] An individual personality could be revealed in the Middle Ages as well, yet it would manifest itself simultaneously on two planes. On the one hand a man was aware of his own ego and made that known while, on the other, he was bound to search out some prototypes with which he might compare himself, models that suited his individual character as it were. Both these manifestations of Sverrir's personality are to be found in his saga. Aware of his role in history, he makes loud assertions about himself and his exclusive importance, and, at the same time, he gives himself the new name of Magnus, goes out of his way to link his sacred ties with Saint Olaf, presents his biography according to biblical patterns so as give him himself much in common with King David, and, completely in tune with the spirit of the times, keeps referring to the will of his Creator.

All the traits of Sverrir's personality that have been noted thus far can be gleaned only from the text of the saga, and the question remains as to the degree to which his personality is actually revealed in the text or to which we are merely enjoying the literary talent of its author. The first is masked by the second and presented to us in refracted form in the saga. Yet Sverrir's personality is revealed not only through his oratorical skills, but first and foremost in the fact that he was a gifted and successful military commander. The proof of this is his victory over superior enemy forces achieved in the end by this unfrocked priest. At a time when Jarl Erling and his son were dependent on the military strength of the noble *lendir menn,* who supported them, Sverrir went out of his way to attract new men into his service, promoting those who distinguished themselves in battle.[22] In large measure, he owes his success to the changes which he introduced into military affairs. The first stone fortresses in Norway (in Nidaros and Bergen) were built on his initiative.

In Western Europe, the twelfth century was the heyday of the knighted class, and it was knightly cavalry that largely determined the outcome of a battle. In the terrain of Norway it was difficult for mounted knights to manoeuvre, and it was extremely expensive to maintain an army of heavily armed knights. Nevertheless, during Sverrir's time, the role of the cavalry became increasingly important and this lent a whole new dimension to the battles he fought. The closed formation of footsoldiers, the so-called 'pig', which marched forward into the attack as a wedge-shaped unit protected by shields, was the tactic regularly used by the Scandinavians; it proved to be far from effective, for such a formation had very little chance to manoeuvre and was not able to deter charges by heavy cavalry. Sverrir abandoned this tactic because it was virtually impossible to control during battle. He preferred to use small detachments that could manoeuvre much more easily. Their advantages were obvious and these were what enabled him to win a number of important battles.

The military reforms which Sverrir introduced resulted in a shift of emphasis in warfare from poorly disciplined and, at times, not very effective groups of fighting men (which were often resented by the peasants who were coerced into joining them) to detachments of professional soldiers. The role of the military commander during Sverrir's reign also changed. According to Ancient Scandinavian tradition, the main fighting unfolded around the king's standard. The king did not so much take charge of the course of the fighting as take upon himself the role of a symbol: fighting alongside the front ranks of his force, he had to provide an example of personal courage. The troops continued to fight for as long as they could see the king's standard: as soon as it fell – signifying that their leader had been killed – the ranks would crumble and all would take to their heels. The king actually embodied military 'luck', and his death in battle signified that this 'luck' had deserted the warriors. In certain situations Sverrir had to assume this role, in particular in a battle near Oslo in 1200, when he was leading a force against insurgent peasants. The position was so desperate that only the personal example of the king himself, fearless astride his horse, as he battled against the peasants, could encourage his comrades-in-arms, who had been demoralized by the unprecedented determination of the foe. When, at the end of the battle, one of the *lendir menn* was killed, and mistaken for the king, panic ran through the army and only the appearance of Sverrir himself, complete with the royal standard, could put an end to it (Chapter 165).

Sverrir did not usually lead from the front, but kept towards the rear and moved about the battlefield to control the fighting. Rather than taking a stand in one particular place, he preferred to oversee the whole campaign. This meant that, even if there were setbacks at the beginning of a battle which, in those days might well have sealed their fate, the *Birkebeiner* were still capable of launching counter-attacks. These tactical innovations, which Sverrir may have drawn from other countries, were important from a military and from a psychological point of view: they provided more scope for the initiative of individual men and lent the commander in battle new and enhanced importance.

Sverrir also introduced new tactics into warfare at sea. In the early Middle Ages the Scandinavians' battles at sea had usually involved two rows of ships, and the fighting men on each side tried to board the enemy's ships and 'purge' each one of its crew in hand-to-hand combat. The ships would be arranged in a single line and some of the vessels moving closely together would be tied together with ropes. This gave defenders more confidence but, at the same time, it deprived the fleet of mobility. Just like the 'pig' formation in land battles, the deployment of the fleet in battle left little room for initiative, and setbacks for one part of the fleet would, without fail, lead to defeat for one and all. Unlike King Magnus Erlingsson, Sverrir broke with tradition here too. He replaced what had clearly become obsolete tactics with others enabling individual ships to manoeuvre more independently.

From the above it is clear that to describe Sverrir as the conservative to outdo all conservatives, as did the English historian G. M. Gathorne-Hardy, is hardly apt. Innovation was not alien to him: Sverrir boldly embraced new ideas that held out the promise of success.

The institution of royal officials entrusted with the administration of specific regions and districts was something that took root in Norway during Sverrir's reign. These *syslo menn* were not from the ranks of the nobility: they were recruited from men loyal to the king and they assumed fiscal, military and legal functions. Sverrir's attitude to the Church and to the clergy also points to the independence of his behaviour: the leading clergy of the day had been opposed to Sverrir almost to a man. Sverrir had been excommunicated from the Church and a papal interdict had been pronounced against Norway. These measures, which had forced more than one powerful monarch of that period to give in, had no effect upon Sverrir.

What can probably be regarded as a further innovation, if we can trust the saga, is that Sverrir often and willingly showed mercy to his enemies, and to some of them on more than one occasion. It is not known whether he did this from a sense of mercy or out of political shrewdness but, in this respect, he differed strikingly from the kings of the period that preceded his reign, indeed, from Magnus Erlingsson himself, who always indulged in traditional vengeance.

The facts that Sverrir had come from beyond Norway's shores, was a man whom, to use his own words, God had sent from a far-off little island, and did not belong by blood or upbringing to the ruling élite of Norway, naturally meant that he did not observe as strictly the traditions which proved so binding for King Magnus and Jarl Erling. This failed priest turned out to be a more successful military commander, politician and organizer than the aristocrats before him. He was able to distinguish himself in Norway relying, to all intents and purposes, on nothing but his own talents and luck and on the help of reckless young stalwarts, the *Birkebeiner*. Yet he won through. His had been no easy victory: for a quarter of a century Sverrir had to wage war almost incessantly against the nobility, the Church and large sections of the country's population.

To assert himself as an individual and to achieve the goal he had set himself, Sverrir did something, the like of which had never been seen before: the saga which he had written not only shaped the view of him and his deeds held by future generations, but also had a decisive influence upon that part of the historiography of the New Age devoted to the interpretation of medieval Norway. Nevertheless, *Sverris saga* was not dictated, as Halvdan Koht would have us believe, by a spirit of party struggle (as were the *Speeches against the Bishops* written during his reign). This was the model for the 'royal saga', a genre which began to emerge in the time of Sverrir but which reached its peak later in the *Heimskringla* (*The Orb of the World*).

There is no doubt that it was easier for an outsider to reveal himself as an individual and to emerge as a unique personality in a number of respects but, although this personality had distinctive qualities, it sought to conceal itself in the shadow of the saintly King Olaf. Sverrir stands out as the most extreme case of individualization of a real historical figure that we know from Ancient Scandinavian literature.

This study of various categories of writing from Ancient Scandinavia enables us to pick out a number of consecutive stages of development. The complete absorption of the individual into the group and his subordination to ritual give way to the emergence of individuals who are more separate and more distinct. It would be misguided at this stage to rush into putting together a picture of the linear evolution of the individual personality. What we have before us is the taut dialectic of two principles that are to be found within the personality of the German or the Scandinavian – the group principle and that of the individual. The unquestioning adherence to values of the family or clan does not in any way

rule out the development of personal initiative and a keen
awareness of the individual. It is possible now to suggest that
the pre-Christian pagan ethos offered the German somewhat
more scope for the discovery of the inner self than the teachings
of the Church that demanded humility and the suppression of
pride. The importance of Ancient Scandinavian sources lies, in
particular, in the fact that study of these reveals to us an earlier
stage in the history of the individual in comparison to that to
be found in continental Europe.

3

The 'Persona' in Search of the Individual

Belonging to a social group is not a trait peculiar to human beings but the fundamental difference between the human group and the herd, swarm or flock lies in the fact that to become part of a social group people have to adopt certain values. A member of society interiorizes a system of cultural 'co-ordinates'. In the human being's consciousness a picture of the world takes shape that serves as the starting-point for all social behaviour.

The individual does, and indeed can, exist only within society. The medieval individual is absorbed into the social macrocosm via the microgroup – family, extended network of relatives, rural commune, parish, seigneury, feudal domain, monastic brotherhood, religious sect, urban *fraternitas* and so on. Each microgroup adheres to certain values which are, in part, specific to the social microcosm in question and in part common to a number of groups or for society as a whole, and the individual becomes part of that culture by assimilating those values. As the individual does so, he or she becomes a personality.

Christianity underlines the importance of the institutionalization of the individual. Christianity is not merely a faith, but a social community, a world built according to the will and teaching of the Creator and Saviour. Between the 'natural' or 'carnal' human being (*Homo naturalis* or *Homo carnis*) and the human being, who has been transformed by the act of baptism into '*Homo Christianus*', there is an enormous gulf that can be bridged only through the act of 'initiation'. The act of baptism constitutes the profound transformation of the very essence of the human being no less, the incorporation of the 'natural human being' into the community of the faithful. Through this act a human being acquires the chance of salvation. He or she absorbs the 'cultural code' of the Christian community, its principles and norms – the human being becomes a person. A text of AD 1234 states 'Through baptism in the Church of Christ a man becomes a person' (*Baptismate homo constituitur in ecclesia Christi persona*).[1]

What the Middle Ages inherited from classical times – anthropologically speaking – was no straightforward legacy. In the Graeco-Roman period the concept 'person' did not exist. The Greek word *prosopon* and the Latin *persona* served to denote a theatrical mask. A mask is not only not a person but probably the very opposite, and the evolution that the term *persona* underwent over the course of many centuries can testify to the efforts that were undertaken by various cultures before Europeans succeeded in investing that term with the content which might express the essence of the human personality. The *persona*, behind which the actor in Classical drama might conceal his true face, did not presuppose any personality, just as an abstract juridical person lacked one: such a person was merely a symbol for legal capability which, in Roman law, went by the name *persona*. Classical thinkers would see the term *persona* as signifying, above all, a social role that had been assigned by society to one or other of its members. This term was used in the world of the theatre or court procedure and was not linked with the field of psychology.[2]

Another concept just as close in meaning to the term *persona* was 'character', which was linked to the sphere of the mind only insofar as it bore an imprint of something, just as some material might have an impression made on it (the word 'character' was interchangeable with 'stamp', 'brand' or 'imprint'). These concepts are distinguished by their static nature and they indicated to people or to groups of people the place allocated to them within the framework of the system.

The identity of persons is determined from without, laid down in advance by institutions and objective considerations, but it does not reflect any subjective elements or shared emotional experiences.

There seems to have been no awareness of individuality in ancient times. People were not aware of themselves as individuals and did not conceive of their pagan deities in that light: they saw them as personified forces of one kind or another rather than as individuals. The individual was subordinated to an impersonal supreme force – fate – which human beings were in no position to oppose. The beautiful, harmonious and well-proportioned bodies of Classical sculpture did not portray individuals: their souls did not reflect the uniqueness of the human being, the vessel containing the divine principle.

The inner psychological essence of the human being in the Greek World was not the object of tenacious quests and investigations.[3] In Ancient Rome the position was slightly different. Certain writers manifested a tendency to engage in self-examination (Seneca, Marcus Aurelius), but the genuine breakthrough to psychological introspection, although it was to remain the only one in that period, was that undertaken by St Augustine.

In the person of St Augustine (AD 354–430) Christianity made a major advance towards penetrating the individual's 'inner space' and in achieving a more profound understanding of the individual. The human ego underwent re-interpretation and came to be viewed as the combination of substance endowed with awareness and a will and a personality capable of reasoning and of emotion. In contrast to the concentration on Fate typical of the Classical era which, as it were, 'freed' the individual from personal responsibility for his or her own life and actions, St Augustine declared: 'I – not fate, not destiny, not the devil' (*Ego, non fatum, non fortuna, non diabolus*).[4] The centre of the world was the ego, face to face with its Creator. St Augustine responds with dramatic emotion to the experiences of his path through life, which led from his sinful excesses as a young man to his discovery of the true God. Self-knowledge was presented as knowledge of God, the path to

God. Even before St Augustine, such works as the *Confession* of Saint Cyprianus (fourth century) or *De Trinitate* (*On the Trinity*) by St Augustine's contemporary, Saint Hilarius, had been written, but it was the *Confessions* of the Bishop of Hippo which introduced into our culture a new paradigm for the self-expression of the individual.

The *Confessions* were known to many authors of the Middle Ages (at least by hearsay or in the form of excerpts) and, where possible, they tried to take them as their model.[5] Yet they proved capable of imitating the external form of the genre rather than reproducing the attempt at profound introspection that they represented. Evidently the specific sociohistorical and psychological situation at that moment of catastrophic upheaval, that overcame the consciousness and emotional world of St Augustine at the transition from the Classical world to a new age, created the unique opportunity for the appearance of an individual of this kind and the biographical account of his soul. The unique nature of the *Confessions* is unlikely to be fully comprehensible if we do not take into account the fact that Augustine was aware of himself not only as an individual, whose conscious mind was struggling with the enigmas of human existence, but also as a witness of and participant in the universal-historical process. In other words, he was a man present simultaneously at the collapse of the old world, with its well-established but outworn system of social ties and values, and also at the dawn of a new age.

The world was split in two and the split passed right through the soul of this Christian neophyte (if it is admissible to paraphrase the words of Heine who lived 1500 years later). At that unique point in history Augustine, as the subsequent fate of his writings was to demonstrate, laid the foundations not only for Christian philosophy of history, but also for the psychology of the individual in its infinite complexity and with all its diverse facets. Indeed his ideas encompass both the sacred and the historical universe (*De Civitate Dei* – The City of God) as well as his own inner world: there is unlikely to be any reason to doubt that this all-embracing view of human existence, shaped by his own existential experience, was what enabled him to penetrate his own soul to such a depth. Nor does he focus attention on a static soul, but on one that is caught up in constant movement and change. Augustine's heightened awareness of historical time is inextricably linked with a deeply personal sense of the passing of time, of the subjective content of the human soul.

During the whole of the Middle Ages nothing else was written after St Augustine which examined human psychology as astutely as he had done: this is not merely because St Augustine's experience was unique (the conversion of a pagan to the truths of Christianity after lengthy searching, and at a time when he had already reached maturity), nor because of an apparent absence of geniuses (compared with other periods in history, there was no shortage of these in the Middle Ages), nor because they focused their interest and attention on other things, nor even because the religious and ethical maxims of the period after St Augustine did not provide opportunities for spontaneous self-expression of a similar kind.

Here it is important to draw attention to a feature of the *Confessions*, that could not fail to stand out, when we compare St Augustine's work with medieval 'confessions' and 'autobiographies'. In all these works the authors are constantly comparing themselves with the heroes of the pagan or biblical past, with figures from the Gospels, history or literature. These comparisons, or matchings, represent far more than that which first meets the eye. When he turns to these models and places himself in their situations, relating their utterances or deeds to himself, the individual becomes aware of himself and shapes his own personality, considering himself against a background of characters familiar from authoritative texts. Here we find not imitation but self-comparison as a means of self-identification. We shall return to discussion of this device on several occasions later on. It is, however, a device that is not used in the *Confessions*. St Augustine refers to sacred texts, but he adopted from them what are, for the most part, generalized maxims rather than concrete examples. He contemplates his own person and makes judgements about it as it is in its own right. He as a person comes face to face with God and is only compared with Him. It is to God that the confessions are made and no other models apart from the Creator are needed.

To maintain that Augustine is engaged in a direct dialogue with God means, not only that he was striving towards God, searching for him and longing for him, but also that the Creator loves him and is guiding him towards his salvation. The Creator needs him, his likeness. 'I was eager for fame and wealth and marriage, but you only derided these ambitions. They caused me to suffer the most galling difficulties, but the less you allowed me to find pleasure in anything that was not yourself, the greater, I know, was your goodness to me.' (*Confessions*, VI, 6) This intensive interaction between the Individual and his Creator, and their constant intimate communication, are what underlie the rare degree of psychological tension found in the *Confessions*.

St Augustine had provided the canon which was taken as a model for autobiographical narratives in the Middle Ages. He described in detail his path to enlightenment but, after he became a Christian, his subsequent life (between the moment of his baptism and the time he wrote the *Confessions* more than a decade went by) no longer appeared to him as a subject that gave rise to such intense emotional experiences. His conversion was the central climax in his life. The whole of his development before it was gradually preparing him for that moment, without him being aware of it. I deliberately use the word 'development' because Augustine saw his life as a continuing inner process, temporally and semantically speaking, a process filled with intense thinking and emotion, a series of crises through which his soul passed before it eventually attained knowledge of God. In his memory he pieced together that path step by step. In the autobiographies of Guibert de Nogent, Abelard, Petrarch and others who followed in Augustine's footsteps, we find similar crisis points that determine the course of their lives. Yet after Augustine, no other writers throughout the whole of the Middle Ages succeeded in achieving such a high level of awareness of the integrity and evolution of their own life.

A mere 50 years later, Patrick, the Apostle of Ireland, wrote his confession, in which he describes the history of his 'conversion' and relates certain details from his biography.[6] In Patrick's confession, however, it is possible only to find various disparate pointers to the events in his spiritual life: his thoughts are focused on God, and, while Augustine engages in intense dialogue with his Creator, Patrick probably does not do so. This does not mean that he is not interested in his own persona, and he enquires of God: 'Who am I, Lord, and what is my vocation?' – a question that writers asked constantly throughout the whole of the Middle Ages as they strove to achieve self-awareness. Nor does Patrick conceal his wish that his 'brothers and kinsmen' should know what he is like and what his motivation is. We should not be led astray when we read in his writings (as we also read in those of many other Church writers) insistent assertions that he is rough hewn, ignorant, sinful and a nonentity (it is in these terms that his confession begins): set formulae for self-humiliation could mask quite different feelings and intentions. After all, this 'unworthy rustic' (the term he himself uses) was singled out by the Almighty as the chosen one and he completed the mission entrusted to him by the conversion of the inhabitants of Ireland to the true faith. Naturally he does not forget to say that his elevation by the Lord was not in any way deserved and that he does not tell of it for reasons of ambition or vainglory. Yet we do not come across St Patrick indulging in an analysis of his own personality with the same kind of inspiration as St Augustine does.

What therefore was the interpretation of the individual in medieval philosophy or, to be more precise, in its quintessence – in theology? The question is worded inappropriately though, because theologians were concerned not with the individual, but rather with *persona*. The definition of the latter remained highly abstract throughout the Middle Ages. 'The persona is rational indivisible essence' (or the 'individual substance of rational nature' – *persona est rationalis naturae individua substantia*): such is the definition provided by Boethius,[7] which satisfied the requirements of theologians for many centuries, although some thinkers did introduce their own specifications into this definition or even suggested their own alternatives. The indivisible, integral nature of the *persona* is also stressed in what by then was the widespread etymology of the word 'persona': *per se una* ('united on its own'). The scholar's attention, however, was naturally centred on the rational aspect. According to St Thomas Aquinas: *'persona* signifies what is most perfect in the whole of nature, i.e. what is embodied in rational nature' (*Persona significat id quod est perfectissimum in tota natura, scilicet subsistens in ratinali natura*).[8]

It is important not to be misled as to the nature of the chief preoccupation of the theologians who formulated these definitions: they relate for the most part, or even exclusively, to God, the *persona divina*, because their thinking was centred on the Creator rather than on Creation. Considerations of the *personae* of divine hypostases were an essential component of the debates about God's Trinity (*tres personae – una substantia*) and of the dual nature of Christ, that is divine and human.[9] In this context the Classical understanding of the word *persona* as a theatrical mask or a player in the legal process had been replaced once and for all by the new interpretation. At the same time, it shifted the focus from humanity to God, yet did, to some extent, centre on humanity because God and humanity were united in Christ. When maintaining that humanity was not just part of nature, theologians had in mind the fact that it formed part of a divine hypostasis: humanity stood at the boundary between the natural and the supernatural, and the Divine *persona* shaped the *persona* of the individual.[10]

This was the situation, not only at the beginning of the Middle Ages or in the twelfth and thirteenth centuries, but also at the end of the period: Nikolaus von Cües (fifteenth century) when considering the *persona*, again approached it in relation to Christ. When he writes of the *individuum*, he is contemplating an abstraction of the most general kind ('what has become single and inimitable, like any individual'). The human personality attracts Nikolaus von Cües only in so far as it is linked with the Divine: '. . . the basis for the existence of the greatest humanity is the divine persona . . .'. He reminds us that 'Christ did not die to the extent that his personality perished' and Nikolaus von Cües refers to this personality as 'the centre in which his humanity lay'.[11] The medieval metaphysician striving after the Absolute is unlikely to bring the historian a great deal nearer to an understanding of the object of his or her investigations.

If we turn our attention away from specific authors and look at the status of the individual in general, then it is essential to recognize that, in the Christian era, the *persona* acquired an individual soul, an indestructible metaphysical core and a moral foundation. The human being was created in the image and likeness of God, and the whole world was created for humankind – the high point of creation. Not only did the human race share with the rest of the animal world the capacity to exist, live and feel but, at the same time, it had been endowed with the capacity to understand and to reason like the Angels. As can be seen, great emphasis is laid on the human being's rational nature, the capacity to reason. The scholastics and theologians lent that quality central importance and set more store by it than by all others: the capacity to reason constituted the essence of their profession – the capacity for logic and the inclination to arrive at rational judgements. Central to their analysis of humanity was the question of salvation. Individuality, on the other hand, was seen to be more of a misfortune than an advantage – a 'disease of the soul'.

Yet this portrait of a philosopher – moreover, one drawn by that philosopher – does not yet give us a picture of the medieval individual. Nor can we progress much further with the definition of humanity provided in the eleventh century by Notker Labeo: 'Man is a rational animal who is mortal and capable of laughter' (*homo est animal rationale, mortale, risus capax*). This monk then asks himself: 'What is man?' and replies that he is a creature capable of laughter and laughable (*Quid est homo? Risibile. Quid est risibile? Homo*).[12] Why do we find such a strange combination of qualities: rationality, mortality and a capacity for laughter? Can this not perhaps be explained by the fact that only laughter can reconcile reason and the human being's mortal nature? Like a defensive reaction to the fear of death or to the dark and unknown aspects of existence, laughter in the face of what is terrible provided, so to speak, a mediator between death and reason.

The definitions of humanity and the individual in the anthropology of medieval thinkers made no further progress.

The reason, I repeat once again, lies in the fact that it was the idea of God that was uppermost in people's awareness, and reflected light shone on humankind by then.

In texts of a secular character, the term *persona* often served as an equivalent for *homo* ('someone', a 'certain person'), but it did not signify the individual human personality or a theatrical role. More often than not it was used in relation to those who possessed a particular social status. The concept *persona* was firmly linked with the concept of high office or rank: 'a layman of high rank' (*laicus magnae personae*). Alanus ab Insulis provided a similar definition of the concept *persona*: 'he who occupies a respected position' (*Persona dicitur aliquis aliqua dignitate praeditus*). His treatise, written in England at the beginning of the eleventh century, which explains the functions, duties and rights of representatives of various social groups and holders of office, is entitled *Rectitudines singularum personarum* (*Correct Conduct of Individual Persons*). In this case, the term *persona* is also used in relation to persons of low status, including serfs.

It is not merely in the theology of the age that the anthropological aspects of the individual are not elaborated in detail. If we turn to the history of western European languages, it is not difficult to realize how slowly and with what difficulty all the words signifying personality, individuality and the human character were incorporated into common usage. Concepts linked with the psychology of the individual have only relatively recently taken root and come to be used on a regular basis. Words with the prefix 'self-' denoting the attitude of the individual to self or awareness of self have proliferated only since the Reformation. It was then also that the range of words indicating the aims of the individual and emotional states began to be widely used. Human feelings, which throughout the Middle Ages were regarded as some kind of independent forces with an existence all of their own that either filled or were absent from the individual's soul, gradually came to be interpreted as emotional qualities of the individual that were an integral part of that person. Words designating personality (*personnalité*, *individu* etc.), which have been known since the time of the Renaissance, came to be actively used only in modern times.[13] Behind all the imperceptible shifts in linguistic values and the emergence of new words in our day-to-day existence nowadays (*personnification, individuel, individualiser, individualisation, individualisme* . . .) lie the psychological processes involved in the individual's awareness of self.

A long and difficult process was involved before the mask could develop into the individual. It is quite clear that the changes noted above in the values expressed in the concept *persona* were not the result of the autonomous development of a lexical, theological or psychological kind. All these linguistic mutations were linked with transformations within human groups and with changes in the awareness of the world achieved by the people who made up those groups.

It would not be over-hasty to conclude from the above that the Middle Ages did not produce a clear concept of the individual and that the word *persona* was to remain a term relating exclusively to God. We shall see later on that as early as the thirteenth century a breakthrough occurred making it possible to arrive at a more profound understanding of the individual (*see*: 'The Parable of the Five Talents', page 156).

4

Biography and Death

L'homme devant la mort was the title given to the major work of innovatory research produced by Philippe Ariès, yet for me these words appear to be appropriate for expressing the general situation with regard to human consciousness in the Middle Ages. In that age, as in any other, people lived, worked, fought and prayed, loved and hated, mourned and revelled, yet however much they might have been totally swallowed up by earthly cares and pursuits, their active and emotional lives inevitably unfolded against a background of death. Death can rightly be viewed as an essential component of life. 'Where are those who once lived?' (*Ubi sunt*), 'Be mindful of Death' (*Memento mori*), '*danse macabre*' – these are not simply designations for what were then fashionable and widespread genres in literature and art. These themes, that doggedly pursued people's consciousnesses, were something in the way of leitmotifs, which left their specific mark on religion and philosophy, on art and everyday life and, to a large extent, shaped people's thoughts and behaviour.

The fear that gripped people of this age was fear of sudden death, a death that they had not prepared for with prayers and other 'good deeds', death at a moment when they had not had time to confess, repent of their sins and receive remission of the same. At that period it was crucial to be constantly mindful of death. Preachers did not tire of insisting that people should not postpone their repentance and atonement for their sins until the very last moment and that timely repentance was pleasing in the sight of God. The *danse macabre* that was depicted in church frescos was terrible, above all because the dancing representatives of various social estates and classes could not see who was leading their dance, and therefore they did not know when it would be interrupted.

Ariès, on the other hand, wrote about 'tamed death' (*la mort apprivoisée*),[1] death that one anticipated and expected, which the head of the family encounters surrounded by close relatives and heirs after giving the last instructions and asking for forgiveness from everyone. A person would pass over into the other world at peace and lamented, without fear or regret, because life's cycle was complete and care had been taken of his or her soul in good time. Ariès imagines that death really was like that all through the early Middle Ages, and continued like this until as late as the modern age in the world of the peasantry. I fear that Ariès has taken on board without question descriptions found in folklore and in literary works. Yet these narrations are in themselves interesting and important: this was how people imagined death after having been taught to fear an unexpected departure from earthly life when they were still bent under the weight of their sins and therefore had little hope of salvation. Unwilling to accept what Ariès had to say, Arno Borst pointed out that the people of the Middle Ages experienced an acute fear of death, because their fear had not merely psycho-physiological and existential roots, but religious ones as well for, as they faced death, no-one could be certain that he or she would be able to avoid the torments of Hell.[2]

The legend concerning such well-timed and seemly death had other implications, too: it meant that a person died leaving behind positive memories. In the Middle Ages, the genre of sermons concerning the dead (*de mortuis*) was popular. When the Pope or some other Church leader, a secular monarch or aristocrat, died, a sermon would be delivered in church, in which respect would be paid to the deceased: his merits and deeds would be described and, at the same time, more general themes would be touched upon, in particular death and the need to prepare for it, Paradise, Purgatory and Hell: models of Christian behaviour would be cited and those present would be told how the living might alleviate the lot of the souls of the dead.

The question arises as to how far it was possible to go in such a sermon towards revealing features of the individual personality of the deceased to whom it was dedicated. Of course, the actual genre of remembrance makes it imperative to assume that, if a word-portrait of the deceased was being provided, his or her positive qualities would be the ones recommended as models for imitation. This is clear a priori. Nevertheless it emerges that these sermons *de mortuis* were by no means mere icons. After studying the texts of such sermons composed until 1350, David d'Avray points out that, despite all the unavoidable stylization, mention is made in them of pivotal features of personality, and some of these word-portraits are interesting throughout.[3] Yet the preachers quite obviously set themselves very different goals, and the descriptions that singled out individual traits of character, which in their turn testify to the authors' astute powers of observation and the attention that they were paying to that individual, not just to his or her role in society, were all simply swallowed up into the moralizing text. The medieval preacher was unlikely to have been ascribing great importance to genuine features of personality, so precious for the scholar, for their own sake: they were not an end in themselves, merely an auxiliary means for making the moralizing clearer. Not so much the specific nature of an individual, but rather the chance to compare that person with some kind of model (taken from the Bible or classical literature) was the focus of the preacher's attention. I should like to stress once more, that the author was sometimes capable of seeing the particular and distinctive in the individual's character, even of noting the changes in appearance and behaviour that took place in the course of that person's life, but the actual genre of the sermon placed certain limits on the preacher's scope for doing so. As in other genres of medieval literature, so too in sermons *de mortuis*, the individual is depicted mainly via what is common to people of a particular category and not via features peculiar to that individual alone.

Contemplation of the world in the Middle Ages is distinguished by its focus on two worlds at the same time. Life does not end with the human being passing into a complete Void: after its sojourn on Earth the human soul passes into a different world. In that new world a new stage of the soul's existence begins – no longer an existence in time but an existence in eternity. Yet, has the deceased renounced earthly interests and cares for ever and a day and have the emotions that seethed within that person during his or her lifetime grown cold? On visiting the Kingdom of the Dead, Dante noticed that many of them continued to be stirred by their previous passions. People are capable of taking love and hate with them to the grave. These pictures of passions on the boil in the next world are not just the fruit of the poet's imagination: we find similar motifs in the popular imagination as well. Two peasants living next door to each other were constantly at each other's throats. It so happened that they died at the same time and that they were buried together. And what next? . . . It turned out that, even in the grave, they continued to beat and kick one another. In many tales of the wandering of souls through the world, that were recorded throughout the Middle Ages, motifs of this kind are to be encountered – the idea of the interaction between the two worlds is ever-present in medieval culture. It is therefore quite natural that ideas concerning existence in the world beyond the grave reflected basic ideas about life in general, about the nature of people and their personalities.

Between the two worlds there existed constant, animated, two-way communication. The living would go out of their way to find means of influencing the souls of the departed to relieve their torment or to shorten the period they needed to stay in Purgatory: masses and prayers for the deceased, offerings to the Saints, alms for the poor and the purchasing of indulgences. Some of the departed were able to visit the world of the living and interfere in their affairs. In some cases the living would summon them forth, while in others those who emerged from the other world did so on their own initiative. More striking still was the way in which certain individuals died merely for short periods and, after wandering through Hell or Purgatory on their way to the gates of Paradise, would return to life on Earth and testify to what they had seen beyond the threshold of life. Enormous and unswerving interest is shown in all that takes place beyond the grave. Indeed, what could be more important than to know what fate lay in store for the human soul after the death of the body? We read that it was a widespread custom for friends to agree between themselves that whoever should die first would return later to the friend remaining on Earth to relate how his or her soul had 'settled down' in the next world.

In short, according to the convictions of medieval people, the life story did not end with death. Indeed it is possible to go still further: a true assessment of the individual cannot be given on the basis of the deeds carried out during a lifetime (as had been held by the Scandinavians of the pre-Christian era: they believed that after a person's death all that remained was the glory of the deeds), for there exists a supreme Judge, who will pronounce a sentence for every soul and in the light of His sentence it will at last become clear once and for all what a particular individual really was: a sinner or a righteous person. Everything else was superficial and insignificant: earthly concerns were nothing when compared with Eternity, and only on the very threshold of Eternity would the true 'value' of a soul be revealed.

After pointing out with good reason that the final reckoning regarding the value of an individual's life could be made only at the Last Judgement in that system of religious beliefs, Ariès stressed that right up to that moment, a person's life story remained incomplete. Yet when will that Judgement come about? The second coming of Christ, the resurrection of the dead that was to accompany it and the judging of the whole human race were, according to the Church's teaching, to coincide with 'the end of time' that would take place at some unknown point in the future, because only the Lord knew exactly when. Between the moment of an individual's death and the pronouncement of his or her sentence at the End of the World comes a span of unknown length. The life story of any individual is split in two: earthly existence and God's judgement are separated by something like a dream, in which the dead have to languish until the Second Coming of Christ.

All this is well known from theology, but what does it all

imply if we look at the question in connection with analysis of the individual's self-awareness in the Middle Ages? For that, it is important, according to Ariès, to probe more deeply into the depths of the collective consciousness. In his opinion, the idea of the inwardly complete individual was missing from medieval culture until a specific period. Only in death did the individual reveal his or her individuality. At that moment there took place the 'discovery of the individual, the individual's awareness at the hour of his death or when thinking about death of his own identity, his personal history, both in this world and the next'.[4]

Ariès' idea concerning the link between concepts of death and Judgement beyond the grave with the individual's self-awareness, is, without doubt, profoundly reliable and provides much food for thought. Its explanation using one specific example, on the other hand, cannot withstand criticism. Ariès' mistakes result, on the one hand, from his overlooking important levels of medieval sources and, secondly, from the fact that this scholar, despite all his innovatory methods, could not see beyond the theory of linear progress. Judge for yourselves.

Ariès assumed that the image of the Last Judgement had not yet taken shape at the beginning of the Middle Ages, when the allegedly dominant belief was in effect that the deceased slept the sleep of the dead and would continue to do so until the Second Coming. According to him, it was only in the twelfth and thirteenth centuries that this concept took shape, at the time when scenes depicting the Last Judgement appeared at the west doors of cathedrals. Later Ariès went on to maintain that the idea of a separate judgement of the soul of each person taking place at the moment of death dated only from the fifteenth century, since it was then that engravings began to appear depicting such judgements: angels and demons would be shown at a deathbed disputing the soul of the individual concerned. In this way, the Last Judgement, when Christ would judge the whole human race, is replaced at the end of the Middle Ages by the idea of a separate judgement of each individual. This change – the substitution of 'small (i.e. personal) eschatology' for 'great eschatology' – is explained by Ariès with reference to the growth of individualism, the 'liberation of the individual' from traditional psychological fetters.

Closer scrutiny of the historical sources would lead us to
draw rather different conclusions. In the first place, the idea of
the Last Judgement is to be found in Christianity from the very
beginning. Indeed, the Gospels mention a judgement which
shall take place 'at the end of the world' after the Second
Coming (Matthew, 24: 3 ff.; 25: 31-46; 26: 29; 13: 39 ff., 49-
50; 19: 28 et al.), and also punishments for sinners and rewards
for the righteous, which shall follow immediately upon the
death of the individual: Christ says to the thief crucified at the
same time as himself: '. . . Verily I say unto thee, To day shalt
thou be with me in paradise' (Luke 23: 43; cf. 9: 27). Immediately
after his death a beggar finds himself in Abraham's bosom and
a rich man in Hell (Luke 16: 22). The fact that Matthew is
referring to the Judgement for all after the Second Coming,
while Luke is referring to the decision as to the fate of an
individual's soul immediately after death did not give rise to
any striking contradiction, because the early Christians expected
Christ to return to them very soon and saw themselves as
people living on the threshold of that great event.

The gulf between the ideas of the 'great' and 'small' (or
personal) eschatology became far wider later on, particularly
in the Middle Ages, when the end of the world seemed a far-
off prospect. Ariès is misguided in his assertion that the idea of
the Last Judgement had not taken shape in the early Middle
Ages. In fact, the tradition for its depiction in medieval
iconography goes back at least as far as the fourth century and,
by the period of the Carolingians, such depictions were already
quite numerous.[5] The Last Judgement was an integral part of
Christian consciousness from the very beginning of the medieval
period.

In the second place, ideas concerning the Last Judgement
pronounced over the individual were also widespread in
Europe from the beginning of the Middle Ages, and we can find
these in the writings of Pope Gregory the Great, Bede, St
Boniface and other writers of the sixth, seventh and eighth
centuries, and from then on. In the works of these writers, we
find such scenes as the following: angels and devils gather at
the deathbed of a sinner and display lists of the person's merits
and sins, and, after wrangling between the two sides, the soul

of the departed immediately makes its way to the appropriate sector of the world beyond the grave. The genre of the didactic *exemplum*, which was in its heyday after the beginning of the thirteenth century, provides particularly extensive material on this subject. When a person dies, he or she immediately comes to stand before the Judge, either to be condemned or to gain entry to the Kingdom of Heaven. Despite the assertions of Ariès to the contrary, it is clear that in the next world Hell and Paradise were already set in place, and it was not a question of sleep or rest: this is borne out by numerous accounts of visions of the next world and of visits to it by the souls of those who are dead for only a short time.

It is therefore evident that there are virtually no grounds for describing ideas on the subject of the Last Judgement and the world beyond the grave in the way they are presented to us by Ariès: as progression from the peaceful sleep of the dead to the Last Judgement, from universal eschatology to the individual variety, from Judgement 'at the end of time' to Judgement that is pronounced at the moment of each individual's death. The concept advanced by this scholar is based on the idea of the 'discovery' and later progress of human individuality in the course of the Middle Ages. In reality it turns out that the ideas of the Last Judgement for humankind as a whole and for the individual have existed side by side in Christianity since the outset and that 'great' and 'small' eschatologies were not separate stages in believers' awareness of their own identities.

If we accept the notion that latent ideas about the individual find expression in these views regarding death that are incorporated in the 'code' of every culture, then we have to acknowledge that Christianity was focused on the individual from the start, the individual who is personally responsible for his or her own behaviour. This idea was expressed in different ways, however – at the level of esoteric theology and at the level of everyday human awareness, where it assumed a guise all of its own.

Then the question arises as to the way in which there could exist side by side in the individual's consciousness what would appear to be two incompatible ideas of the Last Judgement – 'great' and 'small' eschatology. In my opinion, the contradiction is more obvious for us than for the faithful in the Middle Ages. When they entered a place of worship they would contemplate a sculptured depiction of the Last Judgement decorating the tympanum of the west door. When, from their point of view, would that Judgement be taking place – at the present or in some indeterminate future? The question is a difficult one. One of the 'examples' (*exempla*) of the thirteenth century depicts the following: a lawyer is dying, and at his deathbed are gathered colleagues, other lawyers, and they are listening to his answers given to the Supreme Judge, from which it emerges that the dying man is standing before Christ at the Last Judgement and trying to justify himself in the face of the accusations brought against him. The dying man calls to those standing around him with the entreaty: '*Appellate!*' (Appeal!), for he wishes to use a legal device so as to win time and have his trial extended or postponed. Those present, who appear as witnesses at the Last Judgement, as it were, are standing there in terror. Yet the ruses of the pettifogger achieve nothing where Christ is concerned, and with a howl, 'You were too late with your appeal: I am condemned for ever!', the sinner expires. From this it is clear that the Last Judgement is seen to take place at the very moment of the individual's demise.

Let us now turn to another *exemplum*: a cleric has died and shortly afterwards he comes back from the other world (as he and his friend had pledged to do for each other) to tell him that, on the very day he died and found himself in the next world, the Last Judgement took place. The friend objects with the words: 'You are a well-read man, how could you imagine any such thing?' What kind of answer is given from the world beyond the grave? 'All my learning was of little help to me . . .' An astonishing reply! The Church taught that the Last Judgement would take place 'at the end of time' but the personal experience of the man who had already been judged testifies to the opposite. The most interesting point of all is that the author of the *exemplum* does not adopt any final position on this issue: it is not clear to him who is right in this argument which, for a passing moment, exposed one of the fundamental dichotomies in the medieval religious consciousness.

The images of both types of Judgement, that for the individual soul which follows upon death and the universal one after the Second Coming, are interwoven within one consciousness. As we have been able to see, the complete life story of the individual is unthinkable before the Last Judgement, according to official theology, and the individual is not an integrated whole either temporally speaking or in essence until then. From this it follows that it is impossible to give a final assessment of the individual beforehand. This assessment is also one that is not given by people but by the Judge on High. Yet another idea had also made its way into the medieval consciousness: the judgement for the individual is pronounced at the very moment of death, thus bringing the individual's life story to its completion. The contradiction is clear for all to see.

Yet the religious consciousness is not daunted by contradictions: in a mysterious way it succeeds in combining the two eschatologies and one is envisaged through the prism of the other as it were. In connection with the question of individuality it is very important to stress the following: people find themselves in a situation in which their life stories are interwoven with the universal-historical process, which they experience in a symbolic way as the history of human salvation. Through the mediation of the Church and the liturgy the individual becomes aware of his or her own personal involvement in that history, for each human individual occupies a particular place in that history, even if it be only the most insignificant. At the point where the individual's life story intersects with history, the overlapping of the 'small' and 'great' eschatologies becomes possible, even inevitable: at the same time, this overlapping accentuates the importance of the individual and incorporates that individual in the current of historical time.

5

Autobiography: Confession or Apologia?

In their search for the individual, scholars naturally turn to 'autobiographies' written by religious writers. According to Georg Misch, autobiographies underwent marked development during the Middle Ages. Indeed, during that period, a good deal of writing appeared in which the authors touched in one way or another on the details of their own lives, dwelling on certain episodes and depicting their mental and emotional states as they did so: in a number of cases it appears as if they were deliberately trying to reveal the nature of their inner world.

Yet medieval writers as a rule do not seem inclined ,or perhaps able, to depict their lives in a consistent way, and, in this respect, the works that Misch has scrutinized differ significantly from modern autobiographies. If they are autobiographies at all, they are autobiographies of a most unusual kind, and, judging by what they wrote, their authors pursued specific aims, the implications of which need to be examined carefully. After drawing attention to the large part that motifs involving confession and repentance play in them, Mikhail Bakhtin refers to these works as attempts at self-justification or confessions. He points out that the Middle Ages had not yet been acquainted with 'biographical values', and the basis which those provided for examination of a person's own life took shape only at the very end of the Middle Ages.[1]

Despite their unusual and 'unpolished' qualities, medieval 'confessions' and 'autobiographies' do not lose their importance as valuable testimony regarding the individual. The first experiments in 'autobiography' appeared in the West in the tenth and eleventh centuries,[2] but, at that time, they were rare exceptions. They were encountered more frequently in the literature of the twelfth and thirteenth centuries.

Nowadays, the middle centuries of the medieval period are attracting the attention of scholars specializing in this period more and more, and there are good reasons for this. It is worth mentioning two of these reasons: in the first place, it was precisely during those centuries that the West began to develop beyond the state peculiar to traditional societies and, to a far more noticeable degree than before, to light upon the potential of that development which enabled the West to assume a leading role in world events. Without doubt, the seeds of this potential had been sown in the previous period (the Classical and Christian legacy on the one hand, the distinctive nature of the Germanic barbaric world on the other, and then the decisive condition for this breakthrough, namely the intensive synthesis of both principles) but they came into their own only in the twelfth and thirteenth centuries.

Secondly there was a major extension in the range of sources at the disposal of scholars in that period, a circumstance which, in the final analysis, had resulted from the historical breakthrough described above. The content of the new writing was changing: it was becoming possible to reach a somewhat clearer understanding of the human inner world which, prior to that, had been almost totally hidden behind literary clichés and the rituals of early medieval religion. Several phenomena were to be observed at that time which testified to an increase in the individual's introspection and to an acquisition of partial autonomy within the framework of the group to which he or she belonged.

Scholars focus particular attention on the fact that, at the beginning of the thirteenth century, the confession acquired new significance: it was laid down in a decision taken by the IV Lateran Council (1215) that every Christian should make a confession to the priest once a year. Regular individual and secret confession presupposed self-analysis on the part of the believer: one was required to consider one's own behaviour to decide what was sinful and what was righteous about it. Actual practice sometimes had little to do with analysis of the consciousness of the believer and easily degenerated into profanation of the sacrament of confession, because the majority of believers did not prove able or inclined to carry out self-analysis of this sort, and many confessors were unable to help them, thus reducing the activity to no more than a superficial ritual. Nevertheless, the principle had been established and signified an important stage in the evolution of the Christian's religious awareness.

This tendency towards self-examination was the result of the interaction of many forces – both social and intellectual. The High Middle Ages were an age in which social relations underwent profound change, and the structure of society became more complex. Religious writers were required, in a more urgent way than before, to come to terms with the question of society as a whole and the relationships between the various members within that entity. The development of craft-production and trade demanded more initiative and rational activity than agriculture did. The individual was now confronted with a greater variety of opportunities, albeit mainly in the towns, and yet, at the same time, greater demands were being made by day-to-day life. People were obliged to meet new challenges and new means were required to enable them to cope. A world of hallowed traditions, customs established for ever and a day, and magic rituals was now being ousted by a world in which rationally based actions were playing an increasingly large part. Belief in miracles remained unchanged, but it now cohabited in the minds of educated people with the idea that there was a well-ordered pattern of events to be observed in Nature. After collecting together in his treatise entitled *De diversis artibus* (*On Diverse Skills*) various rules applying to the practice of professions and instructions for craftsmen, a German writer using the pseudonym Theophilus (*c.* 1100) directed attention first and foremost to people's minds.

Later we shall be turning to such outstanding men of the

twelfth century as Abelard and Abbot Suger. It would be pointless to look in their writings for precise dates or for information of a numerical nature regarding the phenomena described above. They make do with vague expressions such as 'a large number', 'some', 'at one time', 'a few months later'. This reflects the traditional medieval attitude to numbers, which meant that either no numbers at all would be found in a text or quantitative estimates would be of a fabulous nature and, in effect, 'picked out of a hat'. Yet gradually calculations became more important. In the thirteenth century, works appeared by authors who were clearly preoccupied with numbers and measurement, and frá Salimbene (of whom more later) was able to manipulate precise numbers and dates with facility: indeed, when recounting the sinking of the Pisan fleet by the Genoese, he refrained from providing his own figures on the grounds that he was waiting to obtain more reliable ones. It is with every justification that scholars refer to the emergence of the 'arithmetical mentality' in that period.[3]

Literacy was still the privilege of the select few, mainly clerics, and yet the written word was beginning to exert a constantly growing influence on the thought of even those who could not read.[4] New social, political and economic needs made it imperative for schools to be established not merely for members of the clergy, but also for lay people. In a world which, as before, was based on the religious world outlook, a gradual reappraisal was taking place with regard to the correlation between faith and reason, and the foundations of scholasticism based on logic were beginning to take shape. Theology was expected to be based on rigorous analysis of concepts. People perceived space and organized it differently by now and they had come to attribute more importance to time. The first mechanical clocks in towers appeared at the end of the thirteenth and beginning of the fourteenth centuries.

A restructuring of social groups can be seen as the process underlying all these changes in the spiritual life of that age. The number of groups grows and they become more diverse: members are no longer totally absorbed into their group but stand out as separate persons within it. The opportunity to select one of a number of 'rival' groups appears and, in these conditions, a growth of individual self-awareness was inevitable.

Among the writers of the twelfth century, who later came to be seen as embodying the spirit of the age by anyone examining the inner world of the individual and the gradual revelation of the secrets of spiritual being, were Pierre Abelard and Guibert de Nogent. The great philosopher, known as the 'father of scholasticism', and the abbot of a provincial Benedictine monastery became akin to classic 'models' in the process of the 'discovery of the individual' in the Middle Ages. Despite all the differences between them, Guibert de Nogent and Abelard were both aware of the need to leave descriptions of their lives behind them, each in his own highly personal way.

To what extent do their works allow us to achieve a closer understanding of the authors as individuals? It is not easy to answer this question because, in medieval literature, there existed almost without fail a 'screen of rhetoric' between the author announcing his sincerity and readiness to confess and his intention to introduce the reader into his own inner world on the one hand and his actual work on the other. This literary device, which might have seemed designed to reveal the thoughts and feelings of the writer, at the same time constitutes a barrier that conceals true motives and character. Generalizations, clichés, quotations from 'authorities', traditional turns of phrase, well-known formulas for the expression of humility and repentance, and other rhetorical devices constitute a kind of 'defence mechanism' that prevented the reader from glimpsing the actual human personality of the writer and the writer's real motivation.[5] Was this not the state of affairs we find in the works of Ratherius, Bishop of Verona (*c.* 890–974)? Several works of a confessional or penitential nature have survived from the pen of this highly educated Church leader. Nevertheless, analysis of these writings does not enable us to gain a closer understanding of his individuality which is concealed beneath a veil of literary conventions. Ratherius is, of course, an extreme example, but all the same an example which serves to illustrate a general rule.

To express his own feelings or depict a specific life situation he has experienced, the author resorts to comparing himself with a figure from the Bible, the early history of the Christian

Church or from the Ancient World, and such comparisons are not straightforward but something more significant and with deeper implications. The author identifies himself with the figure selected for comparison and becomes totally absorbed within that model. In an attempt to recreate his own character from 'bits and pieces of the authorities' the subject becomes 'mindful of himself in another'.[6]

Guibert de Nogent

Among many other works, Guibert de Nogent (*c.* 1053–1125) left behind him one entitled *De vita sua, sive monodiarum* (*On his Life, or, of Monodies*): a monodia is a song for one voice, which is performed when the singer is alone). Many scholars have attempted to classify this work as belonging to the autobiographical genre and, for us, it is of particular interest.

Let us start though with Guibert's criticism of relic worship. Historians who regarded Guibert de Nogent as the founder of modern source study did not take into account the fact that Guibert, who wrote very sceptically about the worship of holy relics in his treatise *De pignoribus sanctorum*,[7] quotes dozens of accounts of miracles in *De vita sua* including some concerning miraculous healing attributed to the relics of saints, without expressing as he does so any doubts about the worship of saints and their relics, but merely about its abuse. Like a number of other medieval writers, Guibert was worried about the increasing worship of holy relics that was not controlled in any way by the Church. He does not raise objections to that practice as such and, in *De vita sua,* he writes with a good deal of sympathy about the journey undertaken by French monks to England, where they displayed holy relics to collect money essential for restoring the shrine at Lâon after the destruction that took place during a rebellion there. When, for example, one of Christ's milk teeth was displayed in one French monastery and, in another, his umbilical cord or his foreskin removed at the time of his circumcision, Guibert protested against 'holy relics' of this kind because he had grave doubts about their authenticity: after all, during his childhood, Christ had not been worshipped as the Saviour and the Son of God.

There is no justification whatsoever for viewing Guibert as a 'new, modern man' or 'rationalist' such as Rabelais, Calvin or Voltaire (as Abel Lefranc has done). His scepticism is selective and the miracles of which he approves are recounted by Guibert without any criticism at all.[8]

It is interesting to note, however, that the very same scholars who justifiably object to the modernization of Guibert's views and insist on the need to 'restore' him to the context of the medieval mentality, sometimes fall into the same trap. After rejecting Lefranc's interpretation, John E. Benton puts forward a Freudian explanation for Guibert's attitudes. He sees him as possessing an exaggerated sense of guilt and 'fear at the prospect of sexual mutilation', and he chooses illustrations for his edition of the 'autobiography' that give weight to his thesis. It is with this 'complex' that Benton links Guibert's criticism of the sexual degradation to be observed among the aristocrats of his day: he sees symptoms of psychiatric disturbance in references in the 'autobiography' to the punishments that Guibert was subjected to as a boy by his teacher; Benton attributes the dreams Guibert describes to his 'homosexual tendencies'; Benton underlines the crucial role played by his mother with her 'puritan ideas of sex' in shaping the attitudes of the future abbot, who, since birth, had never known his father (he, incidentally, suffered from impotence in relations with his wife for a number of years); if we add to this Guibert's 'narcissism' then we can appreciate the full extent of his 'irrational fear of punishment, death and mutilation (self-castration)'. According to Benton, the hero of *De vita sua* was a 'disturbed man'.[9]

I dwelt at some length on this psychological, or rather psychopathological, assessment of Guibert de Nogent's personality because it is not an isolated example but a rather common symptom. People are anxious to understand the personality of medieval people but approach it from a modern angle. While, at the turn of the century, there was a tendency to assess thinkers or writers of that era by applying modern ideological criteria (scepticism, rationalism, free thinking), now scholars try to discover fashionable sexual complexes, especially in their subconscious. Yet they do not take into account the fact that it was not possible to make people of the twelfth century lie down on the psychoanalyst's couch and probe the hidden layers of their psyches. This is why all Freudian interpretations of medieval texts inevitably remain superficial.

Guibert refers to the 'inner man' (*interior homo*) within himself (in the spirit of the teaching of Saint Paul, Epistle to the Romans 7: 22), which he contrasts with his sinful *persona* focused on the external world (*persona ad saeculum idonea*), and his awareness of this juxtaposition is the source of the constant psychological uneasiness which Guibert experiences, as indeed did other monastic writers of the twelfth and thirteenth centuries. Many of these aspects of Guibert's mind, which Benton interprets as symptoms of an individual's deviations, should rather be interpreted as indications of the religious-cultural situation of the era. The special features of Guibert's mind fit easily into the general picture of contradictions and moral conflicts stemming from the doctrine of sinful human nature and from fear of God's Judgement and unavoidable punishment.

Guibert de Nogent's *De vita sua*[10] consists of three books, and the first is devoted to the story of his life or, to be more precise, to its initial stage before he was appointed as Abbot of the monastery at Novigentum. Guibert turns to his Creator and tells him about his early years. It represents a kind of confession. The work opens with the words: 'I confess to Thy Majesty, O Lord, of my countless errors'. Yet a real confession presupposes self-scrutiny. Guibert goes on to write: 'While gaining knowledge of myself, I strove to gain knowledge of Thee and as I drew nearer to Thee, I did not lose awareness of myself'. The confessional genre demands that specific rules be adhered to as the narrator gives his account of himself: the central focus of the exposition should be the repentance of his sins, and Guibert dwells in detail on his inner impulses and deeds. At another place in the book, he returns to the reasons that led him to write it, stressing as he does so that it was not his pride that prompted him, but his desire to repent of his own transgressions. He sought to be useful to other people by narrating his successes and setbacks (*fortunas et infortunia*).

This indication of the moral goals that he is allegedly pursuing is, however, more likely than not a concession to literary tradition. When he described his childhood and early years in detail, Guibert appears to be trying to understand for himself that difficult time and to introduce some sort of order into the chaos of emotions that he experienced then.

Guibert's account of his childhood is unique for that age. This son of a knight had not known his father who died in captivity when Guibert was just an infant. For the modern reader, it is striking that, when Guibert describes his childhood, on which he dwells in more detail than the later periods of his life, he does not regard it as imperative to supply either the time or the place of his birth, nor even the name of his father. (His father's name is mentioned much later in the tale of his vision of his mother, when she turns to the ghost of her deceased husband: but when she addresses him as Evrardus, he tells her that the souls inhabiting the world beyond the grave do not use names.) Still more striking is the fact that we are not told the name of Guibert's mother either, even though he was deeply attached to her and constantly turned to her in his thoughts. Nor does he give the names of his other relatives. Is this the approach typical of a monk who, after cutting himself off from the world, severs all family ties in his mind as well? His brother was at the same monastery, but no information regarding their relationship is provided. All that we know about the brother is that he behaved in such a way as to merit punishment after death.

The details of Guibert's birth predetermined his destiny in the Church and as a religious writer. His parents' marriage had been barren for seven years because, apparently, a relative of his mother had placed a *maleficium* (curse) on their sexual relations, so that Guibert's mother-to-be remained a virgin. It was only after kinsmen of Guibert's father, worried that he might not have an heir, demanded that their marriage be annulled and that he take monastic vows so that they might gain possession of his estates, that the spell was broken and Guibert was conceived. His parents vowed that their child would devote his life to God. Thus the boy did not take part in the games customary for the sons of knights and devoted himself not to military pastimes but to study. Guibert's mother, who was to exert such a powerful influence over her son, found him a teacher, who was not particularly well educated. This man obliged Guibert to work very hard and, from love for the child, subjected him to extremely harsh punishments. Despite this, he did not dampen the boy's enthusiasm for learning, and Guibert admits that he would have remained devoted to it, even if under the threat of death.

Guibert admits that his tenacious approach to his studies was not originally the result of devout motives, but stemmed from his thirst for fame. He was carried away by the urge to write works 'in imitation of Ovid', 'using immodest and even shameful expressions', so much so that his teacher was given a warning in a vision during a dream. Yet, Guibert acknowledges, neither fear of God, nor his own sense of shame, nor his teacher's vision enabled him to see reason or dissuaded him from writing songs (that seem to have been like those of wandering minstrels). Later on, as is familiar from hagiography, came the moment when the sinner returned to the path of righteousness. Guibert then devotes himself to more respectable and serious pursuits: he writes a commentary on the Holy Scriptures and studies the works of Gregory the Great and other old and highly respected writers, which he interpreted 'from an allegorical, moral and anagogic point of view'. In these devout pursuits Guibert was supported by Anselm, Abbot of Bec, who was later to become Archbishop of Canterbury. Moreover Guibert gives his readers to understand that the intellectual exchange of ideas with Anselm was his main reason for visiting the famous theologian.

When he starts thinking about his mother again,[11] Guibert notes that, though illiterate, she had been extremely devout. What filled her with fear more than anything else was the prospect of the ruin of her own soul, and this was why she was constantly and ardently repenting of her sins, the gravity of which was known only to Guibert. She seems also to have nurtured this fear in her son. The terrible dreams that haunted him, with their visions of devils, are far more likely to have stemmed from her phobias than from his alleged Freudian complexes.

Visions, which played such an enormous role in the emotional lives of the people of those times, usually constitute an essential part of their biographies, regardless of whether these are descriptions of the lives of saints or autobiographical confessions written by lay people. This was the traditional technique for depicting the inner world of the individual: these visions are a reflection of the individual's attempts at self-identification. The psychic experiences of monks of that age, mentioned in a number of Lives, are almost identical, whether the subject be Raoul Glaber, Otloh von St Emmeram or Guibert de Nogent. Usually visions preceded decisive moments in the life of the person concerned and constituted stages in that person's 'conversion'. Guibert's 'autobiography' contains accounts of as many as 50 visions: some of them are visions that Guibert experienced at various stages in his life: some are those seen by his mother or by others.[12] The visions shed light on the mysteries of the other world and, therefore, they have a powerful influence on people's lives and personalities. In them are concentrated all kinds of fears and depressive states, suppressed urges and desires, to which the person who sees the vision is not prepared openly to admit. For this reason it is not easy to decode the hidden meaning of the visions, of which those who experienced them were themselves unaware.

Guibert's successes in the field of learning aroused envy from monks whose knowledge and zeal to obtain knowledge were outstripped by his. He was subjected to attacks by monks and by demons, but the Holy Virgin always protected him. It was because of his worth and his learning that, between 40 and 50 years of age, Guibert was placed in charge of the monastery at Nogent near Lâon, a monastery that had been founded only a short time before. To all intents and purposes that is the moment when his autobiography terminates because, in the second book of this work, Guibert has less to say about himself and turns to a description of the monastery that he ruled. It does not, however, contain any information about the monks in his charge either.

What does appear in this book is a whole host of miraculous stories about the Evil Spirit, who was constantly interfering in people's lives and who did not even leave monks in peace.

Scheming as they did to make merry within the human body, devils preferred the fat and wealthy, who would enable them more easily to eat their fill. There were some demons who were content merely to mock, but there were other truly evil ones who caused more harm. It is at this stage that Guibert's antisemitism also comes to the fore. He mentions a Jew who is well versed in medicine but who indulges in *maleficia* (wickedness): this Jew led a monk to the Devil, and, in exchange for teaching him the art of magic, the devil demanded that he abandon his faith in Christ and bring him by way of an offering sperm, 'the most precious thing in man'. Guibert did not confine himself to retelling fables about the wily nature of Jews; he gives accounts of pogroms with unconcealed sympathy for their perpetrators. When in Rouen men assembled to set out on a Crusade, many were grumbling: 'We intend now to march against the enemies of God into distant lands, yet here before our very eyes there are Jews who are bitter enemies of the Lord'. With those words they attacked the Jews, with no respect for sex or age and allowed to remain alive only those who had abandoned the faith of their fathers and 'overcome their evil nature'.

Our writer, whose French patriotism was never in any doubt, (the French are described elsewhere as 'a people that is noble, wise, courageous, generous and refined') does not reserve all his distaste for Jews. He seems not to like the Germans who, according to Guibert, cannot be compared with the French, and he takes offence at the words of an archdeacon from Mainz who refers disparagingly to the French as '*francones*'. In one of Guibert's accounts of mischief perpetrated by devils, the latter assume the guise of *Scotorum* (Scotsmen). Christianity in the West was the common heritage of all, yet peoples were different and their self-awareness assumes the form of self-glorification at the expense of their neighbours.

In general, Guibert is sparing in his positive descriptions of the figures he introduces into his writings: gloomy tones are those which predominate in his portraits of the people he happened to encounter. The world is for him both attractive and threatening: it is this attraction-cum-repulsion that can be traced throughout the whole of *De vita sua*.

Guibert possesses a particularly acute sense of time. For him life does not stand still and time brings changes with it. He writes that in the past nobles had been generous and hospitable and their morals had been stricter. When Guibert had been a young man, women had behaved modestly and set store by chastity, while now depravity reigned: a lady without a lover regarded herself as unfortunate. Extravagant fashions had appeared on the scene, while the level of morality had sunk, particularly among the privileged. Lamentations regarding moral decline and references to the 'good old days' were commonplace in ecclesiastical and monastic literature of that period. Guibert discerned, however, not only moral decline but progress as well. He recognizes, for instance, that there were more educated people at the time he was writing *De vita sua*.

It is interesting to note at the same time, however, that, while in his *Gesta Dei per Francos* (*The Works of God as executed by the Franks*) Guibert praised a Crusade as a unique and important event, in *De vita sua* he managed to ignore it almost totally: it was almost as if he had not perceived that there was a connection between this event and his own life. It is possible even that Guibert was present at the Council of Clermont in 1095, when the Pope announced that there would be a crusade, but this fact is not mentioned at all in his autobiography.

Once again it should be stressed that there is nothing biographical in the second book of Guibert's work. Just like his young contemporary Suger, the Abbot of Saint Denis, whose own personality is virtually absorbed into the life of the monastery, Guibert also forgets about himself. The description of Nogentum, its location and history, the list of those who donated lands and other valuable commodities for it, the description of the ancient tombs that have survived there and, most important of all, the wide range of miracles and visions completely oust the personality of Guibert himself. What we are confronted with in this work is a specific type of consciousness that is rare today. The individual is absorbed into the surrounding world. Guibert's viewpoint is such that his own figure, which is quite clearly discernible at the beginning, becomes more and more blurred as the narrative draws nearer to the time when it is being written, and then it disappears altogether.

Indeed, in the third book, the author's personality has shifted even closer to the periphery of the narrative. Its central '*dramatis personae*' are the town of Lâon, the bishops who had administered it so badly and the cruel conflict which broke out between them and the citizens. Despite all Guibert's undisguised antipathy for the commune proclaimed by the burghers – 'that new and worst of names' (*communio autem novum ac pessimum nomen*) – he believed that the conflict had occurred because of the guilt of the dissolute prelates who worked against God rather than for him and who were members of the secular aristocracy. At this point, Guibert presents his readers with an unusually vivid and dynamic picture of the uprising of 1112, which led to the murder of Bishop Gaudry and his close associates and also to the burning of his palace. In the course of the unrest, which showed no signs of dying down, the city was plundered by peasants and later by the wealthy. Its fate had been foreshadowed in visions and signs, like those which accompanied the birth of a two-headed infant. Moreover, the only date that Guibert thought it necessary to inform his readers of in this work was the date when the citizens of Lâon had launched their attack.

No-one could say that Guibert was anything if not observant, and many of the scenes that he described took place before his eyes. Yet, in those cases when he relied on the testimony of others or on rumours, Guibert demonstrates his rare skills when he describes the people involved in dramatic events, and we should remember once again that, for the most part, these descriptions were negative ones. A whole procession of villains is led out before the reader – men of the people, representatives of the nobility and leading clerics. He describes, among others, the sect of heretics to whom he attributed ungodly acts – accusations of this kind were standard in medieval ecclesiastical literature (illegal meetings involving orgies of fornication, the ritual killing of newborn infants, whose bodies were then allegedly burnt so that their ashes might be mixed into bread eaten 'as in the Eucharist' and so on). The Church strove to throw these Manichaean heretics into dungeons but the people would accuse clerics of being too lenient and would take them from prison and burn them. Guibert noted with approval, that 'the people of God pronounced its own judgement with great zeal in this way, as it feared the spread of the plague'.

In addition to the description of ordeals, there follows another listing of miracles, the authenticity of which does not seem to raise any doubts in Guibert's mind. One of the miraculous events recounted by our abbot scholars with a penchant for psychoanalytical interpretations would seem as a fruit ripe for picking although it is perfectly in tune with Guibert's times. A young adulterer resolved to set off on a pilgrimage to the shrine of St James in Galicia. On the way to Santiago de Compostela he encountered the Devil who presented himself to the young man in the guise of the Apostle James: the Devil then went on to demand that the man should demonstrate his repentance and earn absolution by cutting off his penis, the instrument of his sins, and then kill himself. The young man duly obeyed and, after dismembering himself, stabbed himself with a dagger. He was saved by his fellow travellers, however, who implored the Lord to restore him to life. On his resurrection, the young man related to his companions that, when he found himself in the next world, his soul had stood before God, the Holy Virgin and Saint James. They had discussed what should be done with him and the Apostle had recalled the pilgrim's good intentions, although these had been tainted by sinful acts (it is worth noting here that Saint James judges the sinner not only on the strength of his sins but also with regard to his intentions, and it is precisely the latter that resolve the issue – it is almost as if the Apostle was acquainted with Abelard's ethics!) The Lord paid heed to the entreaties of the Holy Virgin and decided to show mercy to the victim of the Devil's wiles: he was allowed to return to life on Earth on condition that he mend his ways and tell his fellow men about what had befallen him. This whole story is related to Guibert by an old man, who had seen the pilgrim restored to life, as well as proof of the miracle, namely the trace of the dagger wound on his throat. As for the young man's penis, all that remained was a small hole allowing him to urinate.

Guibert's belief in the miracles that he recounts is total. He even goes further to demonstrate what happens to those who do not believe in them or who just voice doubts. An abbot 'in our times' wished to convince himself that the head of Saint Edmund, King of England, had really grown back again as if nothing had happened after it had been severed from his body. When inside the saint's tomb, the abbot had tried to pull the head towards him while his companion pulled the saint's legs in the opposite direction, and they found that the head and body were indeed one. The punishment for the scepticism they had shown was that their hands were robbed of all strength. In the town where Guibert had been born (the name of which is not given), the hand of Saint Arnulf was preserved, but doubts about its authenticity were expressed. The relic was duly subjected to testing through fire and those present were able to see for themselves that it remained whole despite this. Shortly afterwards a relative of Guibert's fell sick and the hand of the Holy Martyr was placed upon him; at that moment the pain was transferred to that part of the body on which the hand had been laid and the process was repeated until, eventually, the pain was shifted to the sick man's neck and shoulders and then out of his body altogether.

Tales of miracles and visions fill Guibert's autobiography. It might seem that they distract the writer's attention from his main theme, but this is not, of course, the case. Just as they did for his contemporaries, visions and miracles constitute for him an essential part of reality, and it was for this reason that Guibert so readily recounted them. Without them, life would be far poorer and far harder to understand, for they constitute an important dimension of life. Knowledge of these phenomena, acquired either from direct observation and participation or from other people's accounts, enriches people's lives and makes up an integral part of their personal experience. When writing of visions, miraculous healing and other wonders, Guibert does not turn attention away from himself: on the contrary, he reveals more of his inner world.

The information we have on the life of Guibert de Nogent is fragmentary, because we have only details of his early life, after which the writer 'forgets' himself more and more. The reason for this does not seem to be some exaggerated humility, which prevents him from concentrating attention on himself, but rather that he does not see himself as the principal, self-contained subject of his writing so that he concentrates on those topics that interest him far more and distract his attention from his own life. After he had been appointed abbot of his monastery, Guibert the individual ceased to develop and evolve: his aim in life had been achieved and this meant that there was not really anything more to be said about him.

Nevertheless, an observant scholar will find connections between the various parts of Guibert's work. The connecting link is Guibert's memory, a memory focused on confession. If we turn away from the autobiographical model that since taken shape nowadays, it becomes clear that memoir and autobiography are not two separate things and that the genre linking memories of events Guibert had witnessed and the story of the outward events of Guibert's life and his spiritual life (or rather fragments of both) is none other than the confession. The first word in Guibert's *monodia* is '*confiteor*' (I confess), and one of the concluding ones is *confessio* (confession). It is within this framework, determined by the religious thinking of the time, that the description of Guibert's life unfolds.[13]

Abélard

Pierre Abélard (1079–1142) was a younger contemporary of Guibert de Nogent. In his philosophical writings he developed further ideas that were sometimes unfamiliar for medieval thinkers, and formulated a number of theological questions in a new way. In an effort to reconcile faith and reason without renouncing the pre-eminence of the latter, Abélard countered the principle 'I believe, in order to understand' with the principle 'to understand in order to come to believe'. Faith for him was not blind, unthinking adherence to the commandments, based on the whole range of sacred rites, which do not directly effect a person's soul or reason, but rather the content of his inner world.

Underlying Abélard's ethics was a principle that was new for that age. Whether or not an individual's behaviour was correct or free from sin was determined in Abélard's eyes not by that individual's acts and their consequences but exclusively by inner motives. Abélard provided philosophical substantiation for the tendency to an internalization of faith, as opposed to a predominantly ritual-based approach to questions of salvation which was characteristic of the period.

This principle represented a fundamental break with the tradition intrinsic to the preceding period, when people had been condemned for their acts without any attention being paid to their intentions or emotional state: all that was taken into consideration was the act in itself, viewed objectively, while the mind of the person concerned was ignored. One of the expressions used to designate that traditional approach was the ordeal of 'Divine Judgement'. A person's guilt or innocence was determined on the basis of a legal procedure which combined sacred and secular principles. God's intervention, which manifested itself in a tangible act (torture involving red-hot irons, or water or a court-room duel), would determine the outcome of each case examined. The result of the trial would not be considered in connection with the individual concerned or with the mind of the person being tried. The individual receded into the background during such an ordeal behind relations between families, clans or other groups. Ordeals of this kind restored peace between social groups in conflict situations and averted lengthy, bloody and interminable vendettas.[14]

Yet Abélard understood sin as acceptance of what was evil or wrong: in other words, central to his analysis was the individual's wish. Whether the individual embarks upon the path of sin or renounces it depends upon the moral choice made. Abélard regarded as free from guilt persons not familiar with the Gospel, who did not know the moral laws contained in it. Even those who had judged and crucified Christ or subjected Christians to persecution could not be regarded as guilty, according to Abelard. After all the members of the Sanhedrin, the Roman soldiers and the imperial officials saw themselves to be persecuting an impostor and rebel: this meant that the values they adhered to were very different from the Christian ones and their deliberate aims did not involve any sinful violation of divine law as they understood it. They were acting in accordance with their consciences while Judas, who betrayed his Master, was aware of his guilt, repented and hung himself. In Abélard's interpretation sin becomes something subjective.

From this it followed that confession and repentance were not significant in themselves as ritual or obligatory procedures, but exclusively as the expression of sincere emotional distress, resulting from the awareness of a sin that has been committed. The individual sees himself or herself confronted by the prospect of the Last Judgement and this cannot but have a powerful impact on his or her consciousness. Salvation is within reach, however, only if that person truly wishes to attain it, after inner cleansing from sin and deliberate 'collaboration' with God to achieve salvation, not by means of any external actions which make no impression on the individual's mind. Nor does the individual disappear from the philosopher's field of vision in those cases, when Abélard addresses figures who have long since turned into symbols. In his *Lamentations* (*Planctus*) Old Testament characters are not presented as Christ's forerunners (in the medieval tradition it was generally accepted that the Old Testament served to pave the way for the New), but more often as real individuals caught up in tragic situations: for example, Abélard was the first writer to see in the biblical figure of Samson a suffering human being.

This channelling of the philosopher's thought in the direction of the human personality comes to the fore in Abélard's writing more clearly than in that of his predecessors and contemporaries. The term '*persona*' is used by him with a variety of meanings (he writes 'this word persona is used with three, or four, or more meanings') – in theological texts in relation to the Holy Trinity, in others to designate leaders of Church and State, and less frequently in relation to human society and the individual,[15] although, as has been noted by historians of philosophy, Abélard, when considering the question of universals, does not analyse the concept of individuality .[16] Nevertheless, when discussing the general question of the 'awakening of consciousness in medieval civilization', M.-D. Chenu begins his analysis with the writings of Abélard and presents him as an example of one of the most striking phenomena to be found throughout the period 1120–60: 'Man discovers himself as *subject*' (*L'homme se decouvre comme sujet*).[17] Abélard begins his *Introductio ad theologiam* (*Introduction to Theology*) with a phrase in which the verbs '*ut arbitror*' and '*existimo*' are used (I assume, in my opinion, I consider). The basis of this new knowledge is made up of personal experience, personal observations and reflections.

Finally, Abélard's own personality, his insuperable penchant for actions that were out of the ordinary, for unusual and unconventional behaviour, his egocentrism and urge to assert himself – surely these all point to a 'discovery of the individual'? To answer this question let us turn to the 'Crown Witness', that is to his 'autobiography'. In the opinion of Georgii Fedotov, it is precisely Abélard's personality and self-awareness that constitute the greatest interest for the historian: they are more interesting than his 'works', than his philosophical achievements: '. . . the historian cannot pass by this cataclysmic explosion of an individual's self-awareness in the very heart of the Middle Ages'.[18]

Historia calamitatum mearum (*The Story of my Misfortunes*),[19] written between 1132 and 1136 (but accorded this title much later),[20] was addressed to an unnamed friend, whom Abélard allegedly sought to console by recounting the story of his own misadventures ('so that you, comparing them with mine would see your own misadventures as negligible or insignificant and would find them easier to bear'). There can be little doubt about the fact that this format is no more than a technique or literary device selected by Abélard as an excuse for his exposition of the events of his own life. If so, then this work has to be seen as stemming from the philosopher's need to bare his soul and recount what weighed heavy upon it. Is it not most revealing, however, to note that the author had to seek justification of this sort for writing an autobiographical work of this kind? No less revealing is the fact that this is not so much an autobiography as a confession, because the account of specific life situations and events has been subordinated to some kind of 'higher purpose'.

We then need to ask what that purpose was. As we acquaint ourselves with the text of *Historia calamitatum mearum*, it soon becomes clear that the author, who turned to his addressee at the outset, soon 'forgets' about him until the very end of the work, where Abélard repeats the words he used at the beginning, adding to them some general ideas about Divine Providence, according to which everything will end in a triumph of supreme justice. Abélard is completely absorbed in himself and his endless and most serious misfortuncs.

Differences with leading theologians and philosophers of his time, with whom Abélard fought to win over the minds of scholars and defend his own original ideas; arguments with influential clerics; quarrels with monks, among whom he had to live, exposed to real and apparent dangers; the crisis experienced by a young man in the prime of life, after his illicit liaison with Héloïse, his 'marriage out of wedlock', as it were, for which he paid with castration, the disgrace that went with it, and then the taking of monastic vows; the public condemnation of his theological 'delusions' at the provincial Council and his incarceration in the monastery: in the light of all this it can truly be said that an inordinate number of hardships and misfortunes befell Abélard, that could well have broken a man of different character. Not Abélard though for, despite all his lamentations, he remained true to his calling of scholar and teacher.

In essence, the central theme of *Historia calamitatum mearum* is the conflict between the individual and the surrounding world, the institutions of the Church to which the individual belongs. It would be wrong to take a one-sided view of that conflict, namely that it was a clash between an individual breaking out from the framework of universally binding conventions and a social entourage that is alien and hostile to him. Abélard did not have, and indeed could not have had, the intention to turn his back on his social estate and the role within society that had been assigned to him. What he did try to do, however, was to carry out his duties in a way that was different from that of his predecessors and contemporaries. Is it not revealing that Abélard interpreted his struggle against the theologians and heirarchs of the Church (as we shall see later) in the light of tradition and categories from the domain of hagiography? In this virtually interminable conflict, Abélard's will is steeled and he becomes increasingly determined oppose generally accepted rules of behaviour, being convinced of the exclusive nature of himself as an individual, of h destiny and of his capacity for struggle.

Abélard's wide use of military terms in his writings (dialectics are referred to as the 'arsenal', arguments in a quarrel as 'weapons', debates as 'battles' or 'jousts') can possibly be explained in part by his knightly forebears. The influence of knightly attitudes can also be discerned in statements by a contemporary of Abélard's, Bernard of Clairvaux, who would appear to be his opposite in almost every other way. The source of Abélard's military metaphors should most probably be sought in his natural inclination to engage in struggle, the innate aggressiveness with which he defends his ideas and, even more tenaciously, the principles he followed in life.

To whom does Abélard decide to tell his numerous misfortunes? It could well be assumed that he felt a strong need to explain his life complete with all its adventures to himself, and to justify the path he chose to follow. The writing of *Historia calamitatum mearum* was an act of confession, of self-justification, self-analysis and self-affirmation. Abélard addresses himself first and foremost. Yet, at the same time as the picture of his life – turbulent, both in its external events and inner experiences – is unfolded, he attempts to justify himself in the eyes of others as well and perhaps, through this work, to pave the way for an eventual return to Paris, to active academic work and to a professorial post. It is, however, difficult to rule out the idea that the writer of *Historia calamitatum mearum* did not have the younger generation in mind as well. It has been noted by scholars that this work follows the pattern typical for Lives of the saints. The emphasis on his own sinful ways before his disgrace and atonement following on from the physical and emotional sufferings he had undergone, and which had enabled him to 'set forth upon the path of righteousness', shows how Abélard is using traditional motifs of hagiography. There are several Lives that he could have taken as models. The intentions behind a work composed in accordance with patterns that reproduce models from the world of hagiography are clear.

Abélard is constantly comparing himself with great and glorious saints such as Athanasius and Jerome.[22] When he recalls his enforced flight from his refuge at the Paraclete, he declares: 'The envy of the Franks drove me westwards, just as the envy of the Romans had driven Jerome eastwards'. The monks in the monastery where Abélard was abbot tried to poison him 'as had been the case with Saint Benedict'. Enemies subjected Abélard to persecution 'just as the heretics had persecuted Saint Athanasius'. His own condemnation at the provincial Council immediately reminded Abélard of Christ being judged by the Sanhedrin. Origenes, who had been castrated of his own free will, was a source of comfort to him in face of his own humiliating impotence. This placing of himself side by side with authorities from eras long past is an important means of enhancing his own self-awareness, something to which medieval writers resorted constantly. Abélard's personality is unusual and highly individual, yet he 'constructs' it from fragments taken from archetypal 'models'. The same can be said of Héloïse. She compares herself with Cornelia, wife of Pompey, after his return from defeat. Cornelia offers him her life, which could be used to calm the anger of the Gods, and, in exactly the same way, Héloïse, ahead of Abélard, enters the monastic life of her own free will.[23]

At the same time, the fact that the narrative is in the first person distinguishes the *Historia* from Lives of the saints (as does the fact that Abélard experienced his struggles not isolated from the world but in the very thick of it) and gives it closer affinities with another model – the *Confessions* of St Augustine. While St Augustine expounds his spiritual biography filled with a tense struggle with his own self, with his doubts, and his *Confessions* are filled with introspection and uninterrupted analysis of his own ego, Abélard is not inclined (or perhaps even capable) of such self-absorption.

It would be a mistake to assume that Abélard's 'autobiography' or 'confession' were really permeated with a spirit of repentance or humility, or that he accepted God's punishment as deserved retribution for his sins. Not in the slightest! Abélard is truly distressed by his sins, to which he gave himself up for a long period of his life, but this distress and repentance constitute only the first, external level of his account. While repenting for the sins of pride and of succumbing to the delights of the flesh and then forgoing dissipation (*luxuria*), the opportunities for which had been literally cut from under him by the knife of men in the service of Canon Fulbert, uncle of his beloved, Abélard was still a long way from overcoming his pride and, in his franker moments, did not see any real need for eventual achievement of such a goal.

There exists a widespread convention, seen as obligatory for all, demanding that one should be humble, modest, repent of one's sins and even make false accusations against oneself, to be still surer of earning salvation. In his writings, Abélard does not tire of acknowledging the truth of this convention. In particular, it is difficult not to call into question his assertion to the effect that, from the very beginning, it had not been desire alone that had drawn him to Héloïse, but true love: it all sounds very much like the retrospective interpretation of a eunuch and monk, who uses in his *Historia calamitatum mearum* Ovidian motifs, that echo the monastic negative view of love as a sinful temptation of the flesh. (Love, not only in the eyes of Abélard but also in those of Héloïse, is not yet love in its lofty sense, as would soon be expressed in the works of Provençal poets). In this way Abélard provides (deliberately or subconsciously) a reason for repentance. In the same way, he is anxious to appear humble and distressed by his own pride. Behind the generalities that mask his true personality, there is a second plane in the *Historia calamitatum*.

Indeed, it is easy to pick out passages in this work such as: 'I was convinced that there did not exist any philosopher in the world other than myself' or 'Having a high opinion of myself that did not befit my age . . .' and so on. It is only if we lift such admissions from their context that we can appreciate their true import, for the sentence immediately preceding the words quoted above reads as follows: 'It was here [as a result of the triumphs of young Abélard, who had just appeared in the school of Magister Guillaume de Champeaux, engaging in debate with him – A.G.] that my misfortunes began, which continue to this day: the wider my **fame** spreads, the more **envy** of me flares up'. The words *gloria* and *invidia* were emphasized by the author (A.G.), because it is they and they alone that are the key words. Immediately after that sentence there follows an account of Guillaume's machinations against the talented young scholar who is a threat to his authority, and Abélard provides a far-from-ambiguous explanation for the Magister's actions: 'envy'. Later he goes on to say: 'From the very beginning of my work as a teacher the reputation of my mastery in the field of dialectics began to spread so wide that the fame not only of my fellow pupils but also that of the teacher himself began to dim somewhat'. What causes his opponents' envy are Abélard's talent and unique personality: with no hesitation he applies a quotation from Horace to himself: 'Lightning strikes the mountain tops'; and also words from Ovid: 'What is highest is the target of envy – the summits exposed to storms'.

Such is the context in which we should read Abélard's statements about how he regrets his pride. Envy of his glory drove his opponents, while Abélard's authority was so great and spread so quickly that, wherever he went, he acquired not only admirers but also enemies. What therefore seemed to be the only thing he needed to regret was the fact that he was so talented, clever and eloquent, for those were the qualities that gave rise to his glory and also the envy that inevitably went hand in hand with it. What made it easier for him to speak of the envy that filled his opponents was that he himself was not prey to envy and looked down on his contemporaries from above.

It is not easy to find a page of *Historia calamitatum mearum* on which those two key words cannot be found. Guillaume de Champeaux is beset by unbearably acute envy and disappointment on account of Abélard, but the more he dogged Abélard with his envy, the more the latter's authority grew. The next conflict was with Anselm de Lâon whose fame, according to Abélard, was attributable not so much to his brain or memory but to his long years of teaching: his discourses were 'extremely poor in content and lacking in ideas' and 'As he lit a fire he would fill his house with smoke but not bring to it the dawn of light'. On closer examination, Abélard declared him to be 'a [barren] fig tree cursed by God'. In relation to Anselm, as indeed to his other opponents, Abélard did not spare sarcasm and cruel jests: his penchant for irony was an essential trait of his character and this 'untamed unicorn' (as he used to call himself) could not resist the temptation of far-from-innocent buffoonery and insulting puns, even in those cases when he risked attracting revenge on the part of the person at whom they had been directed – his mind moved '*a jocis ad seria*' (from the frivolous to the serious').[24]

The contempt that Abélard had shown for Anselm's lectures filled the latter with hate, which waxed greater still after Abélard had publicly and impromptu displayed his skill at interpreting the most obscure passages in the Bible. Once again the same pattern emerged: fame – envy – hatred – persecution.

The next sentence about repentance ('prosperity always makes fools arrogant, while a carefree peaceful life weakens a man's spirit and can easily steer him towards the temptations of the flesh') is once more squeezed into a passage concerned with the growing fame and material well-being of the young philosopher. Then follows the price that has to be paid for all this: 'I toiled, totally engulfed by pride (*superbia*) and voluptuous pleasure (*luxuria*) – and only divine mercy, despite my will, cured me from both these diseases' namely from seeking after voluptuous pleasure by depriving him of the means to enjoy it, and then from his great pride 'by humiliation through the burning of the very book which had been the source of my greatest pride'.

In its external structure, Abélard's narrative follows the hagiographic canon: the crisis Abélard experiences cures him of his sins and he is reborn to a new, less sinful life. Yet to what extent has Abélard really been cured of temptations, and, at the time when he was writing his 'autobiography', was his condemnation of those temptations really sincere and genuine? There then comes a sentence in which Abélard recalls what a handsome young man he had been at the time and how his fame had made him irresistible to women ('I did not need to fear rejection from any woman, on whom I might have wished to confer my love'). Not only does he recall with pleasure the delights bestowed upon him by young Héloïse whom he had seduced, but he does not conceal the fact that, when their relationship was finally discovered and the lovers were forced to part, he experienced not so much sorrow as disgrace: the castration that followed upon the resumption of that relationship was for him above all a source of shame and bitter awareness of the fact that he had been deprived of his great reputation ('as news of my great disgrace would spread throughout the world . . . what face could I now present to the public?'). The decision to enter the monastic life came to him 'not for the sake of piety, but because of my confusion and shame'.

As for conflict with prelates of the Church, Abélard sees the cause of this to be not so much the actual content of his theological writings, because he could find no heresy or even hint of the same in them, but once again envy, which resulted from his ever-growing popularity among his pupils and followers, whose numbers grew with the same speed as that with which the audiences of his opponents shrank. 'Envy', 'hatred', 'vexation' are what drove his opponents, who themselves were alleged openly to have admitted that 'the whole of God's earth would not be able to refute his [Abélard's] proofs and sophisms!'. It was for no other reason that, if we are to believe *Historia calamitatum mearum*, Abélard's theological treatise on the Trinity was condemned 'without any consideration' at the Council of Soissons (1121): not only was it decreed that it should be burnt at once in public, but its author was obliged to commit it by his very own hand to the flames. Moreover, Abélard was also required to recite the Creed 'like a small boy' and then he was locked away in a monastery 'like a criminal'. The struggle between the leaders of the Roman Catholic Church and the new trends in philosophical thought expressed in Abélard's work had given way to a conflict of purely personal interests.

In the account of this condemnation the ear of any medieval scholar could easily have picked out echoes of motifs from the Gospels: in exactly the same way, Christ had been judged by scholars and Pharisees. For this it is sufficient to compare the following excerpt from *Historia calamitatum mearum* with a

passage from the Gospel. Abélard writes that the people and
clergy present at the Council 'began to deliberate amongst
themselves: "Now he is speaking openly before all and no-one
is objecting to him about anything. The Council will soon
come to an end and it was convened after all mainly to oppose
this one man. Have the judges really acknowledged that they
have strayed from the truth more than he?" This was why my
rivals became more incensed with each passing day' while the
Evangelist tells us: 'Then said some of them from Jerusalem, Is
not this he, whom they seek to kill? / But, lo, he speaketh
boldly, and they say nothing unto him. Do the rulers know
indeed that this is the very Christ? / ... The Pharisees heard that
the people murmured such things concerning him; and the
Pharisees and the chief priests sent officers to take him.' (John
7: 25-26, 32).

The author's main sin is pride. While establishing this fact,
we apply to Abélard's personality the criterion that was the
distinctive characteristic of this twelfth-century man, namely
we 'judge' him according to a law which he himself
acknowledged. From the *Historia calamitatum mearum* it is
clear how little the punishment meted out to the philosopher
succeeded in 'curing' him of his lofty view of himself. His
account of that decisive and tragic episode in his life ends with
the words: 'I was far more dismayed by the fact that my good
name had been discredited than by the fact that my body had
been mutilated: on the former occasion I had myself been to
some extent to blame, yet now I had been subjected to blatant
violence on account of my pure intentions and my love for our
Faith, which had led me to write'. Throughout the text
Abélard's innate talent (*ingenium*) is constantly being contrasted
with generally accepted custom or routine (*usus*).

Abélard was, however, soon able to have himself set free and
to embark once more on work as a teacher: as before, this
brought him fame and fanned his pride, just as it led again to
envy on the part of his less talented rivals. 'The whole world
went out after him, and we not only failed to profit from
pursuing him, but added still more to his glory' was what the
rivals declared, according to Abélard's own testimony. He
does not conceal the fact that, when news came to him of

meetings held by Church dignitaries, he had the impression that they were convening to condemn him once again. His sense of persecution became so acute that Abélard wondered for a time 'whether he should seek Christian refuge among Christ's enemies'. Instead he made his way to Brittany, 'a barbarous region' inhabited, according to Abélard, by 'a wild and untamed people': the monks of the monastery, where he was appointed Abbot, were constantly plotting all kind of intrigues against him, even to the point where they attempted to kill him. One of the monks died after inadvertently eating food that had been poisoned to do away with Abélard.

As he moved from one monastery to another, Abélard was not able to settle down anywhere. His presentation of himself as the hero in the account of a saint's life was probably the result of his adherence to literary convention rather than a reflection of his actual path through life. At the time when he had just finished *Historia calamitatum mearum*, Abélard was unable to find himself a place where he could be calm and take refuge from his enemies inside a monastery or out. In his reply to a letter from Héloïse, which she had written after reading his 'autobiography', he asks her and her nuns to pray for his soul, if death should overcome him.

Nevertheless, Abélard soon returned to Paris and, once again, found himself in the centre of the capital's intellectual life. Reference has already been made to the suggestion that this event in his own life was something which he had sought to pave the way for with his *Historia calamitatum*. In 1140, however, his most outspoken opponent, Bernard of Clairvaux, succeeded in having Abélard condemned as a heretic at the Council of Sens and in having all his writings banned: in a papal bull ratifying this sentence, it was decreed that Abélard was banned from making any statement, his books were to be burnt and his supporters to be excommunicated. He himself was once again to be removed to a monastery. Abélard succeeded in avoiding incarceration thanks to the Abbot of Cluny, Petrus Venerabilis, who provided him with a refuge that was to prove his last.

Let us now return to the *Historia calamitatum mearum* for the evidence that can be gleaned from it about the personality of its author. Many of the facts that Abélard provides in this work do not call forth any doubts, while others seem to be presented one-sidedly. Spiritual life in France in the first third of the twelfth century is depicted as revolving round the figure of Abélard. It is almost inevitable that a man who is subjected to persecution places himself in the centre of events and perhaps does so even without meaning to. This is understandable from a psychological point of view particularly because, in Abélard's case, there were fairly substantial grounds for such a course of action. What is also worth noticing is that by repenting of his pride from time to time, Abélard complies with the demands of the confession as literary genre. Yet his confessions and repentance only underline how his sense of superiority is ineradicable. That was how a man felt whose intellectual abilities and achievements did indeed raise him above those around him, and the disasters he endured not only failed to rid him of this sense of superiority, but painfully reinforced his awareness of his own exclusivity. Erwin Panofsky refers to him, far from justly, as a 'paranoid genius'.[25]

As we read *Historia calamitatum mearum*, it emerges that Abélard was lonely in the extreme. Firstly and most importantly, he does not feel close to God. To use G. P. Fedotov's expression, he has no 'voice of inner revelation'; his religion is too cerebral, it is based on knowledge and not on an integrated personal faith, as in the case of Bernard of Clairvaux. For Abélard 'Christian' and 'philosopher' are the same: he sees truth and reason as religious categories. This is why, at moments of crisis, Abélard is not aware of a supportive God and, after each setback, is filled with a sense of terrible abandonment and rejection (*desperatio*).[26] To use Héloïse's expression, 'gall with wormwood' is Abélard's predominant mood.

He is also, however, lonely in the human world. Unlike Guibert de Nogent's *De vita sua*, *Historia calamitatum mearum* is almost devoid of any reference to Abélard's childhood: very little is said about Abélard's father, still less about his mother and, although there were brothers, we are not even told their names. Perhaps these omissions are merely symptomatic of the monastic mind? Bernard of Clairvaux, for example, was ashamed of the grief he showed at the death of his brother, seeing it as a manifestation of 'blood-ties' inadmissible for a monk. Nor is there any mention of a friend in *Historia calamitatum mearum*! Apart from Héloïse, there is nobody. Yet for Abélard even Héloïse, according to his own albeit belated admission near the end of his life (as she herself was to note with pain in her own letters to him), was first and foremost the object of his desire and the source of sensual delights, rather than a friend he regarded as any kind of equal. Héloïse loved Abélard devotedly, whereas he merely responded to her emotions. Abélard's love was devoid of any refinement, it was the very opposite of knightly love, and Héloïse meekly accepts the 'rules of the game' thrust upon her: she is his 'slave', 'concubine', 'maid-servant' – a lesser being. They had a son and what are we told of him in this 'autobiography'? 'She bore a son, who was named Astrolabius'.[27] That is all.[28]

Further on, if we can believe his 'confession', Abélard emerges as being lonely as a member of society as well. Although he was born in Brittany, he did not know the Breton language and had a very negative view of the population of his native province, which he described in most unflattering terms, referring to his fellow Bretons as '*bruti*'. His pupils he lumped together in a faceless mass: if any names were mentioned these would be mainly names of enemies and opponents. A name index for *Historia calamitatum mearum* would be virtually empty, if it were not for the names of ancient authors, heroes of classical mythology and biblical figures. The latter have 'replaced' Abélard's contemporaries and especially his friends and pupils. When disaster befell him and he was castrated, the next morning, according to Abélard's own account, the 'whole city' came flocking to see him, but the sympathy shown him by priests and pupils only caused him the deepest shame, from which he did not know how to take refuge. 'Where could I go after that? How could I show myself to the people?' He saw expressions of friendship exclusively as encroachments on his individual liberty. He took monastic vows and withdrew to a monastery, although his mutilation did not deprive him of the right to continue his career in the Church or to be in charge of a school. It was the act of a desperate man. It was not until a good deal of time had elapsed that he resumed his teaching activities.

What we are confronted with here is a philosopher to whose lectures, delivered on Mont Sainte-Geneviève at the edge of Paris and elsewhere, not merely French scholars flocked but Italian, English and German ones as well; an intellectual whose fame exceeded that of all his contemporaries and whose pupils included a wide range of men such as John of Salisbury and Arnold of Brescia; a man who found favour with many different women attracted to him by his handsome appearance and love songs; . . . yet who, in spite of all, lived out his life in complete isolation. There is no mention of any feelings he entertained towards any other individual – with the exception of course of Héloïse – apart from his enemies. There is no inclination on Abélard's part to examine the minds of those enemies, the motives behind their behaviour or their characters.

It is worth pointing out in passing that, after arriving in Lâon to visit Anselm soon after the communal uprising in that city had been crushed (an event that stunned his contemporaries, including Guibert de Nogent), Abélard made no reference at all to that bloody upheaval. Indifferent to questions of politics, he paid no attention to dramatic conflicts which were making the whole of France tremble. He stood back from it all. Abélard was engrossed in philosophical debates, dissensions within the world of scholars and, above all, engrossed in himself as a person.

Researchers have drawn attention to Abélard's inclination to lighten the burden of his own responsibility by shifting it to others around him. Yet, at the same time, he was not inclined to indulge in self-analysis and, in his writings, there are only few reflections concerning his own ego or attempts to come to a closer psychological understanding of it. Perhaps he mentions instead his teachers, the influences he experienced during the period of his formation as a thinker? Not at all! Before us we have an 'autobiography' by a great intellectual, but it is not an intellectual autobiography.[29] Abélard talks in detail about his own philosophical calling but, as a thinker, he is described as a lone figure deeply isolated. What view should we take of this contradiction?

Abélard was, of course, surrounded by people all his life –

supporters and admirers on the one hand, but enemies and those who wished him nothing but ill on the other. To judge by the assessments he made and the statements in his writings, he was extremely egocentric and this total concentration on his own person and destiny left little room in his memories for other people. It is unlikely that Abélard was actually quite as lonely as it first appears: evidently, any thoughts of friends or devoted followers were driven from his mind as he wrote the *Historia* by images of his lonely fight against the hosts of enemies and persecutors.

Abélard's book cannot really be called an autobiography and, despite certain similarities to one, it is not a confession because it is not sincere enough and it is permeated with a spirit of uncurbable pride. It is, rather, an apologia. In the format traditional for repentance, he wrote a self-justification; indeed, he went even further so as to elevate himself in the opinions of others. This is why, after we have learnt a great deal about the events of his turbulent life and his emotional experiences at moments of crisis, we cannot say very much about him as an individual. His personality remains hidden behind a mask, or rather behind several different masks following on one from another, which the philosopher saw fit to don.

Abélard's insincerity comes particularly clearly to the fore if we read his 'apologia' in conjunction with the letters sent to him by Héloïse, in which her profound nature indulges in outpourings that are more detailed and direct, though we cannot say spontaneous because her intimate revelations are, of course, swathed in a carefully thought-out and subtle literary form: moreover, her self-evaluation is nothing other than self-identification with literary heroines and authorities of the Ancient World. This form, however, (involving, among other things, allusions to the *Song of Solomon* (*Canticum Canticorum*) serves to enhance still further the expression of her love that knows no bounds and her devotion to her 'husband' and teacher, making her emotions seem more convincing than ever. Héloïse's epistolary style is perfectly adequate for the content of her missives ('her individuality emerges and takes shape as the implications of the text evolve'),[30] while the style of the 'apologia' her spouse Abélard uses is subordinated to a quite different task: the format of the confession, which should theoretically be an extremely open statement, in fact conceals that which Abélard found himself unable or unwilling to express.

Abélard's attention was directed not inwards but at the psychology of other people or even his own, and at the relationships between the individual and the world around: it is precisely the grim conflicts with the world at large experienced by the hero of *Historia calamitatum mearum* that are central to that work. These clashes, and the disappointments and setbacks born of them, lead Abélard to speak of such emotions as pride, glory, veneration from contemporaries, desire on the one hand and alarm, shame, humiliation, pain and grief on the other. Abélard stands before us as a one-dimensional figure, presented in relation to a world which heaps suffering upon him. This lonely individual, who lives in the thick of events and amid his fellows, needs their attention, support and admiration: this thinker, teacher and preacher is constantly at odds with his own immediate world and cannot be at peace with himself.

Abélard's personality is not easy to pinpoint: his inner world eludes the outsider's gaze. Here are two pieces of testimony provided by his contemporaries. The first is from his opponent Bernard of Clairvaux: 'This man does not even resemble himself – inside he is Herod and John from without: everything about him is ambiguous and there is nothing of the monk about him, apart from his name and his habit' (*Homo sibi dissimilis, intus Herodes, foris Joannes, totus ambiguus, nihil habens de monacho praeter nomen et habitum*). Another account is to be found on his tombstone in a text composed by his friends: 'Here lies Pierre Abélard. He alone would be able to say what he was . .' (*Petrus hic iacet Abailardus. Huic soli patuit scibile quidquid erat . .*).[31]

It is worth noting here that, despite contrasting attitudes to Abélard, both statements single out the same trait of his personality: he is two men in one, has a far from harmonious nature and is ambiguous; he does not 'resemble himself' and only he could say what kind of man he was. Could he have done so? I have my doubts. Throughout the whole of the Middle Ages people who were inclined to self-analysis and who had occasion to write about themselves, persistently asked themselves: 'Who am I? What am I?' This question, that had already plagued St Augustine and was to torment the priest Opicinus de Canistris from Avignon in the first half of the fifteenth century (we shall return to him later), is also considered by a thinker who appears far from medieval, such as Michel de Montaigne: 'In this world I have not seen any wonder stranger than myself. In time it is possible to grow used to any strangeness thanks to constant familiarity: yet the more I communicate with myself and the more I come to understand myself, the more I am amazed at my ugliness, and the less I can grasp what I really am' (*Essais*, 3, XI).

Evidently Abélard's contradictory personality had already appeared as an enigma to his contemporaries and it remains so for us. All we can assume is that, as he extended the dividing line between himself and the rest of the world, protecting himself against incursions from without, Abélard instinctively sought to say no more about himself than he had included in his *Historia calamitatum mearum*. Yet in him a new type of individual emerged -an autonomous individual, who shielded his inner world and was constantly at odds with those around him, caught up in conflict which spurred him on to continue defining himself anew. If we do not accept at face value his words to the effect that everywhere, in the monastery, at school, in the midst of philosophers, in the world of the Church, webs of conspiracy were always being spun around him, then we have to suspect the following: because of the nature of his personality and as a result of his new social status, which he tried to create for himself, he was unable to integrate himself into any group. Hence his ceaseless conflicts and his feeling of being hounded, which, in their turn, explain the guarded, even hostile attitude of society to this individual, who did not fit into any well-established niche.

Abélard was unique. Yet, at the same time, a specific social process found its expression in his particular journey through life – the emergence of the community of professional scholars. People had to wait until the following century before universities evolved and yet already in Abélard's time it was possible to observe the appearance of people who turned their backs on their origins and on the traditional monastic occupations and ways of life, and then proceeded to devote themselves entirely to the search for knowledge, turning their teaching into the source of their livelihood. Abélard, who renounced his rights as the eldest son of a knight so as to pursue learning, announced with a certain amount of pride that he was incapable of tilling the land and despised monastic poverty, while he considered his only vocation to be 'service through his own tongue'.[33]

The emergence of self-awareness on the part of professional scholars, with their specific system of values, their faith in the power of reason and the individual's understanding, and a new type of mentality, took place in advance of the emergence of such men as a social stratum. Despite its many unique features, the fate of Abélard was partly shaped by this wider process.

Suger, Otloh and the others

The descriptions of themselves which such widely differing individuals as Guibert de Nogent and Pierre Abélard left behind them have little in common, apart perhaps from what were traditionally obligatory formulas of self-denigration that should not necessarily be unreservedly accepted. The differences between these two men, even the contrasts, are particularly striking if we compare the way in which Guibert de Nogent does not set himself apart from the social milieu in which he lives but, on the contrary, blends in with it, while Abélard does everything to emphasize, even exaggerate, how he is opposed to the society in which he finds himself, deliberately skimming over facts that might contradict the picture he paints of endless misfortunes and his lonely combat against the rest of the world.

Nevertheless, it is possible to find some general category that could embrace the writings of both Abélard and Guibert de Nogent, and indeed those of other prominent men of their age, such as Bernard of Clairvaux (1190–1153): perhaps the psychological incompatibility of these two men was what really underlay all their differences regarding questions of doctrine and the role of the Church?

Georg Misch suggests that 'morphological individuation' is

typical of the medieval personality and that it leads to a subordination of the uniquely individual to the typical, to what is characteristic of a given estate in feudal society, and that therefore the most important manifestations of that personality are directed towards views and forms that are laid down in advance and are outside it, so to speak: on the other hand, the Renaissance type of personality which succeeded it was a product of 'organic individuation' and the centre of that type of personality was to be found within itself.[33] One of the many cases cited by Misch to demonstrate the viability of this generalization is that of Abbot Suger (*c*. 1081–1151), a contemporary of Guibert de Nogent and Abélard. This prominent Church leader and political figure was famous for the fact that, under his leadership and in keeping with his theological and artistic ideas, the Abbey of Saint Denis (where he had been appointed Abbot in 1122) was fundamentally reconstructed in the fourth decade of the twelfth century.

This abbey was where the relics of Saint Denis 'Apostle of all Gaul' were kept. This saint was venerated as the patron of the king of France. The abbey was the last resting place for Frankish and French kings and one of the first Gothic buildings in France. In the surviving description of the building and of the process of its erection and decoration, which Suger has left behind for posterity, traits of personality do come to the surface and there are good grounds for assuming that here, too, behind the conventional expressions of humility, lurked pride in his achievements, irrepressible ambition, self-admiration and 'humble vanity' (to use Erwin Panofsky's expression). Is it not revealing that among all the numerous details of the decor in the Abbey only one name is mentioned, not that of a builder, nor of a craftsman responsible for the stained glass, nor a sculptor nor jeweller, but that of Suger himself? No less revealing is the fact that depictions of the Abbot are to be found decorating the most prominent parts of the rebuilt church.

It has been said that Suger's personality was completely absorbed into his splendid architectural creation in which the use of light is the dominant feature in the building's overall aesthetic conception, yet it would perhaps be more realistic to maintain the opposite with regard to Suger: in his hunger for self-affirmation, Suger as it were absorbed the building into himself. Panofsky sees the difference between the ambition of Renaissance Man and Suger's thirst for glory to lie in the fact that great figures of the Renaissance asserted their personalities 'centripetally', absorbing the whole world into themselves in such a way that it was swallowed up into their egos, while Suger, on the other hand, asserted his personality 'centrifugally', projecting his ego on to the world around him, denying his own identity, and as a result, his ego was absorbed into his abbey. The paradoxical blend in Suger's personality of unrestrained conceit and humility serves to explain the 'inferiority complex' that he allegedly suffered from, which Panofsky saw as stemming from Suger's humble, as opposed to noble, origins (something he was particularly aware of when among aristocrats) and his unusually small stature. This complex was what Panofsky sees as the driving force behind Suger's urge to 'overcompensate'. Another contributory factor was Suger's childhood experience in Saint Denis, where he had been brought up, which nourished in him the feeling that he belonged to the Abbey like a son, that all his hopes and abilities were intricately bound up with it, and indeed in the end he came to identify himself with it totally.[34]

It is clear that many of today's scholars cannot move a step forward in their analysis of the medieval personality without references to Freud! Suffice it to recall Benton's statements with regard to Guibert's 'complexes': Abélard's personality and the misadventures he experienced after his castration might appear to be crying out for the psychoanalytical approach. There is no need to rule out the possibility that the medieval writers mentioned so far in this study suffered from various neuroses. The tense mental states in question were, however, first and foremost shaped by historical circumstances and coloured by the times. It is precisely the details of the cultural and historical situations in question that should be the focus of the scholars' attention.

It is also frequently the case that 'mental illness' is referred to by scholars analysing the works of the Bavarian monk Otloh von St Emmeram from Regensburg (*c.* 1010–1070). Long before Guibert and Abélard, Otloh left behind interesting notes that are autobiographical in content. C. Morris discerns such illness in the admissions of Otloh to the effect that, over a long period, he was plagued by doubts as to the veracity of the Holy Scriptures and even as to the existence of God: after all, if God really existed, how was it possible to explain the evil in the world? These sufferings which, without doubt, resulted in a profound psychological crisis, were accompanied by visions, in which evil spirits besieged him, forcing him to renounce the Lord and to give himself up to their power. It is not difficult to imagine the sufferings, wrenching at the very essence of his personality, that Otloh must have endured as he vacillated between hope and desperation. He cites the supplications with which he used to appeal to the Lord 'if he really exists' – that He might reveal Himself to His servant and demonstrate His might, thus putting an end to his doubts and the sufferings they caused, which he felt he could no longer bear. From other writings of that age we know that some people, unable to bear such doubts, even went so far as to commit suicide. I would suggest, however, that the problem here is not a matter of psychopathology (a manic depressive, a neuropath or a masochist who seeks temptation in consolation and healing in sickness are the terms in which J. Leclerq[35] describes him), but that the roots of such mental states need to be sought in religion and culture.

It is clear that it was far from coincidental that the scholastic thinkers of the next century began to ask themselves the question: 'Does God exist?' (*Utrum Deus sit?*), and that Otloh's contemporary, Anselm of Canterbury, felt the need to elaborate ontological proof for the existence of the Divine. It was unlikely that this question had resulted from the development of philosophical thought and nothing else: it was a question which had been of crucial concern to many contemporaries of St Anselm. Otloh was not one of the thinkers to whom such questions occurred in a pure form, philosophically or logically speaking. His doubts grew from his eagerness to believe and to achieve peace of mind. The Lord, when he appeared to Otloh in a dream, called him 'a proponent of all manner of doubts' (*amator dubitationis totius*). The selection of biblical texts concerning the hopelessness of human suffering Otloh places in the mouth of the Devil, and the Lord then counters these. The argument remains unresolved, however, and Otloh is once more torn between doubts and illusions on the one hand and insights and hopes on the other.

In addition to theological and existential doubts, Otloh experiences certain others as well: how can love for literature of pagan content (such as the works of Roman authors) be compatible with study of Christian texts? In the monastery where he spent most of his life, he reports that some of the monks used to read pagan books and others the Scriptures. Otloh acknowledges that the choice was not made by them independently, but as a result of intervention by forces from the other world. He writes how, in a vision, he was visited while sleeping by someone who subjected him to beatings (moreover, the wounds and bruises were still to be seen on the body of the sinner after he had woken up), and, only after a miraculous event (which consisted of a simplified version of Saint Jerome's conversion to the true path) when the Lord appeared to him in a vision and accused him of being not a Christian but a Ciceronian, did Otloh renounce his secular predilections.

Although he had written a treatise devoted to the subject of his own life, Otloh, like the writers whose works have been discussed earlier, nevertheless had not, strictly speaking, written a complete autobiography. His work consists of scattered memories of temptations to which he was subjected, and visions, as a result of which he eventually embarked upon the true path. This is clear even from the title of the work: *A Small Book about his Temptations, Changing Fortunes and Writings* (*Libellus de suis tentationibus, varia fortuna et scriptis*).[36] The impression emerges that Otloh, like Guibert and Abélard later on, did not see an autobiography as a structural whole that would encompass a life and in which the events of that life would unfold in a coherent sequence. Just as Otloh sees his renunciation of pagan literature and his return to sacred texts as made possible thanks to the mercy of his Creator, so too he attributes his successes in scholarship to Him as well: interestingly enough, however, he takes pride in his writings at the same time. Immediately after expressing that pride, he points out that a list of his works has been included only so as to turn the lazy monks away from idleness and goad them into action: 'even if they are not capable of anything so great, let them accomplish some easier feat'. Thus, the reader encounters an intriguing mixture of extreme humility and self-awareness.

It does not take long to establish that the 'autobiography' composed by Otloh von St Emmeram was written in accordance with the canons applicable to confessions and Lives of the saints, and that central turning-points in his life are presented as victories over diabolical temptations. The victories enable a 'conversion' to the true path, a conversion resulting not so much from an exertion of the individual's will, and thus representing a logical step in the individual's inner life, but rather from miraculous intervention on the part of divine forces. In such cases, individuality is concealed behind the a priori structure of the text, dictated in large measure by the given genre rather than by actual impressions drawn from life. The same can, however, also be said of Ratherius of Verona, to whom reference has already been made above. In his writings we also found self-criticism and pride intertwined with each other: an attempt by the author to justify himself looks like invective aimed at those around him. From the depths of the tenth century there rises up to us a cry addressed to the Lord from this profoundly unhappy and troubled man: '*miserere mei!*' (Have pity on me!).[37] Yet, once again, the human personality behind the words is concealed from us.

There is little justification for taking the individual personalities of various medieval authors out of their specific cultural context and trying to explain them with the help of Freudian concepts, as is the practice of a number of scholars today. Apart from the fact that such attempts are far from convincing (for the works that historians have at their disposal did not enable them to penetrate to any depth the minds of their authors), the question remains as to the kind of people we discover when analysing the 'autobiographical' texts of the tenth, eleventh and twelfth centuries: without exception, they are anomalous individuals. In that case, to what extent can they be representative of their culture or age? What we are confronted by here is clearly not mental disorders of the various individuals concerned but rather the problems that the individuals came up against, problems shaped by the moral and ideological climate of the times.

The Master and his Self-awareness

Meanwhile, let it be said that the urge to assert oneself as an individual by creating a work of art or literature is by no means a speciality (*differentia specifica*) of Abbot Suger. For centuries, medieval masters – sculptors, architects, builders, book illuminators – left monuments behind them enhancing their work with the inclusion of their own names ('signatures') and sometimes their own images ('self-portraits').

Such 'signatures' and 'self-portraits', which violated the tradition of anonymity, can be found as early as the eighth century. On the gold altar in Milan Cathedral, its creator has depicted himself as a figure kneeling in front of a saint who is crowning him: on that same altar we find an inscription with the master's name '*Vuolvinus magister phaber*'. In a copy of a work by Saint Jerome (late eleventh century), we can find a self-portrait of a monk called Hugo, who illuminated books with miniature paintings: he has included a picture of himself going about his work. The monk Robertus Benjamin also painted himself and signed his name in a manuscript copy of St Augustine's psalms that he had illuminated. On the last page of a manuscript copy of St Augustine's *De Civitate Dei* (*c*.1140) the copyist (*scriptor*) Hildebertus has depicted a whole scene from his everyday life. He is shown attired in a rich garment copying out a book that is displayed on a book-rest, and at his side stands an assistant. The copyist has been distracted by a rat that has climbed up on to the dining table, thrown down a bottle of wine from it and dragged away a piece of cheese. The text contains a curse directed by Hildebertus at the rat. He also immortalized himself in another drawing. Between 1160 and 1170 this monk from Saint Amand left his signature on no less than six manuscripts: '*Sawalo monachus me fecit*'. We need to try to imagine the complex range of ideas and emotions that lie behind such laconic texts.

Gerlachus, a master craftsman in stained glass at the monastery of Arstein (mid-twelfth century) did not forget to include himself, brush in hand, complete with a caption that read: 'O most glorious King of Kings have mercy upon Gerlachus' (*Rex regum clare Gerlacho propiciare*). At the feet of Christ in judgement depicted in a tympanum at the west door of the Church of St Lazare (in Autun, Burgundy *c.* 1140), the craftsman concerned has carved out his name – Gislebertus. An Italian craftsman left behind an inscription in the church of San Cassiano: 'The creation which you see was skilfully created by Biduinus' (*Hoc opus quod cernis Biduinus docte perfecit*). While another craftsmen praised himself in the following terms: 'in his art he surpasses all others'. On a relief in the chancel of the cathedral in Worms we can find the words: '*Otto me fecit*' (Otto made me).

In other cases the actual name of the master is not mentioned, but his art is praised nonetheless. A depiction of the Bishop of Winchester (mid-twelfth century) is accompanied by the words: 'Art comes before gold and gems, but higher than all of these is its creator' (*Ars auro gemmisque prior. Prior omnibus autor*).[38] In a number of cathedrals we can find sculptured 'portraits' of master craftsmen: they look down on us from windows, armed with the tools of their trade.

These literary and artistic 'texts' are few in number. Their brevity is a serious obstacle to the historian's chances of forming a clear and detailed picture of the inner world of the authors of these revelations, of their system of values and self-evaluation. It would, however, be wrong to underestimate the importance of such testimony or to consider it outside the broad social context and the attitudes of the age. In all the cases mentioned (and many other examples could be added to the list), the artist, very much aware of what he personally has achieved and his importance within society, not to mention the religious implications of his work, is realizing his desire to immortalize his own name. In his struggle against oblivion, which time brings in its wake, he asserts his ego.

Many of the examples mentioned so far date from the twelfth century. This period appears to have been characterized by an increase in self-awareness on the part of creators of works of art. Does this mean that artists only by that point in time had become capable of 'discovering' their own individuality? As we have already seen, such aims were not alien to individual craftsmen far earlier, even as far back as the eighth century. Nor should we lose sight of the fact that far fewer works of art have survived from the early Middle Ages than from the twelfth and thirteenth centuries.

Regarding the self-awareness of authors of literary texts, major modifications[39] have had to be made to the idea that most medieval poets sought to remain anonymous. Suffice it to mention in this connection the high self-evaluation and pride in their own work to be found among such writers of the early Middle Ages as Saint Gregory of Tours (*Grigorius Turoniensis*) in the sixth century or the Venerable Bede (*Baeda Venerabilis*) in the eighth. The former asked that his fellow monks might not change anything in the text of his *Historia Francorum* (*History of the Franks*), while the latter concludes his *Historia ecclesiastica gentis Anglorum* (*Ecclesiastical History of the English People*) with a detailed bibliography of his own works.

The same applies to Otloh von St Emmeram who does not hide his writer's pride as he lists his works. In what would seem a jocular rather than serious tone, he declares that he had not included his name in some of these, so as to avoid arousing envy on the part of the prelates of the Church who, on reading them, would not only experience envy but might also be irritated at the humble origins of the author. Thus, what we have here is not unacknowledged authorship and the anonymity that goes with the former but, on the contrary, deliberate concealment of the name of the author of the work resulting from his particularly acute self-awareness.[40] The twelfth-century poet and chronicler Benoit de Sainte-Marie declared, once more with a definite note of pride, that the text which he had created and 'written with his own hand is composed and polished in such a way that there is no need to change anything in it or to make any additions'. Again, in the 1170s, Chrétien de Troyes opened his prologue to *Le chevalier de la charette* (*The Knight of the Cart*) with the words: 'I embark now upon this story, which shall always remain memorable for as long as the Christian world shall stand; that is what Chrétien takes pride in!' While narrating past events the poet's thoughts are directed towards the future.

Yet particular interest in this connection is to be found in the poetry of the skaldic poets from Iceland whose writings, from the very beginning (and they are known to us from the first half of the ninth century), were profoundly personal and, in this and all other respects, markedly different from Eddaic poetry. While the author's name was not mentioned in Icelandic sagas that were part of the epic tradition, the skald, on the other hand, was proud of the art and deliberately cultivated it. As has been pointed out earlier, the personal element was particularly pronounced in skaldic poetry in the pre-Christian period of the history of Scandinavia. In the twelfth century, this element began to make way to some extent for formulas of humility. In this case, however, there are grounds for assuming that the poets, artists and other masters of the early Middle Ages were not lacking in individuality at all: it was just that Christian ethics and the aesthetic that went hand in hand with it placed strict restraints upon individuality.

Jacob Burckhardt, Karl Lamprecht and *tutti quanti* maintained that interest in human individuality appeared in European culture for the first time during the Renaissance. Prior to that, individuality had been despised, because only the 'typical' had always been the centre of attention. It is from this premise, albeit within slightly different parameters, that those modern scholars, who talk of the 'discovery of the individual' in the twelfth or thirteenth centuries, start out. Yet it has long since been established that, as early as the tenth and eleventh centuries, interest in individual traits of character and the individual's appearance can be found in literature and that such interest is to be discovered not merely in annals and other historical works, but even in certain Lives of the saints. The nature of the hagiographical genre, however, was far from ideally suited to the affirmation of an author's individual viewpoint or to the concentration of attention on the individual and what extended beyond the framework of the relevant canon. At any rate, there are no grounds for referring to authors' 'inability' to dwell on what was individual: the only thing that stood in the way of that was the principle intrinsic to hagiography demanding the reproduction of the exemplary and what was. at the same, time ideal and typical.[41]

Generalizations of the 'discovery of the world and man' type in relation to the Renaissance have no foundation in fact. Étienne Gilson made this point most powerfully with regard to Abélard and Héloïse.[42] Yet they were seen rather as an exception to the general rule. Now it is becoming increasingly clear that they were not an exception at all, but human phenomena that constituted an extreme expression of a particular trend.

Yet theirs was just one of the conflicting tendencies to be observed in that period. The tense conflict between the dominant principle of humility and anonymity, on the one hand, and ambitious aspirations in the work of an ever-growing number of authors and artists to leave memorials behind them 'now and for evermore', on the other, appears to have risen to ever greater heights as time went on. The contemporaries of Abélard and Suger were more often inclined to ponder over themselves and their work and had greater opportunities for self-examination and self-evaluation than their predecessors. Yet the means for an individual to express the inner self remained limited. The personal core was wrapped in the stock topics, literary clichés and constraints of tradition, from which generalized models were taken that restricted the scope for individuals to express themselves as such. The unique nature of their personalities and features that distinguished each one of them from other people were viewed as sinful and abnormal, deserving of repentance, even if deep down the author concerned might be proud of such characteristics. As a result the genuine inner self of such authors eludes our gaze.

6

The Parable of the Five Talents

The ideas put forward by intellectuals of the Middle Ages cited so far and others like them with regard to the 'persona' are interesting in themselves, yet they hardly enable us to gain a complete picture of the medieval personality in all its unique historical originality. For this it would appear necessary that we should leave to one side now the theologians and philosophers and move into the thick of society, to where men and women live not by abstractions, but with reference to more concrete, tangible models and where their ideas and interests are of a more ordinary, everyday kind. Is that possible for us? In an age when the oral, as opposed to the written, language predominated, when the vast majority of the population had not progressed beyond folklore and did not yet have access to literacy or books, it might seem that penetrating the thoughts and ideas of the ordinary believer or simple person is a far-from-easy task. But it is not impossible.

There exist genres in medieval literature which, although they stemmed from the pens of educated people, such as clerics and monks, were nevertheless directed not to a narrow and self-contained circle of people familiar with the subtleties of theology and scholastic philosophy, but to all believers. Sermons, books of penitential prayers (*libri penitentiales*), moral homilies providing the faithful with 'examples' (*exempla*), 'visions' of the world beyond the grave (*visiones*), accounts of miracles (*miracula*) and Lives of the saints (*vitae*), popular manuals of theology, and books of blessings and incantations used by the Church were often composed in such a way as to make an impact on the minds of the whole congregation. Therefore, there was an exchange between the thoughts of the preacher, priest or confessor on the one hand and the consciousness of the parishioners on the other: the authors of texts used in this situation could not but talk to their audiences in a language full of images and concepts that were accessible to them, that were in their audiences' own language. This meant that the language was also one that the monk or priest was familiar with (other than that of elevated theology).

So, when we acquaint ourselves more closely with works from the genres listed above, we can hear two voices: there is the voice of the 'simpleton' or the uneducated figure drawn from folklore (*illitteratus, idiota*), in whose mind 'pre-cultural', still ill-defined and inadequately explained seeds of culture emerged and took root, on the one hand; and that of the simple person as the bearer of the antithetical culture of the medieval period who was addressing the 'folkloric simpletons' on the other. The voice of the former is vaguely audible through the voice of the second: glimpses of the consciousness of the ignorant parishioner reach us albeit censored by the confessor and preacher. Nevertheless, here historians can draw nearer to the level of attitudes that are hidden from their gaze in official theology.

It seems strange at first that we are planning to search for the concept of the individual at such a level. Yet we have already been able to appreciate that, in the rarefied atmosphere of high theology, it was difficult to find an answer because, in that sphere, thoughts were totally concentrated on God. So we shall now examine the group consciousness.

My attention was captured by the text of a sermon delivered by the famous German Franciscan preacher of the thirteenth century, Berthold of Regensburg. Turning to the people of the cities and villages of southern Germany and to the inhabitants of those regions of the Empire which he visited, Berthold would explain to them diverse aspects of religion and principles of Christian behaviour, delivering sermons that, according to contemporary testimony, were uniquely popular. Salimbene maintains in his chronicle that the words of Berthold brought forth miracles and that enormous crowds of people assembled to hear him preach. It would be interesting to listen to him speak: what did the preacher talk to the masses of the faithful about? what were the subjects that captured their attention? and what techniques did he use to sustain that attention?

A sermon of Berthold's which is of unique interest in connection with the investigation of the individual in the Middle Ages is entitled *Concerning the Five Talents*. This text, of fundamental significance as I see it, has not yet been accorded due credit by historians. So far as I know, it has not been quoted by scholars examining the question of the individual in the Middle Ages at all. Yet, as regards the level of understanding for the essential nature of social relations and for the organic link between the human individual and what extends beyond the individual effecting society as a whole, this sermon has no parallel, either in Berthold's own writing (several dozen of his sermons have survived) nor in contemporary works from the same period. This remarkable work sheds light on both the potential and the limits of medieval 'anthropology'.[1]

To have a more reliable understanding of Berthold's arguments, it is essential to refer to the historical situation in which those ideas took shape. Berthold was active as a preacher during the interregnum in the Holy Roman Empire. The weakening of power at the centre, the increased influence of the Electors (*Kurfürste*), the increase in civil strife, growing numbers of robber knights, the undermining of civil rights, the ever more arbitrary treatment of subjects by their rulers, the oppression of peasants, the instability of the situation in the towns – these were some of the features of life in Germany in the period between approximately 1250 and 1275, precisely the period when Berthold was delivering his sermons (he died in 1272).

Was this coincidence a mere chance phenomenon? At such critical moments of confusion and disarray thoughts are bound to turn with particular urgency to the eternal questions concerning the essence, nature and destiny of humanity. Nor is it a coincidence that precisely at this period single-minded spiritual searchings in Germany brought forth an interesting flowering of artistic and intellectual activity. At this time the outstanding representative of scholastic philosophy, Albertus Magnus, was working in Cologne, and Thomas Aquinas was among his students. Poets such as Tannhäuser, Ulrich von Lichtenstein, Konrad von Würzburg and Marner were at work in Germany during the interregnum. It would also appear that, at that same time, part of the enormous cycle of songs *Carmina Burana* was written. Germany's first ever 'peasant tale' in verse, *Meier Helmbrecht*, composed by a poet, Wernher der Gartenaere, also dates from that period: the ideas contained in it clearly echo the emotions to be found in Berthold's sermons.

Yet the phenomenon which it is especially important to underline in connection with the question of the assessment of the individual during this period is the fact that the second and third quarters of the thirteenth century were marked by the supreme achievements of German Gothic – the classic creations of the illustrious 'Hamburg artel' of sculptors and architects working in Mainz, Meissen and Naumburg. They created a remarkable sculptural composition in the Cathedral of Saint Peter and Saint Paul in Naumburg. The spirituality of the statues depicting the cathedral's founders and rich donors (these include representations of Ekkehardt and Uta, Hermann and Reglindis) strikes the beholder as psychologically profound and emotionally powerful, and it should be noted that the male faces have been individualized more than the female ones.[2] Biblical scenes in the west choir screen (*Westlettner*) in the same cathedral (*The Last Supper, The Arrest of Christ, Christ before Pilate, Judas receiving his reward*) appear as sketches taken straight from everyday life. Here, for the first time, we encounter real individuals in the art of medieval Germany. It should be noted that, in the decades that followed, Gothic art in Germany did not reach such great heights again. This flowering of the arts did not last very long and was not consolidated in the culture of subsequent generations. Evidently it had been called forth by a specific socio-psychological, cultural and ideological situation in Germany in the middle and second half of the thirteenth century.

This was the environment in which sermons were being

composed. The preaching of Berthold of Regensburg should be considered against the background of all this creative activity and spiritual energy, because it is in connection with this heyday for the intellectuals and increased interest in the individual that the ideas of Berthold of Regensburg acquire special importance.

Before turning to the interesting concept of the sermon as such, we need to note a feature of Berthold's rhetoric. His sermons were based on the principle of the dialogue. The ideas expressed are constantly being interrupted by exclamations, remonstrations and questions, which are presented as if addressed to him by his audience. 'That is what you say, Brother Berthold, but my worries are that . . .'; 'O Brother Berthold, explain to me . . .'; 'I should like to marry, Brother Berthold, but I am a poor man and what shall I do . . .' and so on. In response to the fictitious exclamations of his listeners Berthold always provides immediate answers. This device enlivens his sermons, captures the attention of his audience, lends unexpected twists to his ideas and gives rise to the sense that his flock is being drawn into a conversation. The impression is created that the sermon is based on a dialogue, that his listener is always present in the preacher's mind and that the preacher is striving to grip that listener. I used the word 'listener' rather than 'listeners' quite deliberately. Thousands of people would come together to hear Berthold preach (Salimbene cites amazing figures) but, while addressing enormous crowds, Berthold always spoke as if he was constantly aware of the individual, with whom he was conducting a confidential conversation. Berthold did not see himself as addressing a faceless mass: for him his audience was made up of individuals.

In one of his sermons he provides a classification of sins to which particularly large numbers of people fall victim. At the same time, he differentiates between various social groups and age categories, for young people are more likely to commit sins of dissipation while older people are more likely to fall prey to greed. According to Berthold, simple people are more likely to be caught up in what he calls the 'net of infidelity', because they are poor and far from sensible, while rich people are more inclined to be guilty of conceit and vanity.[3] This tendency to individualize, to use concrete examples rather than the abstract and highly generalized typologies of scholastic writing, manifests itself again in Berthold's description of the social structure of the Germany of his times, which he undertakes in a sermon entitled *Concerning the Ten Choirs of Angels and Christianity*.[4] Although Berthold was a highly educated monk, there is never anything esoteric about his writing. He looks at the world through the eyes of a man who is not far removed from the concerns and interests of his earthly contemporaries but, on the contrary, engrossed by them: the dialogue between the scholar and the simple person proceeds *within* his own mind and it is precisely this feature of his preaching that makes the sermons of this German Franciscan such a uniquely valuable historical record.

Now let us turn to the sermon *Concerning the Five Talents*.[5] For the subject of his sermon, Berthold selected the New Testament parable of the talents entrusted by a master to his servants (Matthew 25: 14-30). He lends it a completely new twist, however, and provides an original interpretation of the parable. What do these 'talents' actually signify? Berthold leaves to one side the part of the parable which tells of the single talent entrusted to one of the servants – in his understanding of the parable, unbaptized children are being referred to – and also the part concerning two talents entrusted to another servant which signify baptized children. What Berthold concentrates on exclusively is the handing over of five talents to the third servant, i.e. to adult men: the preacher reads into this persons who have reached an age when they think before they act and shoulder complete responsibility for their actions. This idea – of the individual's responsibility – is particularly important in Berthold's eyes.

Two versions of this sermon have survived: a Latin version, written before the sermon was delivered, and a German one which was most probably noted down (possibly by one of his pupils or associates) when Berthold was delivering it to the people, or from memory later.[6] These do not exactly correspond and their comparison serves, in my view, to shed light on the development and refinement of the preacher's ideas.

In the Latin 'prototype' the same talents or gifts of God are listed as in the German version, but in a different order. In the 'prototype' they are listed as follows: (1) *res temporales*; (2) *ipse homo*; (3) *tempus*; (4) *officium*; (5) *homo proximus*. In the German text of the sermon, however, the order is different: (1) 'our own person' (*unser eigen lip, unser eigeniu persône*); (2) 'thy service' (*dîn amt*); (3) 'thy time' (*dîn zit*); (4) 'thy earthly goods' (*dîn iredentisch guot*); (5) 'thy neighbour' (*dîn naehster*). Thus, at the outset, Berthold, following the Holy Scriptures to the letter, planned to begin his analysis with property and wealth and only then turn to people and such attributes as time and service: in the final version, on the other hand, he put the individual first and then followed that with service, time, and only then came property and neighbour.

The impression emerges that, as Berthold continued to work on his sermon, his approach to the text of the parable became increasingly free. The 'persona' now came to occupy pride of place in the whole pyramid of meanings and 'dragged after it', so to speak, the service and the time; property, on the other hand, moved nearer to the end of the list. It is clear that this order appeared more convincing to the author of the sermon (or perhaps to the editor of the German record of it). This shift in the order of the talents led to a reinterpretation of the whole content of the sermon: the individual or *persône* becomes its conceptual core.

In another sermon on the same subject – about how man needs to account for himself at the Last Judgement regarding the talents God has given him – reference is made yet again to the five talents. These were written by the Creator on our bodies, writes Berthold, and each time a person recalls the five senses or counts five fingers, these gifts should be remembered. In this second, sermon God's gifts are listed in the following order: (1) we ourselves, our body, our persona; (2) our service; (3) our property; (4) our time; (5) our neighbour, the Christian. Yet, in a subsequent clarification of these gifts, the order has been changed somewhat: we need to account to God regarding: (1) ourselves; (2) our destiny; (3) our time; (4) our earthly goods; (5) our neighbour. When the lists are compared, it emerges that time and wealth have changed places. For Berthold, more important than the order in which time and property are listed is the fact that all five gifts are very closely linked to one another and form a single entity. It is this entity that underlies Berthold's understanding of the nature of the human being, as we shall see below.

In passing, it is worth pointing out that the discussion of the 'five talents' that we are considering here has attracted the attention of scholars only fairly recently: their attention is concentrated, however, not on the entity referred to above, but on ideas of 'work', 'obligation' and 'vocation'.[7] Despite its undoubted importance, this approach would seem not to do justice to Berthold's ideas because it singles out only one theme in the sermon which, for Berthold himself, was of secondary importance. The subject of 'work' and 'vocation' needs to be considered in a wider anthropological context, in the context of Berthold's analysis of the question of the *individual*.

To return to the 'first talent': this, we are told by the preacher, is 'our own person', which the Lord created in his image and after his likeness, and ennobled by endowing it with free will. 'We must account for it before God and deliberately become fond of Good'. The first, and evidently most important, thing that comes to the preacher's mind when he talks about what is best and most valuable in humankind, about what makes each one of us worthy of the name Man made in God's image, lies in the fact that each person is an individual or *persona*. Of course, compared with the modern concept of 'individual', the terms *lîp* and *persône* had rather different meanings at that period. It is important not to ignore the fact that Berthold uses these two words *lîp* and *persône* in conjunction with each other: he clearly does not interpret the term 'individual' as a purely spiritual or rational essence (let us recall here the scholarly definition: 'rational, indivisible substance') but as a unity of body and soul. We have already seen how the Latin word *homo* has been used as an equivalent for these terms in Berthold's preaching ('*ipse homo*'). Evidently, the Latin term *persona* was not to Berthold's liking, because it was loaded with traditional implications of a theological kind (cf. *persona divina*), was not easy for his mass audience to grasp and finally because his sermons were not in the least concerned with divine hypostases. Surely we should assume that this term, which had made its way into the German language from the Latin of theologians, was beginning to be invested with different content?

Despite assertions by those scholars who assume that the 'concept "individual" was never verbalized' in the Middle Ages,[8] I cannot find any equivalent with which to translate the term *persône* other than 'individual'. Justification for this interpretation can be gleaned from analysis of the context in which this concept is used. We should not lose sight of the fact that what we have before us is a **medieval** individual and that the context of Berthold's sermons serves to make this concept more concrete. Of course, the medieval individual in Berthold's day did not possess the same degree of autonomy and independence which were to become its main hallmarks several centuries later. This was an individual created by God and obliged to return to Him. Berthold's interpretation of the rest of the Parable of the Talents immediately sheds light on his conception of the *persona*, for, in my opinion, the other gifts of God constitute from Berthold's point of view no more than a further unfolding of the content of the initial key concept.

The second talent is 'thy vocation (*amt*, office, service), for which God has chosen thee. To each man he has bestowed a service', because no-one should remain idle. Society consists of persons, each one of whom carries out a social function allotted to him or her. In this original form, Berthold develops the teaching of the functional division of labour and duties, without subordinating the picture of diverse 'offices' or 'vocations' to a rigid three-part system proposed at the beginning of the eleventh century by French bishops Adalbéron de Lâon and Gérard de Cambrai, that of the three orders ('*ordines*'): 'those who pray' (*oratores*); 'those who fight' (*bellatores*); and 'those who labour' or 'till the land' (*laboratores, aratores*).[9]

This order, involving three functions, ignored the true complexity of the social edifice, picking out merely the main pillars of feudal society (the priests and monks, the knights and the peasants). The most important thing on which we need to focus our attention is that this system, the main attraction of which is its logical elegance and simplicity (as well as the fact that it is based on the sacred number 3), presupposed that the various *ordines* ('estates' or 'categories') were faceless masses. Berthold, on the other hand, was concerned with **individuals** carrying out one or another type of service. The point of departure for his deliberations was the individual, the **persona** not the estate, class, social or legal category. Such was the principle underlying Berthold's sermons. As he stood before crowds of the faithful, this preacher would constantly turn to individuals, trying to engage them in direct dialogue: it is the individual to whom his words are addressed. One of the distinctive characteristics of Berthold's sermons is that he incorporates the personal element into his dialogues.

I too have a service to perform, Berthold goes on to point out: 'preaching is my service'. Functions and duties are allocated wisely, not as we might wish, but in accordance with the will of the Lord. Many might wish to be judges, while they are obliged to be cobblers. Someone might prefer to be a knight but is obliged to remain a peasant.[10] 'Who will till the land for us, if you all become lords?'. Or again: 'Who will stitch boots, if Thou shalt become what Thou willst? Thou needst be what God desires Thee to be'. One man is created to be Pope and another to be kaiser or king, or a bishop or a knight, or a count and so on. 'And if Thou hast a lowly office (*niderez amt*), thou shouldst not grieve in thy heart and moan with thy lips: "Oh Lord, why didst thou give me such a hard life, while to others thou didst give great honour and wealth?" Thou shouldst say: "Lord, praise be to Thee for all Thy mercy, which Thou hast shown me and art still showing".' In another sermon we read similar words: 'Oh, Brother Berthold, if the Lord would give me at least something!' exclaims his interlocutor. 'No, no,' objects the preacher, 'And dost Thou know why? Thou wouldst be a master, but needs must till the land; thou wouldst wish to be a count, but thou art a cobbler; the same I say unto all workmen. If God had made ye all masters, then the world would be disorderly and in the country there would be neither peace nor order'.[11] Hierarchy and the distribution of functions, ranks and riches were signs that the world was well ordered and they were pleasing to God, who had created cosmic and social order.

Later in the sermon *Concerning the Five Talents* reference is
made to new and illegal requisitions and duties. Berthold calls
for these not to be levied because those who instituted them ran
the risk of their souls dying. Judges are obliged to judge fairly
and equitably according to the law – rich and poor, friends and
strangers, compatriots and relatives – without exacting anything
over and above the legal fines. After warnings against bribes
and other requisitions, there follows advice to the effect that
those who do not judge fairly should rather renounce their
office because, according to God's word, 'it is better for Thee
to enter into the Kingdom of Heaven with one eye than into
Hell with two'. Many thousands have been cast by the Lord
into Hell, because they had not returned their talent to Him
who had bestowed it upon them.

Yet there exist occupations which are not 'offices', namely
which have not been instituted by God – moneylending,
dealing in second-hand wares, fraud and theft. Berthold depicts
a wide kaleidoscope of liars, scoundrels, extortioners and the
workshy. In addition to the general principle that is typical for
any moralist – to see in life mainly its seamy side and to
castigate vices – here it is possible to assume that a whole
situation is being described while it was degenerating during
the interregnum in the Holy Roman Empire, when arbitrary
rule and lawlessness had become widespread.

So, while the first gift of God to humanity was *persona*,
possessed of free will, the second was none other than the
social function of the individual, the vocation in connection
with estate and profession. People did not select their offices in
accordance with their own wishes and should not contemplate
changing their professions or moving from one social category
into another because, in every 'office', they were obliged to
conform with God's design. The *persona*, as understood by
Berthold of Regensburg, was a **socially determined** individual.
The qualities of the individual were bound up extremely
closely with membership of a class, estate and social group.
There was no 'abstract individual' as implied by the term
persona in legal texts, but diverse social types existed – lords,
rulers, knights, peasants, artisans, merchants. The composition
of the personality of a merchant was not altogether the same

as the composition of a knight's personality; in its turn, the composition of a monk's personality was different from that of a peasant. It has to be said that Berthold's ideas serve to express quite clearly the specific nature of the self-awareness of the medieval individual who lived within a hierarchical society consisting of diverse estates and guilds.

The concepts 'service', 'vocation', 'office' serve to embrace a wide range of social functions – administrative, ecclesiastical and political (judges, elders, prelates, priests) right down to labourers and artisans (Berthold, with his taste for the definite, mentioned ploughmen, tailors, cobblers, millers, traders and farm labourers). The category *amt* (office or service) presupposes labour, and labour – and this needs stressing – is not separated from the more general category 'service' because, in the system of analysis used in the sermon *Concerning the Five Talents*, what is most important is not the productive activity the individual is engaged in, but service as a whole – to society – involvement within the system of wide-ranging functions, which are presented as possessing simultaneously social, ethical and religious significance. The individual labours to satisfy both his or her own needs and those of other people, but the labour is carried out before the Supreme Creator and it is precisely that aspect of it which lends it its final validity.

Apart from its meaning of 'work' or 'productive activity', the concept 'labour' (*arbeit*) possessed at that period a number of other meanings as well – 'need', 'punishment', 'torture', 'care'; and the word *arbeit*, with all these nuances, is found in the sermons of Berthold. As a result, it is most important not to forget that 'labour' was not an abstraction: if it did imply economic activity, then as labour on the part of a specific individual. In thirteenth-century texts, the connotations 'service', 'subordination', 'domination' and 'loyalty' went hand in hand with the word 'labour'.[12]

Thus, the Franciscan preacher insists not on ascetic passivity and that people should withdraw from the world, but on the essential nature of labour or socially useful activity as the basis of society's existence. In his eyes, society consists first and foremost of producing individuals, of creators of material prosperity. In this connection, scholars point to the emergence in the medieval city of a new 'ethic of labour'.[13] If all offices have been established by the Creator, they must at the same time be essential for society: through labour each individual helps other people, exchanging with them what he or she is producing. This exchange must, however, be honest and free of deceit. The moral aspect of the economy ('fraternal relations' between Christians) is in the forefront of his attention as Berthold of Regensburg goes about his preaching.

As is clear from the above, Berthold does not presuppose that all individuals are identical and interchangeable: they occupy different positions within society on the basis of social origins, their property and their position in the social hierarchy. Each one has been assigned a particular place.

The third 'talent' that is entrusted to the human being is the time allotted for life. God is anxious to know how that person spends it. Time is granted to people for labours and it should not be spent in vain. Gamblers and dancers, those who swear or curse, drunkards, those who break their marriage vows, or murderers spend their time wrongly. They will be called to account for the time that they did not put to good use. Berthold breaks into invective and curses against all who are 'greedy', for their time is not only spent to no good purpose but spent in sin and in order to sin. Time should be set aside for prayer, fasting, good works, alms-giving, attending Church. The torments an individual will endure in purgatory are reduced each time he or she says the Lord's Prayer or a Hail Mary or gives alms to the poor, and the time that he or she devotes to glorifying God will reduce the time the soul has to burn in purgatory. It is important for a person to spend time in such a way as to obtain salvation, not so as to add to the torments encountered in this world. This is why Berthold exhorts his listeners to make good use of their time!

The fourth 'talent' bestowed on people by God is their earthly property. It is important to use this to satisfy the needs of the head of the family and the spouse and children, and equally those of all other members of the household (*gesinde*). Of course more is vouchsafed to some than to others but, in any case, it is necessary to make good use of possessions. This means that nothing should be given to actors, casual female acquaintances or prostitutes, and money should not be spent on costly garments. What is laudable is to give alms and help to the hungry and the naked. In the sermons of Berthold it is pointed out that those with property are for the most part people directly engaged in production, those who take care to see that they have enough to eat and are prosperous. The ideal propounded by this preacher is the economically self-sufficient family unit. From his point of view, property is that which has been acquired legally through honest work. The views Berthold of Regensburg puts forward with regard to social relations based on property have much in common with those expounded by his contemporary, Thomas Aquinas.

In the conditions of an urban economy and the division of labour, working people cannot engage in any straightforward exchange of services or the products of their labour. The thunderous words Berthold hurled down upon the heads of the 'greedy', 'thieves' and 'scoundrels' were a response to the unequal distribution of property and the misuse of the latter. Abuses of this kind are manifestations of disloyalty in relation to God, who created enough to make it possible for all people to eat. As for inequality in relation to property and the existence of rich and poor, these are not, in Berthold's opinion, so important, and pale into insignificance beside the fundamental equality of all people before their Creator. 'All stems from Him and everything will return to Him in the end.' This was why Berthold did not recognize any complete unrestricted right to property: ownership of property was also something entrusted by God to owners, just like their *persona*, their time and their office, so people are only stewards of their wealth and need to be able to account to God for the way they use their property.

Finally the last of the talents or gifts from God – love for one's neighbour: one should love one's neighbour as oneself. More will be said with regard to this particular talent below.

So these five talents entrusted to humankind and constituting the main values in life, for the use of which people will have to account sooner or later to the Most High, are *persona*, vocation, the allotted time on earth, property and relationships with other people. The question that might well follow after all this is: what about a person's soul? It might well seem that the preacher should have mentioned it first of all among God's gifts bestowed upon humanity. No reference is made to the soul, but it is present as it were in these discussions like some invisible magnet to which all the gifts duly listed are drawn. In each of his sermons, Berthold refers to the soul in one way or another. Yet it needs to be emphasized once again that, after a certain amount of hesitation, he found it necessary to begin his list of 'talents' with the human *persona* – a concept that, in an earlier period, had been used mainly in connection with God considered as three persons in one. The *persona* embraces soul and body. The separation of those two parts of this contradictory unity, which takes place at the moment of death, is viewed as a temporary state: after death the soul makes its way to Hell, Paradise or Purgatory depending upon the degree at which it is weighed down by sins or free of them, while the body moulders in the grave. On the Day of Judgement, however, a person's soul is restored within the body, and the *persona*, finally condemned or vindicated, can then enter that part of the world beyond the grave indicated to it by the Supreme Judge. The body, which Christian ideologues of the late Classical period and the early Middle Ages, tended to scorn as a vessel of evil and a prison in which the soul was temporarily imprisoned,[14] was now rehabilitated as an integral part of the individual.

Returning to the sermon *Concerning the Five Talents*, we need to underline once more that an inalienable quality of the individual is free will, the freedom to choose the path of Good or the path of Evil. On several occasions, Berthold emphasizes this freedom in other sermons and attaches enormous importance to it.

The fact that the list of the Lord's gifts to humanity begins with the *persona* is quite natural because it was the first and most important gift, from which all others follow. The second talent – 'service' or 'vocation' – points to a person's social function. Just as a person constitutes an individual, so that person belongs to an 'office' or 'service', to a social or professional group, category, social estate, that he or she cannot and must not change, because the fact of belonging to it has been decreed from on high. This is why the person must at all costs carry out those duties honestly and see them as a vocation. The significance of 'vocation' or 'service' is accentuated in every possible way in this sermon. In fact, if we consider the order of concepts to which 'service' is assigned, then it stands out as just as inalienable a quality or characteristic of a person as his or her very *persona*. The individual's *persona* cannot be reduced to a psychological entity, merely to a soul-body combination: it includes the individual's social function, the service performed in keeping with the Creator's design.

It is perfectly logical for the third gift or talent, after the *persona* and service, to be the time set aside for each individual's life. Naturally time in Berthold's writing is not presented as a secular entity: the 'Church's time' had not yet turned into 'merchants' time'. Here we are concerned with the Lord's time, something that belongs to Him. It is before the Lord that each individual is obliged to account for the way that the time allotted is spent. According to Berthold, the time set aside for a person's earthly life is first and foremost the time assigned to eventual salvation. Even in the early Middle Ages people were well aware of how transient time was: Christianity had always stressed the need to see time in terms of Eternity, and, when Berthold spoke of spending time usefully, he meant primarily that people should take good care to save their souls. In his sermons, he insisted many times that people needed to repent without delay, to expiate their sins and to restore immediately to the lawful owners any wealth they had amassed unjustly. In the eyes of this preacher, time had not become an independent value in our life on earth and indeed could not do that. In Berthold's interpretation of time it clearly loses its value as soon as the subject of Eternity is raised. Nevertheless, the fact that time is included among the central values of human life in the sermon *Concerning the Five Talents*, and therefore as a condition for one carrying out one's service or fulfilling one's vocation, is highly significant and has many implications: time is presented as an essential parameter of the human personality.

It would seem likely that for preachers who belonged to the poorest orders and who carried out their work in close contact with the ordinary citizen, time was just beginning (and emphasis should be placed on the word **beginning!**) to acquire new value, and, although this value was interpreted from a traditional theological angle, the mere fact that the category of the time allotted for a person's life and the categories *persona* and vocation (service) were associated with each other was most symptomatic of the age. We can assume that the high evaluation of time and membership of a guild that was natural for traders and artisans in the towns of the High Middle Ages influenced Berthold's sermon, in which he approached time, office and wealth from a religious and moral angle.

It is revealing that, when he turns to his flock, Berthold was by this time no longer able to speak of wealth only in a negative tone. Property enabled people to satisfy their own needs and those of their families (in the medieval understanding of the word, families included not merely spouse and children but also other relatives, servants and workers). Of course, it was necessary to help the poor and the needy and to do good works but there was no need to forget oneself at the same time. Berthold returns several times to the idea that riches were not distributed equally, and that some people had great wealth while others had little or even no money. Then the question arises as to what practical conclusions should be drawn from this state of affairs? If one man, for instance, has two or three good cloaks, while another does not even have one or only a single torn garment, is the rich man obliged to give one of his cloaks to the beggar?

While considering the idea 'Love thy neighbour as thyself', the preacher is encouraging an imaginary interlocutor to object and say: 'Alas, Brother Berthold, thou thyself art most unlikely to act in this way. I am thy neighbour, but you have two fine garments, while I only have one cloak, but nevertheless thou art more likely to leave me in poverty than thyself'. 'Yes, that is true' admits the preacher, 'I have clothes but do not give any to thee, yet I should like thee to live no less well than I do or indeed better. Loving thy neighbour is to wish him the same as thou might wish for thyself: if thou wouldst attain the Kingdom of Heaven for thyself, desire it for thy neighbour no less'.[15] This thought is extremely important for Berthold and he repeats it word for word in other sermons as well. There is no mention of the ideal of poverty as found in the Gospels or of the desirability of distributing wealth to others so as to save one's own soul, as advocated by preachers of an earlier period, and indeed Berthold's contemporaries as well time and time again.

In Berthold's mind, wealth was so closely linked with the *persona* and its 'office' or preordained vocation, that 'love for thy neighbour' assumed far less significance than it had done hitherto. There is surely little doubt that this reassessment of Christian values reflects a hidden influence of the new ethics underlying work and ownership that was beginning to emerge in the towns of the day? The ideals of this preacher, whose activities were concentrated mainly among town-dwellers, were radically different from traditional monastic ideals. During Berthold's lifetime, appeals to those who possessed two shirts to share their possessions with their poor neighbours were already considered heretical, and the preacher pointed to such a demand as an indisputable sign of sedition.[16]

Thus, the *persona*, service or office, lifetime and property are all brought together in the sermon as an indivisible whole. All these things should be used for the benefit of the individual and, at the same time, in the interests of society as a whole: moreover, these interests are represented in this sermon in a familiar religious form as the fulfilment of the will of God – the owner of the 'talents' that are entrusted to humanity so that they might be put to the best possible use. Behind the traditional theological form, new earthly content lies hidden, even, it would seem, from the consciousness of the preacher himself. It goes without saying that, in Berthold's exhortations, God is not a mere pseudonym for society with its purely earthbound concerns. God retains His complete independence unassailed, and His importance as the decisive regulator of all that exists, as Creator, as Lord of the world and humankind and of the goals to which people should aspire.

Nevertheless, in the sermon *Concerning the Five Talents*, there is a certain contradiction to be discerned, something in the way of a tense relationship between the familiar theocentric picture of the world and the world picture that was stealthily creeping into the social consciousness of the merchant class, in the centre of which, unofficially at least, stood people and their earthly aspirations. The new world picture did not in any way deny the role of the Creator and, in this sense, it was also theological, yet latent within it there were already new possibilities. Berthold of Regensburg could not but be aware of these impulses stemming from the merchant circles of the day. Remaining first and foremost a theologian and preacher, he abided by the letter and essential meaning of medieval Christianity. Yet that very meaning was imperceptibly changing: there were shifts of emphasis at work and new wine was being poured into old bottles. These shifts were to become far more noticeable in the fourteenth century but, as we shall see, premonitions of them and their prerequisites were already to be discerned in the work of this German preacher of the mid-thirteenth century.

We have before us an unusual, but quite clearly expressed, 'sociology' and 'anthropology' in the writings of a medieval preacher. Berthold felt himself obliged to give a clear answer to the principal questions connected with the existence of humankind, standing at the same time before God and society. Our Franciscan differs from other preachers and authors of Latin *exempla* because of the astute way in which he formulates these questions and the clarity with which he resolves them. It is tempting to assume that the dire state of German society during the interregnum of the 1250s and 1260s, a society that was bogged down in anarchy and internal feuding and was incapable of protecting its members, especially the labouring masses and the poor, from ever worse tyranny and oppression, must have led this preacher to ask himself: what is man? how should he behave within society? what are the main values in his life? and then to look afresh at those eternal questions in the crisis situation that was taking shape. The reflections of Berthold of Regensburg are particularly interesting in that they are to be found, not in a philosophical or theological treatise written for a narrow group of the enlightened, but are expounded in a sermon addressed to everyone, particularly commoners.

Christian preachers have always turned to the common treasure-house of ideas as far back as the Bible and the Fathers of the Church, but they all made use of this legacy in their own ways, reading something new into the sacred texts. Despite their profound respect for these authorities, the preachers of the Middle Ages placed their own accents on the nuances and thought patterns of their predecessors, which corresponded most closely to the demands of their own times. When we examine the sermon *Concerning the Five Talents*, however, we encounter a profound and radical reinterpretation of the content of a parable from the Gospels that lends the original quite new implications. A new concept of the human individual is put forward in the guise of a traditional exegesis of the Holy Scriptures. Most importantly, into this new reading of a passage from the Gospels, there erupts the idea of the human individual until then absent from such commentaries.

7

Knights and Merchants

Among the social types of the Middle Ages that manifested the most marked individualistic tendencies, the knight and the town-dweller should be singled out. Their ways of life and attitudes stimulated human characteristics bound to promote the cause of the individual. The characteristics in question were, naturally, very different for the two categories.

The process of transforming the early medieval warrior into the knight of the High Middle Ages was a process that also served to render him a poetic hero, even a figure of myth. *Chansons de geste*, genealogies of noble families, 'Mirrors of History' (*speculum*), knightly epics and romances, the poetry of troubadours and minnesingers – each of these served in its own way to build up the ideal of the knight. This ideal, that sublimated warfare, was not formulated as any kind of 'system' of specific knightly exploits: it was implicit in the logic of the knight's social behaviour and, at the same time, could not but influence that behaviour. Yet there was an enormous gap between the reality and its poetic representation. The adventures, wanderings and heroic deeds undertaken by knights; their selfless search for exploits and opportunities to protect the weak; their elevated love for the beautiful lady beyond reproach; their ideal – *mesure* or *maze* (balance and moderation) and *courtoisie* or *hovescheit* (courtly manners), that embraced the ideas of *prouesse* (valour) and *sagesse* (wisdom) – and their code of honour are also the stuff of literature,[1] as are the comparisons of earthly warriors with the soldiers of the Lord. Violence, plunder, unrestrained thirst for booty, vindictiveness, unbridled behaviour, the combination of the idealization and spiritualization of love on the one hand and coarse sensuality on the other, arrogance with regard to other social estates, perfidy towards those lower down the social ladder and contempt for those not of noble birth were all part of the harsh reality of feudal society. Comparison of the genres of knightly poetry listed above with the chronicles and other narrative works somewhat nearer to the facts of everyday life sheds light on the gulf between the ideal and actual practice of medieval knights.[2]

The fact that one of the leitmotifs to be found in knightly poetry was *laudatio temporis acti* (praise of the past) can evidently be interpreted as an expression of the gap between the sad reality on the one hand and the lofty ideal of the knights, on the other.[3] Nevertheless, it is possible to understand the phenomenon of the medieval knight only if we consider this social figure caught between the high ideals and everyday reality of the period, on which the ideals did exert a certain influence.

While imbibing to some degree knightly ethics, the warrior of noble birth did not behave at all like the heroes of poetry and prose – that was not possible. For this reason, the historian needs to be extremely careful when turning to literary texts extolling the feats and nobility of the characters depicted in them. Overlooking the gulf between the actual life of a knight and its representation in literature led to Don Quixote's madness: in historical research, the same carelessness led to unjustified idealization of medieval knights.

At the same time, it would be wrong to regard works of chivalric literature as nothing more than fiction. The fictional tales of knights were repeated so often that it has to be assumed they did perform a particular social function in the life of knightly society. Nowadays, historians and philologists have found ways to pick out real features of the age behind the fantastic narratives. The romantic poetry about chivalry did, to some extent, reflect the actual situation in which the sons of noble families found themselves, sons who would look for fiefs and rich brides who might bring them the former. Attempts at self-identification on the part of knights could be concealed behind the searches for the Holy Grail. We shall leave to one side the currently fashionable tendency of certain researchers to look for echoes of Freudian complexes in knightly epics or poetry. Yet, on the other hand, sexual impulses of the young knights may well have found expression in them – in sublimated form – and there is still more reason to assume that such works of literature reflect knights' searches for their own identity, searches undertaken by men who were no longer able to see themselves as part of the family or clan group, such as described in the *chansons de geste*.

One of the characteristic features of the knight was his heightened emotionality, his tendency to lurch violently from anger and temper to tenderness and merriment, his susceptibility to tears or despair. Cruelty and piety cohabit within his soul. The medieval knight (indeed this could apply to virtually anyone in that age) appears to our modern eyes as a man of extremes, prone to violent mood changes. The extent to which these emotional 'excesses' were to be found in medieval literature served to define the fictional individual and his inner world. Yet these facets of the knight's character are also borne out in other sources: we are confronted with a real psychological phenomenon, or rather with a socio-psychological one, because certain forms for the expression of emotions were, of course, part of social etiquette and ritual that determined how they were manifested. In any case, it can definitely be said that these manifestations of the knight's mental attitudes distinguish him very clearly from courtiers of subsequent historical periods, who learnt from their surroundings at court to control themselves and to rein in demonstrations of their feelings. Spontaneous 'outbursts' give way to calculation, reserve and hypocrisy.

Although they belonged to a family or clan group, with all the traditions that bound such groups together, the knights also manifested traits of individualized behaviour. In battle, a knight had to rely primarily on his own strength and valour, for he was usually fighting on his own rather than among other fighting men. He was protected, not by a compact battle formation, but by chainmail or armour, and the speed of his own reactions and his mount's training. On horseback, a knight resembled a self-contained mobile fortress. Yet a knight was active and independent only for as long he was able to stay in the saddle: once unseated, he became an easy target for his enemy because of his clumsiness (his heavy cuirass or coat of mail restricted his movements).

A knight can, however, be termed an individual only with major reservations. All aspects of his social life were subject to strict rules and a high degree of ritual. Rites of initiation to the rank of knight, fighting on the battlefield or taking part in a tournament, lyrical poetry and fashion, modes of speech and behaviour were all subject to codes that were permeated with symbolism and universally binding. The knight saw himself as, and felt himself to be, a fully rounded being only when he was 'centre stage' in society, particularly among other knights, because to assert himself he had to act out his social role. For a knight, being himself meant presenting himself as a representative of a noble *ordo* (social stratum or estate). The social function he performed had to be expressed as 'theatre'. Tournaments, in particular, were spectacles. A knight would be anxious about how he appeared in the eyes of those around him – his fellow knights and the fair ladies present. It is difficult to say how inclined he really was to self-examination, but what can be stated without any hesitation is that his behaviour was directed at, and geared towards, spectators.

In an attempt to rein in the belligerence of the knights and make it serve its own ends, the Church concentrated its attention on 'God's peace' so as to limit bloodshed and slaughter. Elements of Christian symbolism and ritual were introduced into vassalage and elevated knights' aggression by channelling it into the Crusades. Yet, while leaving religious orders of knights to one side, we shall still probably have to acknowledge that the Church did not succeed in rooting out completely the original lay, or even 'pagan', ethos of the knightly estate. In the space that falls between God and the world of men, 'between the saint and the butcher' (Jacques Le Goff), knights did begin to develop individualistic tendencies.

The historical moment when the knights began to perceive of themselves as a class (*ordo*) apart, with specific social functions to perform, was the thirteenth century, and this was also the time when knights began to see themselves as individuals. That is the century of the rise of knightly culture, when epics appeared that extolled knightly valour and particular heroes such as Roland, the lyric poetry of Provence and the German *Minnesang*. Knightly ethics gave rise to new values: courtly manners and courtly love which elevated individual passion to unprecedented heights; knightly honour and nobility, perceived not as chance attributes of birth, but as a whole range of moral qualities characterizing the individual. The ladies extolled by the troubadours and minnesingers were not individualized ideals of female beauty, but the knightly poets' efforts to penetrate their own inner world more deeply and concentrate their attention on the emotional experiences of love, albeit limited by the artificiality and stereotyped nature of the poetic characters, did signify a landmark of no small importance in the development of the medieval knights' self-awareness. Suffice it to remember that Abélard described his infatuation with Héloïse to become aware of the depth of the upheaval in the world of feeling, which would take place in the generations to come.

Medieval lyric poetry was very far removed from the poetry of the modern age. The lyrical 'I' in courtly poetry is presented almost without concrete biographical or 'anecdotal' signs of life: it appeared as a mere convention. According to Paul Zumthor, the '*je*' in this poetry is strictly 'grammatical': it has been universalized and stripped of anything that might be time-specific and it is more like a role than a unique subject.[4] This poetry is hardly designed to bring us any nearer to the true personality of the author, for he eludes our gaze beneath the surface of the lyric text. Sometimes the author speaks about himself in the third person but, in those cases when an 'I' appears in a poem, only an illusion of contact with the author as individual is achieved. With the passage of time, the love extolled by troubadours was interiorized a little more and acquired characteristics of personal feeling, rather than simply expressing literary conventions: however, delineation of individual personalities was subject to definite limits as before. There exist accounts of troubadours' lives (*vitae*), yet these contain only a minimum of biographical information.

The situation is rather different when it comes to knightly epics and romances. Here the poet reveals his attitudes to the world he describes and he expresses his psychological aims and his self-awareness via allegory. Comparisons of the macrocosm and microcosm, which had become widespread by that time, led writers to search for ways in which to express the personal through the general: allegory provided a means for establishing relations of the individual soul with the universal principle on the one hand and the Creator on the other. A favourite literary device for achieving this was the narration of dreams; this provided an allegorical reflection of the author's world of ideas and emotions, lending it inner logic and systematizing the ideas involved. Allegorical poetry becomes, to some extent, poetry of individuals.

With this trend in relation to the individual is linked a shift of the centre of gravity in literature (in courtly novellas, fables, *exempla* and didactic fairy-tales) away from a distant legendary past to a topical present, in which the author acquires his own particular place. The *praesens* of the narrative is the author's present. The author becomes more subjective, for his sense of time is more acute and the resources of his individual memory are being drawn upon. His hero's adventures do not consist solely in his wanderings or in the feats he has performed, they also include 'internal adventures' – self-discovery. As he moves and functions within a particular social landscape, the hero of a chivalric romance at the same time creates or remoulds the mental landscape of his own personality.

What really changes is the *chronotopos* or the 'space-time continuum' – the perception and experience of time and space. These cease to be merely external attributes of the world surrounding the characters in a romance and they become 'subjectivized'. Time moulds the hero but, at the same time, he moulds time because the life of the individual lends time new importance and meaning. Time in the medieval romance had not yet become totally detached from time as represented in myths, and several aspects need to be singled out when efforts

are being made to interpret it. Time is represented in romances
in a contradictory and rather ambiguous way.[5] Nevertheless,
certain specialists in knightly romances talk of 'biographical',
subjective time in relation to their characters. From an individual
perspective, space is also perceived from an individual
perspective in their work in exactly the same way.[6]

The use of allegory and memory lent new meaning and
importance to the author's ego in such works as *The Romance
of the Rose* (*Roman de la Rose*). In this respect the medieval
courtly romance came to represent a kind of *Bildungsroman*
(educational novel).[7] Yet even this work presents us with
abstractions and allegories rather than characters drawn straight
from life. It is necessary to wait until Villon appears on the
scene (fifteenth century) before a poet's '*Je*' (I) gives voice to its
own emotions and makes statements about life as it really was.

The heroes of such romances would be wandering knights,
looking for adventures and exploits to perform, in which they
might come into their own and find their true identities.
Shrewdness, ingenuity, cunning and even the ability to deceive
others (*engin, ingenium*) are demanded of a knight: he has to
rely mainly on himself and on his own spiritual and physical
powers and skills. At the same time, he is cut off from the world
of ordinary society and cannot help but feel alienated from it.
This sense of alienation sometimes leads to outbursts of frenzy
on his part, lapses into a wild state. Heroes of these romances
pass through these extreme, 'borderline' states before they can
be at peace with themselves, their ladies or with God. In the
characters of Tristan and Perceval, and others in these courtly
romances, we encounter intensive searching by the individual
for his inner ego.[8] The heroes of the romance often hide behind
names that are not their own, but we would do well to ask
whether these are just attempts to outwit other people. Among
them there are some characters who do not even know their
own names (Perceval le Gallois). Are not features of individual
self-awareness reflected in such travesties?

Yet it would be wrong to attribute all-embracing importance
to such 'individualization' and 'subjectivization' of the world
of such heroes in the knightly romances, or indeed to assume
that this trend was gradually increasing. Not in the least! As

has been pointed out by Robert W. Hanning, concentration on the individual, the emergence of 'biographical time' and personal points of view – features to be found in the work of Chrétien de Troyes and certain other writers of the twelfth century – cease to be characteristic of the knightly romance of the thirteenth century, when the image of the individual is pushed into the background by representations of the shared destiny of humankind or descriptions of the downfall of the Knights of the Round Table.[9]

I would suggest that this observation is significant from a methodological point of view. When they observe new trends, historians often hurry to conclude that, once they have emerged, these trends will proceed to grow stronger and develop further. The idea of linear progress is what underlies such conclusions. History itself is rich in all manner of possibilities and unexpected twists. At an early stage in the development of the knightly romance, certain shoots of individualism in the depiction of heroes were to be observed, yet there are no grounds for extrapolating this development to cover the genre as a whole or for expecting that these shoots would continue to flourish later on as well.

We can assume that steps bringing us nearer to an understanding of individuality and subsequent moves away from such an understanding did not occur only in relation to the ideas of the people who composed knightly romances, but that these fluctuations to some extent also reflected shifts in the moods of certain sections of the knights' estate. Changes in a literary genre are not, however, directly linked with the attitudes of that particular social stratum of which the poets sang. Another conclusion can also be drawn: the social and psychological status of the knight was bound up with a specific trend towards individualization, yet this trend had always been held in check until that period.

The medieval knightly romance would appear to have nothing in common with the modern novel, and yet it seems to have passed on as a legacy to subsequent generations the specifications that go with this genre. Novels contain descriptions of heroes' lives and they concentrate on their adventures in life: their plots are focused on individuals placed in specific positions or taking steps to create such positions. Eleazar Meletinsky has pointed out that, unlike the heroic epic, the medieval romance, 'is geared towards the depiction of the self-sufficient individual', no longer bound up so closely with the group: the main interest in the knightly romance is to be gleaned from 'the personal destiny of the hero' and in the depiction of his emotions. After evolving from the epic, heroic lays and fairy-tales and reaching out beyond these, the romance discovers the 'inner man' within the epic hero.[10] Reflected in the genre of the knightly romance is the knight's need to lend meaning to his own destiny and to define his place in the world. In this aspect of the medieval romance it is possible to discern a nascent interest in the individual: does not the fact that the heroes of these romances are often depicted isolated from their social surroundings (apparently to a far greater degree than was actually possible in real life) point to the fact that the attention of the authors and their audiences was now more closely focused on the individual and on the ways in which the individual might achieve self-identification than before?

While the knight was armed with a sword and a spear, the merchant's armour consisted of an abacus and ledger for bookkeeping. These accessories already point to the fact that we are dealing with goals in life and systems of behaviour that are fundamentally different. Martial pursuits and tournaments demanded personal bravery and physical agility and strength, while trade and commercial operations demanded entrepreneurial flair, a capacity for logical thought and the ability to anticipate future developments. Part and parcel of the nobleman's way of life were careless generosity that paid no heed to expenditure, theatrical behaviour and a demonstrative performance of a particular social role that the knight was expected to play. What was demanded of the merchant, on the other hand, was a combination of frugality, financial prudence and attention to detail. The irrationally impulsive behaviour of the knight was the very opposite of the rational and methodical habits of the merchant.

Lords of noble birth did not really need books: if they were literate (this applied more often in the case of noblewomen than that of seigneurs), the ability to read was not one of the essential demands that life made upon them. A merchant could not conduct his business if he had not mastered arithmetic and was not capable of carrying on commercial correspondence. As a result, noble lords brought up their sons as future warriors, and heroic epics, family legends, genealogies and knightly romances were presented to them as models to be imitated. Rich men of commerce, on the other hand, would make sure that their heirs attended school or would hire tutors for them, and they would also send their sons to university where they might obtain knowledge that would be of use to them in their lives as merchants or enable them to enter the legal profession.

All this meant that knights and merchants emerged as two very different psychological types, which in many respects were diametric opposites. The two groups' attitudes were quite different as were their pictures of the world. This contrast was obvious to their contemporaries, and noblemen would always look down upon trader-commoners, while the latter were sceptical or even hostile towards seigneurs although, at the same time, they would try whenever possible to join the privileged classes, especially through marriage. This antagonism found expression in the *schwank*, or *fabliau*, epics about animals and other genres of urban literature: it was here that the despised class of traders took its revenge, representing knights as simpletons, as the embodiment of brute strength, who were outwitted by clever artful dodgers.

Two essentially incompatible systems of precepts for living are expressed in an anonymous allegorical poem *A Good Short Debate between Winner and Waster*.[11] The Winner, the Hoarder – he was first and foremost the Merchant; the Waster and the Lazybones – he was the Knight. The Winner would praise those who spent little money and spent it wisely and who lived modestly cutting their coats according to their cloth: contemplation of his assembled riches would warm his heart. The extravagance of the Waster, reflected in his attire and in his feasting, reached a more or less crazy level and filled the Hoarder with indignation. The list of dishes and beverages served in the house of Lazybones constituted a regular culinary treatise. The Winner was filled with amazement by anyone who, although without a penny in his pocket, would nevertheless go out and purchase costly furs, valuable cloth and other expensive luxury goods. The Winner reproached Lazybones because his gluttony and drinking would squander away his inherited estates and oblige him to cut down his forests. Lazybones paid no attention to the tilling of his land and sold off tools to pay for his military adventures and frivolous hunting.

It was, however, futile for the Winner to try to convince the Waster to cut down his expenditure, to guard against financial ruin and to teach himself and his relatives how to work. He understood, moreover, that what motivated the Waster was his 'arrogance'. The Winner, meanwhile, accumulated wealth thanks to his ability to abide by rules of moderation and to conduct his business properly.

The Waster, in his turn, reproaches the Winner on the grounds that the treasures he has amassed are not of any benefit to anyone and bring no-one any pleasure:

> What should wax of that wealth, if no waste were to come?
> Some would rot, some would rust, some rats would feed.
> Let be the cramming of thy coffers, for Christ's love of heaven!
> Let the people and the poor have part in thy silver . . .
> When Christ's people have part it pleaseth him better
> Than if it be huddled and hidden and hoarded in coffers,
> That no sun may see it through seven winters once;[12]

The Waster insists that wealth is mere vanity and he talks of the evil that it causes: the more prosperous a man is the more cowardly he is. Is it not better for life to be short but happy?

This poem would appear to have been written about 1352 and it conveys the mood of a certain section of English society during a critical situation immediately after the Black Death and the first victories achieved by the English in the Hundred Years' War. The anonymous author selects King Edward III to be the referee in the argument between the Winner and the Waster, but the King is not prepared to take either side and so the feud between greed and extravagance remains unresolved. The Winner and the Waster personify not so much distinct social types as opposed principles for living and systems of values, two styles of life and behaviour. Nevertheless, it is not difficult to recognize the merchant, the man preoccupied with money, on the one hand, and the noble idler and extravagant knight on the other.

The fourteenth century, in which this allegorical poem was written, was one in which rich merchants, bankers and moneylenders were far from unusual; such people had succeeded in accumulating considerable fortunes and in organizing reliable commercial enterprises. They would lend enormous sums of money to nobles and princes but, at the same time, they did not shrink from exploiting humble people. It was thanks to the energetic activities of the merchants and artisans that the towns had risen to prominence and become focuses of civilization which changed the whole face of Western Europe.

Rich trading cities had existed at the very dawn of the Middle Ages to the east in the Byzantine Empire and, at that time, the towns of Western Europe could not be compared in any way with Constantinople or Thessaloniki. The petty and all-embracing control exercised by the bureaucratic central administration of that empire had, however, held back its development, and the cities of the Byzantine Empire were condemned to unavoidable decline. The Fourth Crusade, followed by the plundering of Constantinople, served only to accelerate that degradation. By that time, developments in the West were following a very different path. The cities there succeeded in safeguarding their political and economic autonomy, and their campaign against the bishops and other seigneurs, to win greater freedom, gave rise to the emergence of self-governing communities that acknowledged no other power than that of the monarch. In Italy large towns grew up in the city-states of that period.

In these conditions artisans and men of commerce acquired the chance to expand their activities relatively freely. The difficulties that they encountered at this stage were of a different kind – from within. Rich merchants and entrepreneurs, who enjoyed power and influence in the cities, now came up against serious opposition from ordinary artisans and people of humble origin, and, resulting from this antagonism, there was much unrest and rebellion in the towns. Financiers and moneylenders were viewed with the strongest loathing of all. Everyone needed the money that they were willing to loan only at high rates of interest. Exploitation of small manufacturers served as the basis on which there grew up unanimous public opinion condemning their activities.

Decisive in this situation was the stance adopted by the Church: it prohibited moneylending outright because it was displeasing to God. In the scale of professions drawn up by the moralists in the Church, who divided these into professions permissible and impermissible for Christians from a theological point of view, moneylending for profit was seen as the most base: there was no doubt that the moneylender would be condemned to the torments of Hell. Preachers whose work, from the thirteenth century onwards, was coming to be more and more concentrated in the towns as the main centres where sin was widespread, were happy to use their eloquence to defame moneylenders.

According to the monks and priests, the moneylender was worse than any other sinner or criminal. After all, any villain desisted from crime occasionally: adulterers, libertines, murderers, false witnesses, blasphemers do not sin incessantly, for they grow tired from their evil deeds. The moneylender, on the other hand, sins with no respite: asleep or awake the moneylender's interest continues to accumulate. The Lord commanded that people should earn their daily bread by the sweat of their brows, but the moneylender grows rich without labour. Every believer is obliged to refrain from work on feast-days but the 'oxen of the moneylender', that is, the money that has been invested for gain, 'plough tirelessly', offending God and the saints as they do so. Yet, just as the moneylender is tireless in sinning, so too there will be no respite from eternal torment after death. The moneylender trades in the 'expectation of money', that is in time, by selling the light of day and the peace of night, and for this he will be deprived of both eternal light and peace: his soul will be condemned to an eternity of suffering.

Much use was made of 'examples' (*exempla*) in the sermons of the day and, in many of these, moneylending was reviled. After celebrating mass, a priest would announce that he intended to absolve all the townspeople present at the church service from their sins. Then, he would turn to representatives of various professions: 'let all blacksmiths rise' and absolve them from their sins; 'let the furriers stand' and once again he would absolve them from their sins. Finally, the moneylenders' turn would come round but, although there might be a large number of them in the church, not one of them would dare to stand up: instead they would try to hide and then run in shame from the church jeered at by the rest of the congregation. In another *exemplum*, a stone purse that had decorated the figure of a moneylender in a bas-relief of the Last Judgement fell down on the head of a moneylender as he was entering God's house to marry: in this way he had been taken off to Hell by a demon. In *exempla* of this kind, the moneylender was represented as the cause and as the victim of public scandal.

Money gained through moneylending was impregnated with sin and was evil smelling. According to another *exemplum*, a monkey on board a ship stole a purse from a pilgrim, climbed up the mast of the ship and then began to take coins out of the purse: as it smelt the coins, the monkey began to cast some of them into the waves, while it put others carefully back into the purse. What explained this? The monkey had been throwing out the coins which that particular pilgrim had come by unjustly. The coins of moneylenders were voracious. A certain moneylender entrusted all his money to a monastery for safekeeping, and the cellarer put them away in a chest in which the monastery's money was kept. When the chest was opened, it turned out that the moneylender's money had devoured the money that belonged to the monks. The weight of moneylenders' sins was so heavy that, when one of them died, it was impossible to lift his coffin from the ground and, only after it had occurred to the mourners to summon other moneylenders, did it prove possible to lift the coffin and transfer it to the place of burial without hindrance. The reason for this was that the demons would not allow other people, apart from those working in the same profession, to carry their servant.

A story was told of other moneylenders who tried to take money with them to the next world and whose hands went on moving after they were dead as if they were still counting money: people once believed that toads put coins into the hearts of dead moneylenders and that devils fed them with money. One moneylender was even said to have been recast in a smithy in the shape of a coin.[13]

Stories of this kind were related by preachers to their parishioners and used to shape public opinion, rendering it hostile to the rich and prosperous. For moneylenders and merchants, such stories constituted a source of mental torture and a major problem in their entrepreneurial activities. Even after achieving success in their trade and sometimes managing to exert considerable influence on the politics of their city, they still felt themselves to be rejected by God. Was there a way out of this contradictory situation? A prerequisite for the salvation of a profiteer was to return all the revenues gained to those who had been the victims of dealings. The Church was not prepared to accept partial compensation, and Berthold of Regensburg, when he was threatening all 'greedy' and 'avaricious people' (*gîtigen*), announced in his sermons that those who concealed their unjust profits, even if it be no more than a few *pfennige*, would die without repentance and then 'burn in the flames of Hell for as long as the Lord God would remain in the Kingdom of Heaven' and that no-one would save them – 'neither the Saints, nor the Apostles, nor the Virgin Mary, nor the Prophets, nor the Fathers of the Church, nor the Angels'. Berthold went on to point out: ' Even if thou wast to take the Pope's cross, swim across the sea, fight against infidels, defend the Holy Sepulchre and perish for God's cause and then to lie down in the Holy Sepulchre, thy soul would still perish despite all thy saintliness and it would be easier for thee if wolves were to gnaw at thee at thy mother's breast or if the Earth were to swallow thee up, like Dathan and Abiram'. 'Confound thee, miser! Thy amen shall resound like dogs barking in the ears of the Lord!'[14]

Berthold assigns the 'greedy' to the category of the most

inveterate murderers for, not only does the skinflint bring about his own downfall, but he also kills his child and all to whom he leaves his unjustly obtained wealth, and after his death he kills even more people than during his lifetime. It needs to be remembered that the moneylender destroys not only his own soul but also the souls of all his heirs.

Such was the tone of sermons on this subject. Examination of the lives of merchants and entrepreneurs of that period reveals that such sermons had an impact and that many financiers and traders, after amassing a fortune, began to ponder on how they might save their souls and even went so far as to renounce their wealth and donate it to the poor. This was exactly what the merchant Peter Waldo of Lyons did in about 1170: he led a group of men who adhered to the principle of poverty in the spirit of the Gospels (the Waldenses or 'poor men of Lyons') and, within a short period, Waldensian sects had spread through all Roman Catholic countries. In the next generation Giovanni Bernardone, the son of rich textile merchants and a former member of Assisi's 'gilded youth', renounced his earthly riches after a vision in which Christ had appeared to him; he broke all ties with his family and founded an order for his followers who were ready 'to follow barefoot the barefoot Christ'. The fact that this merchant's son, Bernardone, who came to be known as Francis of Assisi, became a saint who categorically renounced wealth and property testifies to the contradictory, even ambiguous position that merchants occupied in the religious and moral life of Western Europe at that time.

Naturally, Peter Waldo and Francis of Assisi, who made indelible marks upon the social atmosphere of Europe (one as the instigator of a heresy and the other as founder of the most dynamic and influential of the mendicant orders) were extreme cases. The extremely rich cloth merchant from Douai, Jehan Boinebroke, who mercilessly exploited artisans and workers and who did not shrink from any methods in his striving for wealth, was anything but saintly. Yet, before his death (*c.* 1286) he too felt obliged to give thought to his salvation and he left a will, in which he bade his heirs make good the losses of all those whom he had robbed during his lifetime.[15] In the same century, the merchant Homobonus of Cremona, who left all his fortune to the poor, was admitted to the ranks of the saints. And another merchant from Siena, Giovanni Colombini, founded the mendicant order of the Gesuati (known as the Jeronymites) in 1360.

There are no grounds for drawing general conclusions from cases of this kind. Yet merchants and financiers who repented or took fright at the prospect of having to atone for their deeds beyond the grave were a real phenomenon. These were people who decided to renounce their wealth and to break off their ties with their families. Revealing in this respect are the words of a priest, that he allegedly addressed to his parishioners (if we are to believe Jacques de Vitry, the author of a collection of *exempla*): 'Do not pray for the soul of my father, who was a moneylender and who did not wish to return the moneys which he had amassed through usury. May his soul be cursed and may he suffer forever in Hell, so that he might never see the face of God nor escape the hands of the demons'.

As is evident from the cases cited, the contradiction between commercial activity and the way of life led by merchants and financiers on the one hand and the religious and moral demands of the Church on the other could well set in motion psychological dilemmas and these left their mark on such people's activities. Commercial and financial transactions were carried out before God. Was it not better to involve God in such operations and thereby enlist His support?

This was obviously the approach used by Paolo da Certaldo from Florence in the 1560s, who compared humanity's indebtedness to God with a person's indebtedness to creditors. The same can be said of Giovanni di Pagolo Morelli (1371–1444) who began from the conviction that if one conducts one's affairs well, God will stand by that person. Unlike those merchants and moneylenders who were haunted by a nightmarish vision of Hell, Morelli, Certaldo and other people of commerce in fifteenth-century Italy, who left behind them records rich in information about their lives and their families seem to have succeeded in establishing normal relations with the Almighty and were not torn by insoluble moral dilemmas. They were religious people and well aware of the world beyond the grave, but they drew rather different conclusions from those described earlier. First and foremost, as Certaldo pointed out, it was important that their affairs should be completely above board so that, at any moment, a person could come before the Judge without having been caught unawares by death. In his *ricordi*, which were not intended for publication but addressed to his children, we find the practical and sometimes even cynical attitudes typical of merchants who value most highly diligence, tenacity, patience, persistence in commerce and thoroughness. These qualities were held to be Christian virtues. Rather than inherited privileges, a person's own energy, quick thinking and entrepreneurial flair making possible the amassing and multiplication of a fortune are the qualities underlying the essential confidence of that Florentine merchant of the Renaissance.

This new individual set great store by time. The town-dweller paid careful attention to its passing. In the late thirteenth and early fourteenth centuries, mechanical clocks were installed in towers in the cities of France, Italy, Germany and England to enable people to calculate time in a more regular way and at the same time to enhance the prestige of the cities concerned. More frequent laudatory references to time can be heard in which it is praised as humanity's most important and inalienable treasure: on this subject, humanists such as Leon Battista Alberti, preachers such as Bernardino da Siena, political figures such as Giannozzo Manetti, merchants such as Certaldo and Francesco di Marco Datino, and an anonymous Parisian leaving behind instructions for his wife, speak with one voice. A merchant does not waste time vainly: the merchant sees work as pleasing to God and God helps those, who take good care to organize their affairs properly. There is interaction and mutual understanding between the world on Earth and the world on high, and, in many commercial documents of that time, words are addressed to the Creator, to the Virgin Mary and to the saints calling upon them to help the business to flourish!

Yet commercial affairs were bound up with many risks of both a material and a moral kind. It is therefore not surprising that some merchants, in their efforts to reduce such risks, took their money out of commercial circulation or banking, preferring to invest it in property. Many followed this course so as to save their souls, just as they might undertake pilgrimages, fast, or make charitable donations in the interests of the poor and needy. Confidence in themselves and in their abilities was to be found side by side with 'melancholy' in the minds of merchants and financiers, side by side with visions of destiny as an all-powerful and capricious force that could bring either sudden success or, just as easily, unexpected disaster. The bankruptcy of a number of major banking houses, including that of the Bardi and Peruzzi families, and the sudden twists of fortune in the lives of such financiers as Jacques Coeur (*c.*1395–1456), the leading financial magnate of fifteenth-century Europe, made an enormous impact on their contemporaries.

The image of Fortuna, tirelessly turning her wheel, on which people of various social estates first climb aloft and then inevitably fall, became very popular in the twelfth and thirteenth centuries. Alexander Murray links the proliferation of this symbol with the fact that, in that period in Europe, upward social mobility was acquiring new importance.[16] The concept of fate was, of course, far from new: it could be traced back to pre-Christian times, to the Greeks and Romans and to the Germanic tribes. While, in the writings of the ancient authors, the accent had been on *Fatum* or destiny which controlled everything and before which human beings were powerless, in the Germanic view of the world 'fate', 'luck' or 'success' were of a more personal character and people were able to engage in energetic interactions with their fate and influence it.

Perhaps, in the circumstances, it would be permissible to put forward the following hypothesis: one of the reasons why the Reformation, with its characteristic emphasis on the idea of success in earthly affairs as a sign that an individual has been selected by God for salvation (the Protestant ethic), succeeded above all in Germanic lands, while it failed in countries with a Romance culture, was the presence in the 'secret recesses' of social consciousness of an active perception of the role of fate outlined above. The old German concept of 'luck' came into its own once again at the end of the Middle Ages. A merchant from Augsburg wrote that the Lord had rewarded his ancestors with 'mercy, good luck and profit' (*gnad, glück, gwin*).[17] In this alliterative, three-part formula the idea of luck-cum-fate clearly assumes a place between God's blessing and commercial revenue. Wealth is regarded as the result of the interaction between success sent down from on high by the Creator, on the one hand, and the single-minded efforts on the part of the entrepreneur on the other.

Protestantism was not the *sine qua non* in the emergence of capitalist relations, for these also took shape in Roman Catholic countries. In the latter, people had to resort to a certain amount of mental agility so that the individual engrossed in accumulating capital might at the same time feel pure before God. To be rich in the material sense and, at the same time, spiritually poor was, according to St François of Sales (1567–1622) 'a great joy for the Christian, since then he enjoys the advantages of wealth in this world and the deserts of the poor in the next'.[18]

8

Brother Salimbene and Others

We have been looking for outlets created by medieval culture in which the human individual came into his or her own. We have tried to single out specific opportunities for the unfolding of the individual within the socio-cultural system of those times. To what extent these opportunities were made full use of by this or that specific individual depended upon the person concerned, individual qualities, the individual's position in society, on social and property status, on knowledge and education and finally on the extent to which he or she had been drawn into the cultural traditions of the time. The forms we have considered have been essentially impersonal but, in each individual case, they have constituted essential conditions for the formation and the self-realization of the individual: the individual's socialization has resulted from an ability to assimilate categories that were universal for that person's society and times.

If we return now to a consideration of individual personalities, then the historian of the medieval age is faced with enormous problems. When we turn to texts, in which a particular author is expressing himself, then we soon realize that a person's endeavour deliberately or inadvertently to conceal his inner self provided the traditional means for revealing himself to others, paradoxical though it may sound. Perhaps it would be better here to talk of the individual's inability to express himself. Yet that inability is not the result of some mental 'backwardness' or 'ineptitude'; nor is it a consequence of the fact that, in the Middle Ages, people 'were not yet able' to do what they have since learnt to do in the modern age, namely to expose their unique inner world. It would appear that, in the Middle Ages, the individual was self-aware but in a different way and that, because of this specific approach, he or she did not focus attention on those traits of individuality that we regard as so important today. In their efforts to express themselves, people sought out models and would attempt to match their own individual personalities to them. This meant that they did not set store by what was unique or unusual about themselves (even if they were aware of such exclusive traits) but, on the contrary, sought to make themselves match particular *types*. Medieval writers went through the same process when working on other people, whom they needed to describe: they made haste to reduce the specific to the general. Moreover authors of biographies or Lives sometimes showed themselves to be better able to single out individual features of the people they wrote about than authors of 'confessions' or 'autobiographies', in which they were concerned with themselves.[1] Individuals did not seek inner satisfaction by contrasting themselves with everybody else: they found it in subordinating their egos to preselected prototypes.

In keeping with this uncontrollable craving to dissolve the individual in the type by depicting people in particular ways, individuals were described with wide use of clichés and stock phrases, designed to fit them into various categories. This means that, when medieval writers are sketching literary portraits of historical or other important figures, they never tire of using devices adopted from traditional models for depicting their subjects: in particular, they used those inherited from the Classical period. In his *Vita Caroli Magni* (*Life of Charlemagne*), Einhard cannot light upon a more fitting way of describing the life and the character of Charlemagne than by turning to the accounts of Roman emperors composed by Suetonius: insofar as the King of the Franks had proclaimed himself to be a Roman emperor, it seemed quite natural to attribute to him characteristics of his distant predecessors.[2]

Medieval sculptors and painters had, after all, gone about

their work in exactly the same way: kings, emperors, popes, princes, Fathers of the Church and saints depicted in frescos, book illuminations and sculptures are totally devoid of any true individuality. They do, however, all have features that indicate their social, political or spiritual status. What was seen as essential and, therefore the only thing worthy of attention, was all that made an individual belong to a type, **not** what set that individual apart. Medieval biographers, hagiographers and artists were all masters of generalization. They were 'not able' to individualize because they felt no need to do so: they did not see features of inimitable individuality, because their gaze was concentrated not on individuality but on something that, from their point of view, was infinitely more profound – the actual essence of the person in question, whose essence was not to be found in the accidental or chance traits of character of which there might not even be any: essence lay in the fact that the person embodied certain 'vocations', 'offices' or varieties of 'service'. While they analysed the question as to what was fitting for each 'rank', socio-legal status and estate (*ordo*), medieval authors ignored any universal ideal that might apply to the human race as a whole. The individuals whom we encounter in the writing or the art of that period are not 'human beings in general', they are socially specific individuals.

Medieval writers and artists reduce individuals to the *average*, depriving them of individuality as we understand it today. Yet, by doing so, they achieved their main aim from the perspective of their own time: the individual they describe in words, carve or outline with brush-strokes does not appear as an isolated and therefore coincidental human atom hardly deserving of attention: that person figures, as depicted in their art, as a vehicle for socially significant qualities and attributes. The authors of Lives of the saints describe their subjects using clichés which pass on from one work to another and which are easily adapted from a common store of definitions and epithets: no-one is perturbed or annoyed by repeated references to the same attributes of saintliness. On the contrary, they clearly derive satisfaction from the fact that each individual case serves to emphasize the shared ideal. The authors of these Lives

and their readers were not looking for the inimitable
individuality of the saint in question, which that saint may not
even have possessed: the mere fact of saintliness presupposed
that the person had renounced his or her ego and was seeking
to draw nearer to God and to be at one with Him.[3]

Individuality is not valued or approved: rather it is feared,
and not only in others – people are afraid of being themselves.
Manifestations of originality or idiosyncrasy have a whiff of
heresy about them. People suffer if they feel aware that they are
not the same as everyone else.

In view of all this, preoccupation with individuality is not a
characteristic mark of the age. To study the Middle Ages,
concentrating exclusively on outstanding figures, surely means
being off target? The fact that medieval chroniclers describe
the history of their times in terms of monarchs and their deeds
should not mislead us in this respect. Kings, popes and princes
were not of interest in themselves for the annalists and historians,
nor as striking individuals: they were seen as no more than the
representatives of a more profound process directed towards
identification of God's purpose for it was through their deeds
that the Creator's design was implemented. Guibert de Nogent's
Gesta Dei per Francos makes it clear that neither Franks nor
the French make history, but it is the Lord God who makes it
using the former as His instruments! Saints, hermits, mystics
were seen still less as individuals: on the contrary, their glory
lay in the fact that they renounced their own individuality and
sought to become one with God.

In this situation, should not medieval historians also confine
themselves to prominent individuals and focus their attention
on such outstanding figures as Abélard, Bernard of Clairvaux
and Francis of Assisi, Anthony of Padua, Saint Louis, Thomas
Aquinas and Dante? To what extent are such individuals
typical of their age? They stand out from the average and they
are not very useful pointers for those trying to understand the
milieu in which they lived. To be more precise, they are
significant as extreme cases, if we are trying to understand the
limits which individualization could hope to reach. Yet is it not
time to come down from the mountains with their rarefied air,
to look at 'the nameless people in the valleys' with their

everyday cares and hopes?

The brief to study the 'average person' is no new departure for the medieval historian. Perhaps it is of interest for the Western reader to learn that this approach has been used on several occasions by Russian scholars as far back as the beginning of the twentieth century. Almost simultaneously (in 1915 and 1916 respectively) two outstanding specialists in Italian history – Lev Karsavin and Pyotr Bitsilli – published works in which they explained why it was essential to become more closely acquainted with the 'average' representative of medieval society.[4] Karsavin set himself the task of singling out the level of religious awareness, which he referred to as 'the general religious background', from which people derived their beliefs and their conceptions of the world. He presented his readers with a hypothetical reconstruction of those who contributed to this 'background', qualifying them as 'average people'. He attributed methodological importance to that concept: the average person was not a run-of-the-mill philistine, but a typical representative of those who held to widespread beliefs and approached new ideas from a religious point of view. When asked about the representatives of the 'religious background', Karsavin was inclined to list prominent individuals because, in his opinion, they are also completely, or at least in part, typical individuals'.[5]

Bitsilli shares Karsavin's point of view to some extent but, at the same time, he stresses that it is impossible to study prominent personalities alongside mediocrities and build up a comprehensive picture, mixing together traits gleaned from analysis of the first group and characteristics of the second, because what is typical of the one group may be far from typical for the other. The difference between an outstanding individual and the 'average person' is, according to Bitsilli, not a 'quantitative one'; nor is the difference to be found in the fact that Saint Bernard, for example, is 'more of a mystic' than someone else, but rather in that he is 'a different kind of mystic'. That is why, if we concern ourselves only with great people, we shall not learn very much about the life of medieval society as a whole. Unlike Karsavin, Bitsilli focuses his attention on one figure, the Franciscan monk Salimbene who wrote a number of works, including chronicles, into which his own lifestory is incorporated. Bitsilli studies Salimbene's chronicle, which had been written in 1282–87, using it as a means of studying Salimbene's personality – the personality 'of a representative of a specific cultural period'.[6]

I would suggest that the approaches to the study of medieval religious culture, such as those of Karsavin and Bitsilli, are valuable. The store of beliefs relating to that age was not just the fruit of great minds, creations of theologists and mystics, as imagined by older historiographers. Cultural models did not take shape exclusively in the upper echelons of the social hierarchy and then make their way down to broader strata of society (becoming vulgarized on the way). The masses were gradually developing their own ideas of the world, space and time, souls, sin and redemption and life beyond the grave. These ideas by no means always matched official doctrines and, between the two, tension and conflict were often the order of the day. It was within the system formed by those sometimes contradictory beliefs that the individual was emerging.

When we return to the subject of Salimbene, it should be noted that he lived and was writing in a critical period in Italy's history. Chiliastic ideas were spreading among the people in the form of Joachism at that time. Joachim del Fiore had predicted that the age of the Holy Ghost would begin in 1260 and, precisely at that time, the fact that the power of the Hohenstaufen over Italy collapsed gave rise to the idea that the Holy Roman Empire was coming to an end. It seemed that the prophecy concerning the end of the world was coming true. Unrest rose to new heights in Italy and it was in the year 1260 that the movement known as the Apostle Brethren began: the leaders of the movement advocated extreme asceticism and rejected property, labour and trades; in other words, they condemned everything that made people feel they had a place in life. At the same time, processions of flagellants began to appear in Italian towns and villages. At such moments in history, characterized by heightened emotionality or even an unhealthy propensity for nervous exhaustion, it is inevitable that people should become more receptive and observant with regard to the individual. Bitsilli points out: 'From our vantage point it looks as if the dawn of the Renaissance was breaking over Italy at that time, while the men and women alive at the time took the light on the horizon to be the harbinger of a universal conflagration'.[7]

Melancholy, fear, pessimism and the expectation that the unavoidable end of the world was at hand – those were the feelings that gripped the particular individuals who left testimony behind them, and also the masses. Individuals felt that they had been left to their own devices, they felt separate and isolated: this was at a time when the structure of society was growing more complex, when a social situation had emerged in which the individual was drawn into a number of groups that did not overlap and which were based on different principles, so that the traditional microsocieties which had previously formed stable psychological entities no longer provided any support. In this context, and as a consequence of intellectual 'bereavement', the individual achieves new self-awareness which, in those conditions, finds expression mainly as extreme egoism and moral nihilism. These traits are to be found in good measure in Salimbene, too: he lacked any family attachments, forgets to mention the death of his parents and almost overlooks his brother who, like him, had taken monastic vows; he does not love his native town and is not a particularly ardent Italian patriot; he has something positive to say about the Franciscan order to which he belongs but, strictly speaking, only because he has prospered in it, in other words for purely selfish reasons while, in reality, its ideals are alien to him. Individualism that finds expression in egocentrism is surely something that we encountered 150 years earlier when considering Abélard's *Historia calamitatum mearum*. Was not such egocentrism one of the typical manifestations of individuality?

Unlike Abélard, however, Salimbene is writing a chronicle, not an autobiography. For this reason attention is concentrated not on his own person: this is revealed in the pages of his work, without however obscuring the life around him. Caught up in the currents of everyday life and fascinated by rumours and gossip, so that his attention is distracted by all sorts of trifles, Salimbene does not keep his distance as an unbiased chronicler:

like other historical works of that period, Salimbene's chronicle is also permeated by personal experience. He shows keen interest in the customs and habits of various peoples and regions and succeeds in picking out their distinctive cultural features. Mistrust or dislike of neighbouring peoples and the urge to find and expose their weaknesses and funny characteristics were typical manifestations of patriotism in the Middle Ages. They stemmed from what was by this time a more sensitive personal response and from the need to scrutinize people's individual features so that an individual's, or a people's, self-awareness might take firmer root: this was an essential step towards contrasting what was 'ours' and what was 'other people's'.

If we look more carefully at the descriptions of individuals generously provided by Salimbene for people he knew or had heard about, then it becomes clear that his descriptions consisted in the main part of stock phrases. 'A lettered man', 'amiable', 'generous and bountiful', 'scrupulous and honest', 'noble' (*Litteratus homo, curialis, liberalis et largus, religiosus et honestus, nobilis*): such are the clichés that Salimbene applies to an extremely wide range of individuals. Generosity and amiability (*largitas, curialitas*) are consistently contrasted by Salimbene with rough-hewn manners and avarice (rustic, *avaritia*) but, in this respect, Salimbene is not being at all original and does not set himself apart from many other authors of his day. The ideal of noble generosity was extolled in the poetry of the troubadours and had long since been a commonplace. Nevertheless, Bitsilli assumes that the stereotyped nature of the descriptions provided by Salimbene did not demonstrate that he was incapable of singling out individuals, but that it was instead dictated by 'the manners of the day, the rules of literary propriety'.[8]

On the contrary, it is Salimbene's powers of observation that set him apart from the writers of the previous period. People of the Middles Ages were inclined to engage in self-scrutiny but 'were blind and deaf to the world around them'.[9] The reason for this should not be sought in asceticism, which served only to take such indifference to extremes. According to Bitsilli, the people of that age simply did not know how to look at the outside world, making do with random analogies and impressions. Every object was of interest only in so far as it presented them with a challenge, and people tended to see only those aspects of objects which could present a challenge. This explains why many medieval texts contain few images, only pale colours and dry descriptions, and this would apply to all Lives, chronicles or poems.

Is it not revealing that 'autobiographies' were regarded by medieval writers as complete when they reached that moment of a person's life when it seemed to them that that person's ultimate goal had been achieved? Yet what was that ultimate goal? For St Augustine the *Confessions*, which were to prove a model for medieval authors, were a conversion once and for all; for Abélard his goal was the Paraclete, the oratory he had founded; for Guibert de Nogent, as we have seen, it was to be appointed abbot in charge of a monastery; and for Salimbene it was to achieve finally a firm foothold in the Franciscan order. The story in a medieval 'autobiography' was not a whole life, but movement along a path to a goal that had been laid down in advance, ordained by Providence and which shall mark the high point in an individual's spiritual growth. The description of a life is subordinated to a single motif, that of spiritual improvement, or the motif of service. Once that goal has been achieved, the life of the individual has, so to speak, been rounded off – person and story are complete.[10] Attention is focused on the achievement of the individual's earthly vocation, the fulfilment of duty, the approach ever nearer to an ideal type and *not* the singling out of unique individuality that shall never be repeated.

In the *chansons de geste* that describe the life of noble families, it is definitely not an individual who provides the real hero of the poem, but rather the whole clan, the whole *geste*, while specific individuals are merely elements in the collective whole and they are deprived of all individual characteristics, for their characters are passed on from one generation to the next and intrinsic to the whole lineage.[11] The individual is not yet an entity separate from the clan, but still bound by an umbilical cord to the family, and not yet occupying the central place in the author's perception. As for Salimbene's monastic 'autobiography', it is an extension of the knightly family chronicle: while he was noting down the genealogy of his line, Salimbene became imperceptibly autobiographical. Comparison of Guibert de Nogent's *De vita sua* with Salimbene's *Chronicle* is most revealing in this respect: the twelfth-century abbot begins the story of his life and inadvertently goes off at a tangent to describe his monastery and then again to discuss the history of France, as if he kept forgetting about his own destiny, while the Franciscan, on the other hand, who had planned to write a historical work, turned his chronicle into an 'autobiography', *sui generis*. Surely these shifts in opposite directions serve to show that, during the 150 years that separated these two writers, the focus was tending to shift from the general to the particular, to the individual.

It would be wrong to make any hasty generalizations. Let us point out merely that, in the thirteenth century, human ability to observe the surrounding world was becoming steadily better. Individuals, now oriented to practical experience, were using their eyes in a more attentive way and they could see more and remember longer. In this respect certain descriptions of scenes witnessed by Salimbene were of interest: he recorded with precision many details, gestures, poses and movements; he was sensitive to human emotions and compared what he saw with his other observations. No-one escaped his penetrating and mocking gaze. Observations by such a man are very much alive, and in them we do not encounter commonplaces or formulas taken over from literature. Salimbene's endeavour was to move away from the stereotype, and this also manifested itself in the individualization of his characters. One of the ways to introduce individuality into a word-portrait is to compare two different people: whom does the particular person resemble and with whom does he or she have nothing in common? Nevertheless, what we find in Salimbene's writing is merely a tendency to renounce run-of-the-mill clichés: because Salimbene was not acquainted with the whole range of positive characteristics, when he started praising someone he was obliged to resort to stereotypes.

Salimbene was a preacher, and his own inner world and personal emotions are not an end in themselves in his writing:

they are simply material for didactic *exempla*, which would be
used in sermons. We need to look further, though, than to his
profession of preacher. Profound religious experiences are
definitely unfamiliar to Salimbene, and this remarkable observer
of the external world is not able to look deep into others' souls
nor, it would appear, into the deep recesses of his own. Nor,
probably, does he even feel the need or inclination to indulge
in such introspection. Is this a peculiarity of Salimbene alone?
Unlikely. 'Medieval man was not interested in his Ego as such.
His soul was for him an object worthy of attention only insofar
as study of its movements opened the way to a closer
understanding of phenomena from the next world.'[12] In about
1070 an inscription was carved above the doors leading into
the church of Sant'Angelo in Formis which read: 'If thou
knowest thyself, thou shalt gain the heavens'.[13]

Evidently, this appeal should be seen, not as a demand that
people probe their own individuality, but as an expression of
an urge to find God in oneself, to draw nearer to Him by losing
oneself in God. Yet had not Bernard of Clairvaux said the same
thing? 'In order to humble the soul there is no better means
than to come to know thyself'.[14] How much had things really
changed a hundred years later? Very little. 'In the thirteenth
century people measured themselves by generally accepted
criteria,' maintained Bitsilli, 'and they had not yet availed
themselves of their own yardsticks'.[15] I would suggest that, in
the implicit argument between Bitsilli and Morris (the former
doubts that people of the thirteenth century attached much
importance to self-awareness, while the latter insists that, as
early as the twelfth century, several intellectuals were busily
searching for their own egos),[16] the Russian medievalist is more
cautious in his assessments and therefore nearer to the truth:
he is not inclined to force the pace and 'hoist' the medieval
individual to the norm that has evolved today.

According to Bitsilli's assessment, Salimbene's religion did
not go beyond magic and fetishism: it was 'naive, popular
paganism' and, given that level of religious thought,[18] it was
impossible to expect any kind of psychological depth in his
autobiography. The self-satisfaction with which this Franciscan
was brimming over and his tendency for self-glorification

determined the limits within which it would be possible for the individual concerned to reveal himself. Frá Salimbene, who came from a family of knights and lawyers, does not conceal his social arrogance in his writings ('the world is destroyed by base men and peasants, while it is preserved thanks to knights and nobles').[19] Such were the views voiced in his *Chronicle*, and he would have hardly been able to develop such ideas any further in his sermons!

Salimbene's *Chronicle* is, to a large extent, no more than a memoir. Most of the events he described are ones that he himself witnessed, and he has no trouble adding personal detail. History and autobiography come together as it were. As we have already been able to establish, the 'autobiographies' of the previous period are primarily confessions. Insofar as humility and repentance were best suited to achieve salvation of the soul, literary confessions often assumed the form of self-denunciation. In his *Dialogue*, Ratherius of Verona provides a detailed account of his own sins, as if he were replying to the questions contained in the confessional ['Excerpt from the confessional dialogue of a certain most profane Ratherius' (*Excerptum ex dialogo confessionali cujusdam sceleratissimi Raterii*) is the name he gives to his work]. Moreover, he takes great care to find in himself (or to attribute to himself?) all the sins listed in the *liber confessionum* although at least one of them cannot apply in the case of monks, namely breach of marriage vows: even here, though, Ratherius finds a way round the dilemma. After all, he had twice served as a bishop and had been deprived of two dioceses, which could be seen as the equivalent of two breaches of a man's marriage vows! How is it possible to penetrate this fictitious confession to reach the true personality of the author? Even in those cases when, as he complains to a confessor he himself has invented about his own lack of will and morbid fascination with self-analysis as the source of his sins, Ratherius would seem to be giving his own assessment of his character, yet the historian is still unable to tell what the bishop was really like. The actual selection of the genre of repentance for self-characterization is, nevertheless, symptomatic.

In the literary confession, what people have searched for

first and foremost have been moral admonitions and examples for imitation, and these works were also lacking in psychological interest of their own. Yet a stimulus to start autobiographical writing is a writer's interest in his or her own personality, which then becomes the object of independent analysis. If we can believe the statements of writers from the early Middle Ages, what they valued about themselves was only their literary activity. This is what we are assured by Gregory of Tours and by the Venerable Bede. In Gregory of Tours, Bede and similar writers, Christian humility goes hand in hand with undoubted self-awareness. The 'bibliographies', which they deemed essential to attach to their main works, serve to summarize what they have accomplished in life. Later on other authors would dwell in more detail on their own lives in their writings (for example, Giraldus Cambrensis).

Mysticism can be regarded as one of the specific medieval manifestations of individuality. By denying ego, eliminating it before the face of God, the mystic is also focusing on inner spiritual experience, on the life of the soul. For mystics of this kind, such as Bernard of Clairvaux, their path through life constitutes a process of the development of the soul and moral improvement. Once more, it is St Bernard of Clairvaux who warned that mystical individualism can lead to the sin of pride. Is that perhaps the reason why the anonymous author, concealing himself behind the name of Bernard, turns to his neighbour when he discusses human dignity: he exhorts him to find himself while facing himself, as if he had encountered someone else; and to bewail himself, to bewail his sins, through which he had offended the Lord. Later he reminds his neighbour that, as he contemplates himself, he will be contemplating his neighbour, for his neighbour is none other than himself. He and the neighbour are, without fail, present the one within the other, for they both dwell in God and in God they love each other.[20] The individuality of the mystic is unimportant: it is the ideal, namely to be like God, into which all individuals are absorbed.

Perhaps emphasis on the moral value of 'simplicity' stems from this fear of the sin of pride? *Simplicitas* implies cleansing from all that is accidental and concerned with everyday life:

achieving simplicity is a step on the path to God. A mystic turns to God with the words: 'I am with myself when I am with Thee: when I am without Thee I lose myself'.[21] This 'psychology' involved penetration into the human soul, which did not lead to more individuality, but brought the individual nearer to God. Such was the character of 'Christian Socraticism': gaining self-knowledge meant renouncing the self for God's sake.

'Simplicity' implies more than ignorance (the definition *simplex* is often used as a synonym for *idiota*, or *illiteratus*) and definitely not foolishness. The quality *simplicitas* embraces different meanings: spontaneity in the service of God, sincerity in devotion to Him. For this reason 'simplicity' is the only admissible form in which a person's individuality and originality might manifest themselves freely and innocently. 'In surroundings where personal awareness was a tragedy for anyone, who had reached that high but was also convinced of his sinfulness and the need to suppress such awareness, the simpleton does not feel oppressed by the awareness of his originality . . .'.[22]

This means that the term 'simpleton' possesses many meanings in the context of medieval culture and religion, and is rich in overtones. A word that might appear humiliating turns out to be ennobling. When Gregory of Tours announces that it was not without fear and after long vacillation that he eventually embarked upon the tale of Saint Martin, because he felt himself 'hardly literate, stupid and a simpleton' (*inops litteris, stultus et idiota*), it would have been rash to take him at his word and imagine that he saw his 'simplicity' to be a vice: indeed, the characteristic way he used to think and express his thoughts, as encouraged to do by his mother when she appeared to him in a vision, was to him the only correct way. 'Simplicity' is true piety. The simpleton is pleasing to God and therefore a person should aspire to be a simpleton, paying no heed to worldly scholarship: 'The Lord has chosen neither orators, nor fishermen, nor philosophers, but peasants in order to destroy the vanity of worldly wisdom'.[23] It follows, therefore, that, according to the Gospel, simpletons are not so much those who need enlightenment, as apostles, chosen by Christ to enlighten the people, and Christ himself lends meaning to the figure of the Simpleton.[24]

Simplicity and spontaneity on the part of the faithful and the vanity of earthly wisdom are contrasted but, at the same time, the simpleton or ignorant 'idiot' and the erudite scholastic who has mastered the secrets of theology, despite all their contradictions, 'greet each other across the gulf of incomprehension' to use Vladimir Bibler's words. 'They are at different poles of thought and they are indispensable for each other . . .', [25] for, within the 'force field' of medieval culture, they loom up as two hypostases of the individual bound together by internal ties. An interminable and insoluble debate goes on between them. In the depths of the popular consciousness, vague images and 'superstitions'[26] take shape: at the level of the people's understanding of the world, they remain as molten magma and are unable to assume definite shape independently or to crystallize. In the discussions of theologians and scholastics, they are viewed as suspicious from the viewpoint of accepted orthodoxy: they are rejected and condemned but, at the same time, those who censor them eventually come one way or another to take in these ideas and beliefs, to rework them into a form acceptable to the Church and then to impress them upon the very same masses. This 'mechanism' of a two-way exchange is possible, not just because the clergy is striving to assert ideological control over the minds of the faithful, but primarily because, in the minds of the masses and of the spiritual élite, the two poles are visible (*see: The Book of the Simpleton* by Nikolaus von Cües: the Simpleton carries on a debate with a Rhetorician and a Philosopher because it is precisely he, the Simpleton, who steers the course of the conversation and lectures his scholarly colleagues).

The enormous distance between the 'chaos' of the simpletons and the 'cosmos' in creations of refined European culture narrows to a point, for the 'popular' and 'high' cultures of the Middle Ages are not different from, and independent of, each other but parts of an integrated culture with its own inner dialogue and contradictions.[27] Intense dialogue is always going on within it. The priest encourages the parishioner to analyse his or her motives and behaviour, and this self-analysis serves to interiorize the dialogue inherent in the consciousness of each individual.

The struggle between extremes that are officially categorized as 'orthodoxy' and 'superstition' or as 'philosophy' and 'ignorance' gave rise to that intellectual space in which the medieval individual emerged. The scholastic, with his logic, and the 'superstitious' simpleton are two aspects of that individual, but each of them is equally important for the individual's existence. The simpleton was hidden within the 'high-minded' intellectual, and even the very last of the simpletons could not ignore the history of salvation. Humanity is torn in two directions between the heavens on one side and earthly life on the other: the human path is caught up in world history. Although bogged down in everyday cares and passions, people cannot disregard the idea of eternity and what that has in store. Prayer, thinking about sin, confession, repentance, consideration of 'final matters' (death, redemption, punishment and heavenly bliss beyond the grave) those were the essential ingredients in the personal awareness of the medieval individual. He 'does not match up with himself: he can and has to look at himself from the side as it were', writes Bibler, 'and that "side" is his own "alter ego": that is the point where powerful social and ideological determination sets in and the individual becomes an individual in the true sense of the word. He detaches himself from the social group and finds that he is capable of shaping his own fate, mind and actions'.[28]

9

'In this Madness there be Method'

A Psychopathological 'Topography' of Opicinus de Canistris

The case of Opicinus, a cleric living in the first half of the fourteenth century, deserves, in my view, to be considered separately, because his *casus* is in many respects unique. At the same time, however, it sheds light on the individual in his age. Tormented by relentless thoughts of the permanent sinfulness of the world and fear that his soul might die and be eternally damned, Opicinus is incessantly struggling with himself, pondering and becoming ever more deeply engrossed in his own ego. While he projects that ego at the Universe, absorbed by his own *persona* as he does so, he is, however, not in a position to explain it. Opicinus' truly manic concentration on the idea of sin and the impossibility of redemption provided the basis for the assumption that what we have before us is an instance of psychopathology.[1] In my opinion, if Opicinus did suffer from a mental disorder, it is a disorder of a medieval individual and, to be more precise, one who was living at the crisis of the Middle Ages. Opicinus is interesting to the historian, not as an ill or anomalous individual, but as a phenomenon of his times: in his mental illness, various historically determined tendencies and conditions for the shaping of individuality at that time duly find expression.

Opicinus (1296–c.1350) was also known by the name

Anonymus Ticinensis: he came from a northern Italian family that was neither noble nor rich, and he lived the life of a wanderer and beggar. After obtaining a religious education, he earned his daily bread by working as a private tutor, copyist and book illuminator. He wrote several books on religious subjects and left behind him a large number of drawings. He did not, however, go down in history as a theologian, thinker or artist. The political treatise, in which he expounded arguments in support of the pre-eminence of spiritual over worldly power, won him favour in the eyes of Pope John XXII, who then granted Opicinus a post as a clerk in Avignon which, at that time, was the seat of the papacy. The best known of Opicinus' works is his description of the topography, history and customs of his native town of Pavia, which stands out because of the writer's powers of observation, which were exceptional for the time.

The main hardships in Opicinus' life were not of an external kind but of an internal, psychological nature. The source of his misfortunes was his own personality. He was constantly troubled by a sense of his own burden of sin and uselessness, and physical ailments exacerbated his condition further. At about the age of 40, Opicinus experienced a crisis. He fell ill and, by his own account, was unconscious for ten days. When he came to, he felt he had been 'born a second time', for he 'had forgotten everything and could not imagine what the external world looked like'. He saw the Virgin Mary and the infant Jesus in a dream, and Mary bestowed upon him 'spiritual knowledge' in place of the bookish knowledge (*memoria litteralis*) which he had possessed before and which he had lost in part as a result of his illness. Moreover, his right arm was paralysed so he was no longer able to work as a clerk. Nevertheless, by some miracle, Opicinus was still able to execute an extensive series of drawings, accompanied by notes and commentaries. He explained unequivocally that this new talent had been bestowed upon him from on high.[2]

This collection of pictures and texts which is, in many ways, unique, consisted of an unusual combination of drawings, geographical maps and diagrams, complete with sketches and self-portraits. With a manic one-track mind, Opicinus keeps returning to the same images and ideas. There is little doubt that he was obsessed with these motifs. For a historian interested in medieval attitudes, these products of Opicinus' imagination provide a rare opportunity to come within far closer range than usual to those layers of personality than anyone would be likely to penetrate via a mere literary discourse. What Opicinus confronts the reader with is a highly unusual piece of psychological testimony.

This work, which was the fruit of 'inner regeneration', is referred to by a modern publisher as an 'autobiography',[3] but it was an autobiography of a kind that is not to be found elsewhere in the Middle Ages, nor probably in the modern age either. Opicinus immerses himself in his own life, in his own ego: he does not, however, do this through a coherent literary presentation of that life. A straightforward narrative is clearly not what Opicinus was seeking. Among the drawings (which are 100 x 50 cm in size), there are symbolic depictions of the Church and the figures of Christ and the Virgin Mary, biblical patriarchs and prophets, the signs of the zodiac, animals and creatures symbolizing the Evangelists, crucifixion scenes and so on.

After careful examination, researchers have established that the creative process underlying these drawings began with a geometrical shape, an oval or a circle (or a number of intersecting circles), inside which some figure or other would then be drawn. Some basic principles that are to be observed in all Opicinus' drawings are a continuation of the medieval principles for the traditional interpretation of the relationship between macrocosm and microcosm. More specific artistic influences and models have also been established. Opicinus uses models that are drawn from the art of his times, from cartography and stained-glass creations and also from contemporary medical and anatomical treatises. Yet the general system into which he fitted his drawings was original and is probably his alone: he selected only specific models that were in tune with his goals and moods. The main achievement – that of transferring elements of cartography or anatomy to a sacred context and the accompanying reinterpretation of such elements which then acquired a new symbolic significance – was his and his alone. Despite the links with his forebears and contemporaries, Opicinus at the same time succeeded in creating his own universe of ideas and images.[4] Texts found in conjunction with the drawings or dotted around them consist as a rule of disconnected notes which can by no means always be deciphered, and some of the drawings also remain an enigma.

The crux of the matter lies in the fact that, unlike his other works, Opicinus made those drawings, not for any outside readers but so as to provide himself with a means of release from his mental anxiety. They reflect the fears that dogged him: self-accusations, including highly personal admissions, are interspersed with expressions of hope of attaining salvation. Opicinus feels not only that it is hard for him to concentrate on theological questions but, sometimes actually during a church service, he is beset by blasphemous thoughts. Uncontrollable urges to burst out laughing during the mass that he was celebrating led him to refrain from carrying out his functions as a priest and to continue asking for absolution. Opicinus also felt oppressed by a sense of his own profound sinfulness. If this haphazard pile of disparate drawings and notes have a common theme, then it is Opicinus himself. The feeling of guilt, which never leaves him, and the resulting humiliation find here an exaggeratedly egocentric form of expression. Nevertheless, what is no less striking is that his repentance and despair sometimes give way to sudden bursts of extreme arrogance: after all, it was not just anyone but he, Opicinus, who had been blessed with the gift of insight into the secret of divine wisdom!

To set out his 'autobiography' Opicinus resorts to an unusual device. He draws a diagram consisting of 40 concentric circles, each of which represents a year of his life, like tree rings. The diagram is divided into weeks, and this unusual calendar is arranged in accordance with the signs of the zodiac, which was a common practice in the Middle Ages. Portraits of the four Evangelists are also included. These 'year rings' are strewn with texts, which provide the main facts of Opicinus' life for the year in question. In the centre of the ring there is a self-portrait. The 'autobiography' contains four other self-portraits, which are stylized and diagrammatic: they depict Opicinus at various stages of his life – at the ages of 10, 20, 30 and 40. These 'self-portraits' do not, of course, convey the subject's truly individualized appearance and, like so many types, they are executed in accordance with medieval tradition (although R. Salomon suggests that the depiction in the portraits of a sickly man with sunken cheeks and a scraggy neck does more or less correspond to the actual subject), but the idea of depicting oneself many times over at various ages is undoubtedly Opicinus' own as a result of his heightened self-awareness. Before him, no-one had come forward with this particular idea.

Weighed down with a sense of guilt and with his own sinfulness, this man was also obsessed with the idea that his creations were none other than the 'newest and the eternal Gospel' (*evangelium novissimum sempiternum*), which was bound to receive the Pope's blessing and be read in all churches. It would seem that Opicinus, like certain of his contemporaries, was not averse to seeing himself as a prophet. The borderline between mystic insight and logic is far from clear here – once again completely in the spirit of the times.[5]

Yet Opicinus and his drawings were presented as part of a wider, all-embracing conceptual system. In one of the self-portraits on Opicinus' chest (or rather in his breast that has been opened) a medallion bearing a map of the Mediterranean can be seen; this has been drawn in reverse, as its mirror image. As in many other of his drawings, the outline of Europe is presented as the bent figure of a man whose head forms the Iberian peninsula, while his chest forms the north of Italy and the south of France – so that his heart coincides with Avignon, the papal seat at that time. The man is leaning over towards a woman, whose silhouette envelops North Africa. She appears to be whispering something into the man's ear (which is at the level of the Strait of Gibraltar). As the accompanying captions point out, these figures symbolize Adam and Eve at the moment of their Fall, while the Strait of Gibraltar is the scene of their Fall. In its turn, the outline of the Mediterranean Sea reminds Opicinus of a terrible grotesque figure, the Prince of this world, the Devil, who has placed himself between the male and the female figures. Seated on a throne, he rules over the world of here and now. The Mediterranean Sea, the centre of the world according to Opicinus, is none other than the Devil's sea, *mare diabolicum*. Finally, the Atlantic coast of France and the English Channel, which separates France from England, assume the shape of a monster symbolizing Death. The world is perceived anthropomorphically; indeed, if readers will pardon the expression, 'demonomorphically' as well. Humankind stands between the Devil and Death.

It is clear that Opicinus is using the traditional medieval diagram of the 'macrocosm-microcosm': man is compared with the Universe and is a reflection of it in miniature. To some extent, the familiar process for reinterpretation is turned inside out here. It is not the figure of a man from the 'little world' who has been incorporated into the 'big world' but, on the contrary, the macrocosm, rendered strikingly human, has been incorporated into the microcosm. The important thing is that this microcosm is not an abstract symbolic figure but Opicinus himself. Within him, within his breast, the whole world has been compressed. This world as a whole, and all its parts and separate elements, are rich with symbolic overtones which Opicinus, with truly manic consistency, tries to find in virtually everything. Next to the medallion depicting the Mediterranean with the male figure of Europe and a female one of Africa, the following words are to be found in Opicinus' breast: 'That is what I am like within' (*talis sum ego interius*)', 'a revelation concerning my motives, which is known to the Lord' (*revelatio cogitationum mearum coram Deo*).[6] Is it possible to express visually a tendency for 'navel-gazing'?

In his searchings for an anthropomorphic picture of the world, Opicinus is most inventive and, in his own way, even logical. It is highly likely that maps, which at that period were regularly being used by seafarers and merchants, served as a model for his imaginative cartography. At the same time, however, he was quite well acquainted with parts of northern Italy and southern France. Meanwhile, the images of people, transposed to the coastlines of the Mediterranean basin, were his own invention, and the map that is the work of his pen charts Opicinus' own spiritual space. R. Salomon refers to his map as a '*carte moralisée*'. It could also well be regarded as its creator's 'medical history'.

According to Opicinus, the world is drenched in sin, and the dominant figure of the Prince of Darkness symbolizes this lamentable situation for all to see. Yet Opicinus' map signifies something more personal and deeply dramatic. Evil is not simply spread all around us: it is concentrated in the soul of Opicinus himself. Figures of the man and woman, representing Adam and Eve, serve at the same time to express the state of this cleric's own body and soul. Next to the cartographic depictions of Europe, we can read the words: 'All this I discovered in my own consciousness, which is to testify against me on the Day of Judgement. Within myself I found the Judge ready to yield me up for conviction'.[7] His essential being is marked out by original sin, and the whole geography of the Universe simultaneously represents the 'topography' of his inner world, a decoding of the profound and ineradicable sinfulness of his personality and the symbol of his destiny 'inscribed', as it were, in the configuration of continents, in heavenly signs, in the circumstances and date of his birth, even in his name and in some statement or other made by Thomas Aquinas (for Opicinus maintains that Saint Thomas will testify against him before the Divine Judge).[8] All these facts unite against him, and everywhere Opicinus finds proof of his unavoidable downfall and justification for his boundless pessimism. In a number of his drawings Hell has been placed at the centre of the world, and the Devil, whose silhouette he picked out in this map, tempts him and does so, moreover, in the very same expressions with which he tempted Christ himself! Opicinus' genuine repentance and despair over his sins are found side by side with incredible vaunting of his own personality.

The figure of Opicinus, dressed in priestly garments and with his arms stretched out symmetrically, had the quality of a monument or statue: if it was taken on its own merits, it might well appear as a symbol of tranquillity and serenity but the inscriptions that surround it immediately demonstrate that such a conclusion would be hasty and superficial. Opicinus is far removed from any kind of emotional equilibrium. He is always asking himself: 'Who am I? Who am I?' (*Quis sum ego? Quis sum ego?*). In one of the comments used to 'sign' a work we read 'In my arrogance I appear to the outsider like a haughty Pharisee'. Near a medallion containing the map of the Mediterranean, that turned out to be a symbol of original sin and the Kingdom of the Devil, we find written: 'In my pride I am like this'. The inscriptions used are highly symmetrical in their meaning and they are designed to reveal the profound inner contradictions and upheavals intrinsic to the author's personality. The problem of how to reconcile the 'inner man' with the 'outer man', which arose long before in the Epistles of St Paul (the first relates to God, while the second belongs to the earthly world complete with its passions and errings) is here turned on its head, just as the world itself is turned on its head in the symbolic map locked in the breast of Opicinus.

To use Misch's expression, let us remember that medieval individuality made itself known 'centrifugally'. Yet, in Opicinus' case, we have to acknowledge a strange combination of the 'centrifugal' and the 'centripetal', for the author is not content with placing himself at the centre of the world: he manages at the same time to enclose that whole world within his own being!

Was this in keeping with medieval tradition? Let us recall, for example, St Hildegard von Bingen (twelfth century). In the visions of this saintly woman, which have also been recorded in texts and drawings, there is a tranquil synthesis and balance to be found between the 'microcosm' and the 'macrocosm'. A sense of harmony and calm order predominate in depictions such as those of this saint. Hildegard herself was also immortalized in the drawings, but where exactly? She is placed outside the microcosm-macrocosm, by the feet of a human figure personifying the microcosm in a contemplative pose and engaged in drawing what Hildegard had seen.[9] Hildegard is an interested beholder, who is not participating directly in the mystery of the harmonious correlation of the lesser and greater worlds, but merely testifying to that correlation by the grace of the Lord. This can be explained by the fact that emphasis of the subjective principle was something totally alien to her, infinitely more than in the case of her contemporaries who adhered to the maxim 'scito te ipsum' ('know thyself'). When expounding her visions, Hildegard effaces herself completely: her attention is totally concentrated on the Creator and his creation. 'The Lord does not love the person' (*Deus autem personam non amat*), she points out 'but those creations which bear His imprint'. The Son of God had said that sustenance was to be found through carrying out the will of his Father.[10]

The position is very different where Opicinus is concerned. In his diagrams we also find, as in those of Hildegard with whose work he was not familiar, circles and ovals, which contain visions of the macrocosm and microcosm: in Opicinus' drawings, however, these figures are to be found in large numbers; they are intertwined with one another and arranged on top of each other. The main difference in the work of the two lies in the fact that Opicinus introduces into his system alarming disharmony that serves to express his own mental distress. His work does not reflect a revelation granted to a righteous person in a vision, but rather tenaciously repeated attempts by a melancholy mind to express its own hopes and fears. While Hildegard is no more than a pious medium, through which communication is effected between the world on high and the earthly world, Opicinus creates images of both these worlds. He is consistently subjective.

Between Opicinus' subjectivity and Petrarch's individual self-awareness there lies a great gulf. It would be possible, for instance, to equate Opicinus' perception of the relationship between the cosmos and the individual with the model elaborated by the humanists.[11] Nevertheless, *mutatis mutandis*, Opicinus finds in the world a point of reference, which lies within it rather than outside it.

The anthropomorphic map of the Mediterranean, placed in Opicinus' breast, is complete with a caption, which reads: 'Revelation of my motives' (*Revelatio cogitationum mearum*). Awareness of sinfulness and a heightened sense of guilt, which at that period had a firm grip on the minds of wide strata of society in Western Europe and were actively cultivated by preachers, are concentrated in the person of Opicinus and, at the same time, projected on to the world as a whole. The Universe is full of sins, yet these are concentrated in the soul of the individual.[12] It is he, Opicinus, who is standing in the middle of the world but, at the same time, incorporating that world into himself: from out of this person emanations of his mental state spread over the whole world. As he draws the world, Opicinus penetrates it with his own ego, his hopes for salvation and, first and foremost, the sense of guilt that never leaves him and his unrelenting fear of his soul's unavoidable death.

If we are justified in perceiving in the revelations of Hildegard of Bingen and the visions of Opicinus phenomena expressing specific spiritual and emotional preoccupations of the twelfth and fourteenth centuries respectively, then it is easier to understand the shift that took place in the self-awareness of the individual in the course of the 150 to 200 years that divide them. Harmony gave way to disharmony: the divine cosmos was replaced by a picture of a world beset by demons. This world had not lapsed into disorganized chaos, but various of its planes, that previously had been clearly defined and separate, had now begun to overlap. The complex and confused system of symbols that Opicinus devised bears witness to the extreme contradictions that filled his mind.

Scholars tend to regard Opicinus' drawings as a kind of confession, through which he fails, however, to be reconciled to his Creator. Moral implications and even, I repeat, demonic ones permeate his symbolic geographical ideas. Gerhart Ladner sees Opicinus' personality and his work to provide a graphic example of 'alienation' of the individual from the world and unsatisfactory relations with God. He also shares E. Kris's[13] opinion to the effect that Opicinus suffered from schizophrenia and was obsessed with unhealthy quests for his own soul and was the victim of manic hallucinations which gave rise to psychosis. Possibly. What is striking is the truly fanatical tenacity with which he keeps going back, picture after picture, to the same images, figures and ideas, repeating the same formulas in the captions that accompany the pictures. In many of Opicinus' notes, it is generally hard to find any sort of sense or logic, because they are so abstruse: unrelated or incoherent associations are piled one on top of the other without any semblance of order, and the key to the puzzle has been thrown away. Any word or name could trigger off in his mind new imaginings and lead him off at a tangent.

An example of such writing is provided by the *Codex Palatinus latinus 1993*. In another manuscript as well (*Codex Vaticanus latinus 6435*), we find a similar accumulation of scattered and unsystematic notes for each day, which provide a focal point for his external and internal experience, religious reflections and scholarly exercises: information about everyday life can be found interspersed with memories. Then again complaints, fear and regrets might be found hand in hand with expressions of hope. These day-by-day notes are acknowledged by the author himself to be 'studies designed to assist the attainment of true knowledge' (*studium ad veram scientiam capiendam*) and 'great knowledge' (*maior scientia*).[14]

While, in the previous work, Opicinus was seen experimenting with space that he reworked into a symbolic map of his own soul, here he was trying to come to grips with time by way of symbols: he resorts to a chronology all of his own and, in connection with each new year during which he intends to continue making notes, he announces in advance his intentions that reflect his prophetic evaluations and hopes: '1335 – the year of expectation' (*annus expectationis*); '1336 the year of retribution' (*annus retributionis*); '1337 – the year of renewal' (*annus renovationis*); '1338 – the year of accomplishment' (*annus perfectionis*); '1339 - the year of discovery' (*annus revelationis*); '1340 – the crowning year' (*annus coronationis*); '1341 – the year of calm' (*annus tranquillitatis*). It is not difficult to understand that these expectations, innovations and discoveries need to be sought not in political or everyday life for the terms are to be understood, from the mystic's point of view, as the transformations of Opicinus' own inner being.

It is important not to lose sight of the fact that, after drawing a diagram for his own life year by year (covering the first 40 years) complete with self-portraits at various ages and with prophecies as to how the years of the near future would elapse, Opicinus sees himself not as something static, but as a historical being subject to change and a certain amount of development. Albeit in symbolic form, Opicinus nevertheless comes close to the idea of autobiography, that is, to the development of himself as an individual in time, and this approach should be

seen as new in comparison to the writings of his predecessors,
to whom earlier chapters of this book have been devoted.

Concentration on his own person is just as crucial a feature
of this work by Opicinus as it was of the previous one.

> Let each man explain his life in the spiritual sense, as he
> can remember it and let him in that same [spiritual,
> symbolic: A.G.] way reveal the importance of his family
> and its deeds, and all those of his dreams which he is able
> to remember. Let him discuss all that with his conscience.
> Then after understanding all that in the light of the truth,
> truth reached through a juxtaposition of deceit with faith,
> with God's help he shall be in a position to form a correct
> opinion of his own persona, following my example
> (*exemplo mei ipsius*).[15]

Indeed, for every event from his own life, even the most
insignificant, Opicinus provides a consistent interpretation in
the spiritual sense or as an introduction to actions that followed,
resorting to literary analogies, sometimes of a rather contrived
sort. His period of service as a young man at the custom-house
by a bridge (*pons*) was a foretaste and 'prototype' for his future
spiritual service (*pontificium*); the illumination (*illuminatio*)
of books meant that, in the future, he would 'illumine' his own
mind; even his wolfish appetite was lent an allegorical
interpretation as a manifestation of his intellectual hunger and
desire to share knowledge with others. All external events in
his life were so significant, from his point of view, that they
required symbolic decoding.

Symbolic interpretation of this kind was commonplace in
medieval scholarly literature. What was special in the case of
Opicinus was the fact that all these allegories were, without
fail, linked with his own *persona*. Returning to the symbolic
geography of Europe, Opicinus identifies himself with the
male figure in the map and declares: 'I . . . with my body testify
to the location of Europe', because the parts of his body
covered with hair correspond exactly to the regions of the
continent that were covered with woodland. That was only
part of it, however: the bouts of constipation that had been
tormenting Opicinus for some time 'signified' the political

collisions in 'the belly of Europe', that is, in Lombardy, just as the rheumatic aches in his shoulder 'signified' the military confrontations between Germany and France, for, in his maps, France occupied the shoulder of the 'Europe-man'. It would hardly be possible to suspect Opicinus of joking or simply playing with words and images, for he was thoughtful and serious and sought to reveal 'spiritual truths'. In those searches, he consistently and ubiquitously found himself. Yet, at the same time, certain parts of Europe turned out, in his view of things, to be sections of the world beyond the grave: for instance, according to Opicinus, the British Isles were none other than Purgatory. It is possible that the legend of 'St Patrick's purgatory' traditionally located in Europe, played a part.

In this work, too, which was entitled *De omnibus et de quibusdam aliis* (*About all things and certain others*), Opicinus provides an extensive series of maps and drawings. In these he returns to a depiction of the Mediterranean basin incorporating a male and a female figure but, in some of the maps, the figures have changed places: Europe is depicted as a woman and Africa as a man. In other instances, it is no longer possible to discern the sex of these figures.

The solipsism in Opicinus' writing creates the impression that, in this particular case, we really are confronted by a mentally ill individual. There is something manic about the way he constantly returns to the same images, about the countless variations on the same theme. The repetitive expressions used are reminiscent of the Old and New Testaments. The words of Shakespeare's Polonius inevitably come to mind: 'Though this be madness, yet there is method in't'). Although Opicinus was quite beside himself, there is still method in his writing. In the writings and, most clearly, in the drawings of Opicinus, medieval scholarship comes clearly to the fore, yet it is, of course, filtered through the disturbed mind of a cleric living in the first half of the fourteenth century. The state of his confused soul was hardly unique, for the people of that period were often profoundly traumatized by an ineradicable fear of the Day of Judgement and the prospect of eternal torment. Precisely at the time when Opicinus lived, these fears were beginning to develop into mass phobias and all manner of psychoses. This should lead us to agree with Ladner, who sees Opicinus' mental illness as symptomatic of a particular historical situation.[16]

The conflict between *ratio* and irrational fear, faith and despair, a sense of deep sinfulness and self-respect, self-abasement and inflated self-importance is a conflict that, at times, is exacerbated to the point of a veritable collision between logic and madness: that was the context in which the individual arrived at an awareness of his or her own personality. The soul was like a battlefield between the powers of Good and the powers of Evil – a concept that was no novelty in medieval culture. On the contrary, the tension between the two was intrinsic to the Christian perception of the world. After all, was not this contradiction already to be observed in the writings of Otloh von St Emmeram and Ratherius, Abelard and Guibert de Nogent? On each occasion in the work of a variety of authors, this conflict expressed itself in its own specific way depending upon the writers' individual characters, the situations in which they found themselves, and last, but by no means least, on the genre of the writings under consideration which facilitated the expression of the dilemma concerned, or, on the other hand, served to conceal it behind a virtually impenetrable screen of literary subject-matter and religious clichés.

In the drawings and texts of Opicinus, this conflict expresses itself to a stark, almost pathological, degree. Comparison of the texts and illustrative sequences would appear to open up possibilities for profound penetration of the secret layers of his psyche. This cleric would appear to be more candid than many of his predecessors and contemporaries. In this case, of course, the question still needs to be asked: does he not give himself away as a repentant sinner who still nurtures hope of salvation in the secret recesses of his soul? That hope is to be found flickering within every confession though . . ..

The problem lies elsewhere: what seems the most important thing to me is that, to achieve self awareness, Opicinus – very much within the traditions of medieval scholarship – needed to 'exteriorize' his inner self, to project it on to a geographical map which, as a result, was immediately transformed into a symbolic image of his mental state, a 'topography' of his soul, his medical history. It is possible that the diagnosis arrived at by various scholars is correct and that, in this case, the man we have before us is a schizophrenic, gripped by an obsession to recreate the world or to put it in order and, at the same time, gripped by fear of its destruction. What is interesting for the historian is not the disease itself, but its cultural-historical interpretation.

Yet that is not everything. In one of Opicinus' drawings, he combines the symbolic map (showing a male figure of Europe whispering to a female figure representing Africa), albeit in a simplified more diagrammatic version, with figures representing himself, Boethius and Philosophy. Opicinus, who came from Pavia, regarded Boethius as his compatriot. Here we also find quotations from *The Consolation of Philosophy* (*Consolatio Philosophiae*) and the inscription: 'What happened to Boethius also happened to Opicinus. Boethius left Ancient Rome and was sent into exile to Pavia; now, by the grace of God, he [Opicinus] left Pavia to go to the New Rome [i.e. Avignon]'.[17] We return once more to a familiar theme: like other writers of the Middle Ages who produced 'confessions', 'apologias' and 'autobiographies' from fragments drawn from other people's lives (lives of ancient heroes and Christian saints), Opicinus hastened to compare himself with an archetype, an 'example', an authority, to identify his own ego. In his mad state a certain kind of logic really does come to light – the logic of the medieval personality, which 'assembled itself' in accordance with rules laid down by the culture of the time.

We can assume that the attainment of self-awareness by the individual in the Middle Ages met with serious obstacles and sometimes went hand in hand with phenomena associated with mental illness. The emphasis in religion on humility, repentance and the expiation of sin, the negative view of the individual's originality and the condemnation of such originality as a source of inadmissible pride led to a situation in which the ego could, paradoxically, express itself mainly via self-negation and self-abasement, or by extending itself to embrace the whole world. If it is justified to speak in terms of Opicinus' mental disturbance, then I should be inclined to search for the source of that disturbance in the striking contradiction between his heightened self-awareness and his sense of his profound sinfulness. It is difficult for the individual to assert himself against the background of such a conflict and in those cases when an individual is not crushed by the weight of religiosity and the sense of guilt that stems from it, his personality may well reveal itself in forms that appear to us as symptoms of mental illness.

10

Dante and Petrarch

The path to self-knowledge was by no means simple or straightforward. Let us turn now to the end of the thirteenth and the beginning of the fourteenth centuries. Is it not the case that Dante (1265–1321) contrived to leave his readers in almost total ignorance of the nature of his inner world and a whole range of factual details regarding his life? In *La vita nuova*, an early work written in 1292 that he referred to as the 'book of my memory', he intended to recreate his youth. The central focus was the story of his love for Beatrice. This love was depicted at two different levels – as an immediate biographical fact and also as a poetic interpretation of the latter. The retrospective account of Dante's love for Beatrice is accompanied by sonnets that the poet had originally composed in his youth. The poems are arranged in chronological order and what we are presented with is not simply a 'songbook' but the record of a life, an autobiographical testimony. Does not this enable us to chart the changes in the poet's moods and feelings? Yet it is unlikely that we are being confronted with real experiences. There is even less of the real woman about Beatrice than is to be found in the ladies extolled by the Provençal poets who were the young Dante's precursors and teachers: at least we find in their songs descriptions of beautiful women, whom they praise and to whose love they aspire, however much these 'portraits' are stereotyped and bereft of individuality. Beatrice is a figment of the imagination, no more than an idea without flesh: her beauty struck the young Dante as soon as he set eyes upon her, but we are left in complete ignorance of her human qualities.

What a contrast with Héloïse! It is not for nothing that certain scholars began to suspect that no such woman as Beatrice ever actually existed. Was she perhaps merely an allegory? Troubadours longed for and desired their beloved, while Dante merely bows to Beatrice – both when she is alive and after her untimely demise. When we compare the erotic power of Abelard's *Historia mearum calamitatum* and the letters Héloïse wrote to him, with the great Florentine's *La vita nuova*, an enormous contrast emerges: in the first case we are offered real human passion and, in the second, extreme spiritualization of a real emotion which, in *La divina commedia*, led to the final transformation of Beatrice from a woman into a theologem. In the same way, the setting, in which the love-struck youth meets his *belle dame*, is deliberately stripped of any tangible features: it is no longer Florence with its squares, streets and churches, but some illusory space.

Dante is, of course, capable of analysing his feelings and looking at himself from outside, as it were, through other people's eyes, yet the world of *La vita nuova* is, for the most part, a world of allegories and symbols, and it is therefore perfectly logical that a prominent place in the work should be accorded to all manner of visions, dreams and supernatural phenomena and that the poet's communication with Beatrice should proceed at a level more elevated than that of the senses. The author's emotions and ideas take on an identity of their own, begin to exist in their own right and are fleshed out, while the living creatures become more ephemeral, mere abstractions without flesh and blood. Dante does more to hide his inner world than to shed light on it.

In view of the above, there can be little justification for referring to *La vita nuova*, as I. I. Golenishchev-Kutuzov has done, as the 'first psychological novel in Europe after the collapse of classical civilization'.[1] The era of the 'psychological novel' was not to dawn for a long time. If we were to seek 'psychology', then it would be more apt to turn to Guibert de Nogent or to Abelard and Héloïse: Dante did not do us the honour of admitting us to the secret recesses of his heart. *La vita nuova* should be linked with medieval spirituality,[2] but not by any stretch of the imagination with the novels of Proust nor the poetry of Valéry.[3] This particular feature of Dante's work can evidently be explained by the fact that it does not constitute a memoir or an autobiography: it has been devised as a poet's commentary on his own verse and, in each chapter of the book, each sonnet is followed by his analysis of it. The sonnet in its turn is preceded by an account of the situation in which it was composed. Thus it can be seen how the autobiographical aspect of *La vita nuova* has been accorded what is without doubt a secondary role. The characters in *La vita nuova* are no less mystical than those in *La divina commedia*.

Neither is the latter work really designed to shed much light on the individuality of the poet. Dante does not remain insensitive to what he beholds in the world beyond the grave, but it would be rash to assume that, as he climbs from Hell to Paradise, he changes as an individual and experiences a profound transformation. *La divina commedia* does not reflect the inner development of its creator but is a grandiose attempt to construct the cosmos as it appeared to the poetic imagination of an erudite Catholic well versed in philosophy and theology at the beginning of the fourteenth century.

The idea of the development of the personality was alien to medieval thought. Dante remains perfectly recognizable despite his sojourn in the world beyond his own. His compassion for the sufferings of sinners (after hearing Francesco da Rimini's story, he swoons) might appear not very 'orthodox': as Honorius Augustodunensis wrote in his *Elucidarium* (or *Illumination*) at the beginning of the twelfth century, the souls of the righteous cannot be distressed at the sight of the torments of sinners judged by their Creator. Yet, in Hell and Purgatory, Dante remains a living being to whom nothing human is alien. On the contrary, he comes to Hell filled with all those passions and predilections that he was prey to previously in his everyday life and in the midst of political struggle.

La divina commedia is the culmination of a long series of visions of the other world. Yet, essentially, it stands outside that series. I refer here not to its language or artistic merits –

in this respect it is difficult to compare it with the plain 'reporting' from the other world provided by Dante's predecessors. Here what should be singled out is not the idea underlying *La divina commedia*. Medieval visitors to the kingdom beyond the grave arrived there after their deaths: as it turned out, their deaths were not final, only temporary, yet they needed to die to make their way to that other world. Dante, on the other hand, wanders through a different world while he is still alive. Moreover, his visionary predecessors passed through Hell and Purgatory, but held back before the Gates of Paradise through which they could not pass. Dante, on the other hand, in his passage through the realms beyond this life – from Limbo to the Ninth Circle of Hell and then as far as the Empyrean – encounters no obstacles. He is the only Christian granted entry to Paradise while still a living mortal.

Does not this 'liberty' taken by Dante reflect extremely high self-appraisal on the part of the poet? We are told how the townspeople looked hard at him to pick out any traces of the fire of Hell on his face: what they should surely have been far more astonished by was that this man had sojourned in Paradise! It would have been unlikely to come across any direct self-glorification or self-abasement in Dante's writing but not because of any lack of interest in his own *persona*. The reason was quite different: namely the medieval ban on utterances of that kind. Following in the footsteps of St Thomas Aquinas,[4] Dante considered self-exaltation or self-censure to be out of the question and explained why that should be.[5] Yet Dante was, without doubt, fully aware of himself as an outstanding individual. This awareness is reflected not merely in Dante's ability to traverse and investigate the whole of the world beyond the grave without any exceptions and thus to be able to contemplate that world as a series of scattered 'places' and as a coherent and harmoniously organized system. It is also reflected in his selection of none other than the great Virgil as his guide through Hell and Purgatory.

After only a short space of time had elapsed, a new autobiographical trend appeared, in the writings of Petrarch (1304–74) and other humanists, which came to oust confessional writing. This constituted a shift towards autobiography in a more modern sense of the word. 'A confessional tone would often intrude into biographical independent accounts of lives in the age of the Early Renaissance. Yet it was the biographical element that won through' noted Bakhtin, referring here to, among others, Petrarch. Indeed, in his message *Posteritati* (*To Posterity*) Petrarch might appear to hover between the stance of the humble Christian and the poet aware of his own worth. The first figure, 'a poor mortal', is allegedly filled with an awareness of his own sinfulness, meekness and humility in the face of the Lord – all usual for the Middle Ages. In keeping with tradition, Petrarch speaks of his 'conversion', his discovery of the Supreme Truth, which radically transformed his whole life and, after turning his thoughts away from all that was sinful, redirected them towards 'sacred knowledge'. The second figure of the poet does not conceal his awareness of the great importance of the champion among poets duly crowned with laurels and gripped by a thirst for fame. After listing the numerous honours that have been accorded him, Petrarch clearly acknowledges that they were well deserved. There is no doubt that he sees himself as a writer of considerable stature.

Both these hypostases – that of the poet and that of the humble Christian – are unlikely to engender any tension in Petrarch's portrait of himself. He refers to his own name as 'insignificant and obscure' and is doubtful as to whether it might 'penetrate far through space and time', yet the poet nevertheless hopes that those to whom he turns 'might be eager to know what kind of a man I was and what fate befell my works, especially those, of which the fame or at least rumours have reached you'. He goes on to write that 'the greatest crowned heads of my time, as they competed amongst themselves, loved and revered me, but what for I do not know: they themselves did not say and all that I know is that some of them set more store by my attention than I by theirs'. The poet is a cunning master of words: he is fully aware of his own worth and looks to ensure his own fame; indeed, that is why he turns to posterity. He is perhaps the very first writer to indicate the day and hour when he first saw the light of day: 'in the year of the age beginning with the birth of Christ, 1304, at dawn on Monday July 20th'.

Just as Virgil had been chosen to accompany Dante through the realms of the dead, Petrarch elects as interlocutor and mentor none other than St Augustine, whom he admired immensely, and then proceeds to carry on long conversations with him in the silent, yet highly significant, presence of Truth herself. In Petrarch's *Secretum*, Augustinus and Franciscus represent, as it were, two hypostases of Petrarch as he seeks to fathom his own inner being. Is it not revealing to note that, while scholars of the preceding era had seen in St Augustine primarily the philosopher, one of the Fathers of the Church, he is of interest for Petrarch from the psychological point of view, as an individual and as author of the *Confessions?*

Petrarch repents of his errings and transgressions, lamenting the decline in morals and the degradation in the world around him, which he neither loved nor approved of, utterly in keeping with the medieval '*Ubi sunt*' tradition. Yet, while declaring himself to be far from perfect, he also sees himself and other poets as belonging to a breed apart. It is with undisguised contempt that he surveys the ordinary people around him engulfed, as they are, in petty everyday concerns. The poet declares that we should leave the cities to the merchants, lawyers, moneychangers and usurers, tax collectors, notaries and doctors (he lists as many as 30 different professions and occupations including not only those of prostitute, foreigner and mime artist, but even throwing in for good measure architects, painters and sculptors). 'They are not of our mould.' After all, Petrarch himself lived on a completely different plane. He used to rise while it was still dark and leave the house as the first rays of sunlight appeared: he would contemplate, read, write and consort with his friends. Yet, who were his friends? They were not only the individuals with whom he came into contact in his day-to-day life, but also those who had died centuries before and who were known to him only through their works. 'I assemble them from any place and any age . . . I am happier to converse with them than with those who imagine themselves to be alive, for they indulge in coarse utterances and hot air. In this way I can wander free and at peace, alone with companions of my own choosing.'

Petrarch sees himself as belonging to 'extended time' (to use Bakhtin's concept): he is able with infinite ease to move from era to era feeling at home wherever he goes and with either his predecessors of the distant past or with posterity.

The poet's self-awareness, be he Ancient Greek or Roman, Scandinavian skald or Italian humanist, *mutatis mutandis*, seems to matter little. He is unable to create without an awareness of himself as an exclusive being of great individual worth, bound to concern himself with his reputation both in the present and in the future. Yet in the context of Christian culture he cannot avoid the formulas of humility.

The above does not, however, encapsulate exhaustively the phenomenon of Petrarch's personality. One way or another, all the medieval authors of 'confessions', 'apologias' and 'autobiographies' were concerned with presenting their own images and justifying their actions: to varying degrees, they would deliberately select episodes from their lives to mould that 'image'. This inevitably led them to resort to models or '*exempla*', that is, to illustrious figures of the past, and indeed it was only by likening themselves to such figures that they could acknowledge the natures of their own personalities. In Petrarch's case, however, we are presented with what would appear to be something quite new. He not only compares himself to various prototypes but consistently elaborates the myth of his own life.

Petrarch saw the whole *raison d'être* of his work to be the single-minded construction of his own Self, and indeed his principal achievement was the moulding of his own magnificent image. In April 1341, at the age of only 37, he succeeded in being crowned with laurels as first among poets although, at that time, his major works had not yet seen the light of day. The occasion is also marked by a striking coincidence: Petrarch assures us that, on the very day when he was invited to come to Rome for this crowning, an identical invitation came from Paris but he, of course, declined the latter because he wished to have the laurel wreath placed upon his brow in no less a place than the Capitol of Rome! Later we shall see that this was not the only astonishing coincidence in the course of the poet's life.

Petrarch made a place for himself in the history of literature primarily because of the sonnets dedicated to Laura and his love for her. Yet did such a woman actually exist? Was she as tangible as Dante's Beatrice, or was her name a derivative from the word for laurels – *lauri* – which the poet constantly dreamed about and eventually won? The question is perhaps of only secondary importance for those engaged in assessing Petrarch's poetic genius, but it is far from irrelevant in connection with the myth Petrarch created of his own life. It is not possible to provide a totally convincing answer, but the reply Petrarch himself gave to one of his correspondents, who expressed doubts as to Laura's actual existence, was that his idea of St Augustine is as much of a fiction as the love of that lady.[7] The reply has rather an ambiguous and ironic ring to it: this was a poet more inclined to pose riddles than to solve them.

On 26 April 1336 Petrarch scaled Mont Ventoux (near Avignon) to admire the surrounding landscape from its summit. On his return home that evening, Petrarch disregarded his weariness and described the experience for one of his friends. In his letter, reference is made to the following episode: the wind that was blowing on the summit of the mountain opened the copy of St Augustine's *Confessions*, which Petrarch had taken with him on his journey, on the very page where the poet was to read the following words: 'Men go out and gaze in astonishment at high mountains, the huge waves of the sea, the broad reaches of rivers, the ocean that encircles the world, or the stars in their courses. But they pay no attention to themselves!' (*Confessions* X, 8). From this it is clear that even this ascent of Mont Ventoux (regarded by scholars concerned with the New Age as marking the beginning of mountaineering and as the first sign of a 'modern' attitude to Nature, of aesthetic appreciation of it for its own sake, which would have been most unusual in the writing of Petrarch's precursors) was something which the writer did not forget to present as an allegory of humanity's spiritual climb towards enlightenment. Reality and imagination appear here welded together as one.

This testimony to the strange dovetailing of the poet's climb up the mountain and the 'intervention' by his spiritual mentor,

St Augustine, is contained in a letter which was lent its definitive form only 17 years later. This is no isolated case. Throughout almost the whole of his life, Petrarch was writing letters to his friends, and he continued work on the texts of many of them at different periods: it is from these missives, addressed not so much to specific individuals as to posterity, that we learn much of what is known about the events of the poet's life. This, however, raises the question as to the extent to which these letters of Petrarch's, that were being written or edited over years or decades, actually reflect the real experiences of his life or were the products of his imagination directed towards the creation of a biography. 'The life as work of art' is the phrase used by an English expert on Petrarch to describe this phenomenon: after using that phrase, however, he immediately added 'If this letter [about the climbing of the mountain, A.G.] is a fiction, it is a fiction quite as significant as any experience, which may lie behind it'.[8]

This approach by a writer to his own life, constructed according to classical models, but no longer in the form of scattered fragments (as had been the case in the Middle Ages), rather as a continuous whole, was a new phenomenon. It does not appear as a symptom of an unprepared or unorganized individual that is being pieced together from a whole series of models: on the contrary, in Petrarch's case, there would appear to be to hand a properly devised strategy embracing this particular life as a whole. Petrarch is clearly anxious not just to be a man of his times, but – and this is obviously far more important – to be a man of the Classical past, which he is bringing back to life ('I am alive now, but would have preferred to be born in another time') and at the same to be able to link himself with the Future. Should this not be seen as a strategy aimed at bringing forth a new type of human individuality?

11

The Historian in Search of the Individual

The method used in this book for seeking out the individual in medieval Western Europe was a combination of two approaches – an individualizing approach and a generalizing one. The first involved the study of testimony regarding certain individuals who left behind them autobiographical works or confessions. St Augustine, St Patrick, Otloh von St Emmeram, Guibert de Nogent, Abelard, Suger, Salimbene, Opicinus de Canistris, Dante, Petrarch . . . this wondrous procession of individuals was unlikely to produce an elegant evolutionary sequence, yet closer acquaintance with those lives enabled us to some extent to immerse ourselves in the psychological atmosphere of the period. The other, generalizing, approach has I hope made it possible to single out certain general conditions pertaining to the emergence of the individual in medieval society.

Nevertheless this attempt to delineate the human individual in medieval Europe has had other consequences as well: it has served to demonstrate the difficulties that historians encounter when setting themselves such a task.

The crux of the matter is that all attempts by the individual to describe himself or herself are inevitably profoundly subjective. To start out from an individual's direct personal references when searching for essence is a risky undertaking and it would be just as dangerous to rely without question on such individual admissions as it would be to reject them out of hand. Far more can be gleaned from what is **not** said directly, but is to be found 'underlying' the words and deeds described, the meaning that is taken for granted or spontaneously shows through the 'outward expression'. During direct personal interaction, an observer can reach a definite judgement about an individual: this, too, will be subjective but it will be based, not merely on the words uttered, but also on many other signs – behaviour, expressions, the person's whole appearance. Our knowledge of any other person depends to an enormous degree upon outward factors. Our knowledge is, of course, shaped by our ideas and feelings, as it also is by judgements that have been made by other people about the individual concerned. Do we not, in the final analysis, project our own selves, complete with our criteria, tastes and prejudices on to the 'screen' of the other individual?

The historian, however, is in a more complicated situation: he or she has no chance to observe at first hand the personality of an individual who lived centuries earlier. Dialogue, that is always presumed to be part of any human interaction, is severely limited within the framework of historical investigation. The only possible dialogue is through texts, and the immediacy of direct contact between two persons is missing. All that the historian can, at best, hope to have at his or her disposal are the individual's own utterances or information provided by other people. Moreover, deciphering such utterances and information is made even more difficult by the fact that historians first need to immerse themselves in the language of the source material and to make the transition from an unfamiliar system of concepts to another (their own).

In historical research, when historians are trying to penetrate the hidden depths of a personality, room for manoeuvre is narrowed down by all manner of commonplaces and clichés with which texts abound: breaking through the system of conventional expressions to the true personality behind them is far from simple and, if we are honest, virtually impossible.

At this point I can almost hear my critics saying that trying to come to understand an individual 'as he really was' is to attempt something that is an unrealistic and spurious task because the individual, as expressed in the context of a range of cultural formulas and concepts, constructs a personality from those very same formulas and concepts. In its turn, the structure of that personality was determined in the Middle Ages by a well-established and intricately ramified network of rituals, patterns of behaviour and customs. Consequently, the language through which the individual expresses himself or herself constitutes the essence of that individual. It is futile to search for anything beyond the text; there is nothing left to be concealed behind it.

Are such objections justified? Would such logic not lead to the conclusion that the personality as such is something empty, that it is no more than a mould filled with whatever the language of culture thrusts upon it? Here Henry James's story *The Private Life* comes to mind: in this, we encounter, besides the split personality of the writer, one of whose manifestations leads an idle worldly life, while the other – quite separate from the first – is secretly preoccupied with writing: ('One goes out, the other stays at home. One's the genius, the other's the bourgeois, and it's only the bourgeois whom we personally know'),[2] Lord Mellifont, the particular figure I remembered in this connection. The problem of personality is presented by James in an extreme form in this work. This gentleman with perfect manners, Lord Mellifont, who is a leading figure within his own circle, exists only, as two other characters in the story discover much to their surprise, when he is in public – in a salon, in society, with his wife (who suspects that something is wrong but admits this to no-one) or in the presence of servants. When he is on his own, on the other hand, he temporarily dissolves: he does not become absorbed 'in himself' or withdraw to be 'on his own' (as a writer), but simply disappears, vanishes! Only the appearance of other people and communicating with them brings Lord Mellifont back from the void.

The idea behind James's story, if I have grasped it correctly, is that, on his own, Lord Mellifont possesses no personality: his self is entirely dependent upon his communicating with other people. His individuality exists only in so far as it is perceived by someone else. This particular value of Western civilization – privacy or the need to withdraw and be 'on one's own' (the very title of the story is concerned with privacy, not 'private life' in the ordinary sense) – is grotesquely transformed in the case of this British aristocrat into a void, not a spiritual void, but emptiness in the literal sense of the word. When no-one sees him or interacts with him, Mellifont loses his material shape. His personality, in so far as it is possible to use the term in this particular case, is totally dependent upon his communication with other people. His very existence is determined by worldly conventions, rules of gentlemanly conduct, the social part he plays so impeccably: outside these there is no essence that might be defined as personality.

His opposite – the other main character in the story – is a writer totally self-absorbed, who possesses a double or 'alternative identity', his 'other self': indeed, they 'had nothing to do, the so dissimilar twins, with each other . . .'.[3] He is always in the public eye: the mask of the gentleman is a substitute in his case for the face and for the personality. The contrast James has built up between these two characters in such stark relief brings out the weakness of the Lord as a human being: there is nothing more to him than his manners, his regular changes of attire, his sophisticated chatter and the various ways he passes his time in public.

The 'case' of Lord Mellifont takes us back, as it were, to that stage in the history of the concept of the 'persona' when, in Classical theatre, it meant a mask that an actor would don so as to conceal his own face. Subsequent cultural development led initially to the persona-mask turning into a 'character', in which actor and mask came closer together, so that the actor would 'feel his way into' the part and identify himself with it: finally, the concept 'persona' acquires the new meaning of 'personality'. Yet the social role-playing, to which the aristocrat in James's story devotes so much time and energy, rules out so effectively all that is personal, or linked with the inner self, that there can hardly be any question here of a real personality. From time to time, the Lord tires of his own all-absorbing worldly role and then he 'ceases to be' – or, to use James's expression, there follows an *entr'acte*. The Lord – unlike his opposite the writer who has a double – not only has no alter ego, he is bereft of an ego altogether.

James uses paradoxes and contrasted extremes to bring out

the ambiguous and contradictory essence of the human personality: one head of this Janus is turned towards society, while the other is hidden, focused within. When studying texts, the historian is contemplating outward manifestations of a personality, its 'accidentals', while its 'substance' usually remains concealed from view. Lord Mellifont has no substance: he exists only in one 'projection' directed towards a milieu, towards other people, for he is empty inside. This is the artistic fiction created by the writer. Yet, I would stress once more, he raises an important issue for, in real life, including the real life of history, we are concerned both with the outward manifestations of an individual and with the 'substance', the hidden content. Can we penetrate that far?

We see ourselves in categories drawn from our own culture, and when, for instance, Abelard describes his life as a series of delusions, from which he has set himself free after being subjected to all manner of vicissitudes before finally embarking upon the true path, it may appear that there was little more to his essential personality than his emulation of heroes and their destinies drawn from hagiography: it was indeed from such elements that the figure presented to us was composed. Yet, as we saw, the truth was rather different, because this comparison of himself with prototypes, even if perfectly sincere, was concealing (perhaps even from himself) the pride which, despite his various declarations, Abelard was unable to put behind him. In other words, behind the humility, the repentance, the identification of himself with Sts Jerome and Athanasius and Christ himself, and behind the emulation of the model provided by the *Confessions* of St Augustine, something quite different was lurking: a high degree of self-awareness turning the confession into an apologia.

In exactly the same way, when Suger appears to let his own identity be absorbed into that of St Denis, we are obliged to assume that no repression of his personality by the abbey he has rebuilt and embellished has taken place, but rather the opposite: this has been an act of self-affirmation that reaches the point when Suger's persona has come to embrace the abbey he has nurtured, when the abbey has been engulfed by that personality.

In such cases it is essential to look beyond the 'plane of expression' – through direct and sometimes deliberate utterances – to the 'plane of content'. These two 'planes' cannot really coincide. This is particularly true in Christian culture because this religion, which condemns the sin of pride, thereby renders impossible the spontaneous expression of self-awareness for the authors of these medieval 'autobiographies', and leads them to conceal their genuine attitudes behind formulas of humility and self-abasement. The verb 'to conceal', which I have used here, does not necessarily imply hypocrisy: the individual interiorized these formulas, which provided him with the only accessible means of self-awareness at that time. Yet, in the hidden depths of his inner self, which the individual was often unaware and which he did not discuss in precise terms, there lurked 'something else', an elusive remnant of something irrational. As a result, the personality, even on those relatively rare occasions when it made itself known, was not able to reveal all of its facets. The doctrine of the dichotomy between the 'outer' and 'inner' person (*interior homo*), to which the Apostle Paul referred (Romans 7: 21-25; II Corinthians 4: 10; Ephesians 3: 16) brings out this essential problem, this ineradicable contradiction inherent in Christian ethics. The Christian religion is a personalized religion and, at the same time, manifestations of individuality that defy control are regarded as sinful.

Affirmation of the individual's ego unrestrained by moral taboos of this sort is possible only in two cases. Firstly, it is possible in settings where Christian morality has not yet triumphed, where it co-existed and 'competed' with other ethical principles. This would appear to apply in the situation of King Sverrir. The impostor, who had fought for the Norwegian throne, had been raised as a Christian and, as we saw, made wide use of biblical and Christian motifs when substantiating his claims to the throne. Yet he was operating, at the end of the twelfth century, within a society in which the Viking ethos was not yet dead at the end of the twelfth century. This meant that he could contemplate fairly open self-affirmation, and he (or the author of *King Sverrir's Saga* who put such words into his mouth) was able to declare aloud about himself: 'a great change of times has taken place and the place of the Archbishop, the King and the Jarl has been taken by one man and that man is I!'.

If we go back to an earlier period of Scandinavian history, then we shall have to admit that skaldic poetry – pagan in spirit and origin – testifies to the fact that, in the pre-Christian era, no impediments existed to obstruct open assertion of an individual's selfish interests, that basically matched the moral demands of family and clan. The most egocentric of skaldic personalities is to be found in *Egills saga* and its poems. It is, in a certain sense, an extreme case, and Egill's inner self is presented in the saga as containing something demonic: as was the case with his grandfather and father before him, characteristics of a werewolf are glimpsed in Egill which provide hints of his 'wolfish' nature.

Secondly, in the Christian era, breaking through the ideological and moral taboos and inner restraints was something possible only for those individuals whose mental and emotional make-up was such that they constituted deviations from the norm. Without going so far as to share the inclination of several modern historians to search for signs of psychiatric anomalies or complexes in virtually every author of a 'confession' or 'autobiography', I should nevertheless be inclined to agree that the 'case' of Opicinus de Canistris can be interpreted as testifying to profound emotional disturbance. The obtrusive repetition of the same ideas and images, the unrelenting fear of emotional collapse and terror born of an ineradicable sense of guilt and sinfulness are what guide Opicinus' pen as he continues to draw his diagrams of the Universe, the Mediterranean and his own biography, occasionally accompanying them with barely intelligible notes, into which he pours out his emotions.

Yet, the case of the cleric from Avignon, who lived in the period immediately before the Black Death (the presumed year of his death being 1350 raises the question as to whether he in fact fell victim to the terrible plague), is, of course, of interest, not in connection with his possible mental illness, but because his writings bring us an unusual manifestation, in the mind of a disturbed individual, of certain tendencies in the culture of what can truly be termed a period of crisis. At this time, profound changes were at work within patterns of social and religious attitudes. Interpretations of the correlation between the human being or microcosm on the one hand, and the world or macrocosm on the other, reflected in Opicinus' drawings, were undergoing radical changes, and these changes could be viewed as symptoms of the individual's growing sense of his own worth. Opicinus was no longer prepared to accept the equation that had been traditional in the Middle Ages, when humanity and the world had been viewed as homologous: not only did people place themselves at the centre of the Universe, they also absorbed it in its entirety into their own being because their sense of sinfulness, though focused on the individual, was extended by Opicinus to cover the whole world.

Does not this cosmic egocentricism provide expression, albeit in an unusual and highly individual form stemming from Opicinus' morbid imagination, of new principles regarding the individual? Yet these new trends in the development of the individual, which assumed such exaggerated form in Opicinus hands, remain essentially medieval in content. The pride bursting forth from the depths of his being, the paroxysms of megalomania (even to the point where the Devil appears to him, tempting him with the very same temptations with which he had tried to subvert Christ), are immediately punished by Opicinus himself: he preaches on and on about sin which is sweeping over the world, but which is also rooted in his own individual being. In this way the emotional complexes of the individual bring us back once again to the fundamental contradiction in Christian ethics, which continues to furnish an obstacle for those engaged in singling out the individual. Perhaps Opicinus' very abnormality serves to explain why, in his case, the secret recesses of personality emerge somewhat more clearly than usual?

So the spontaneous outpouring of individuality breaks through, not so much within the confines of Christian medieval culture, but rather on its fringes – in those places where ethical control, as expressed in the demands for self-restraint and humility, either has not yet taken firm root as an imperative (as, for example, in surroundings that had not yet been fully

Christianized) or had been undermined as a result of an individual's own psychological idiosyncrasies.

I acknowledge without hesitation that, in my attempts to 'dig down' to the hidden core of the medieval personality, I have risked moving off the firm ground of my own historical analysis. Arguments have of necessity become strictly hypothetical. *Individuum est ineffabile* ... nevertheless, I shall risk one last conjecture.

Let us turn to the case of Martin Guerre, an episode in the history of the peasantry of southern France in the middle of the sixteenth century. In terms of strict chronology, this period falls outside the scope of the Middle Ages but, in its essence, it was still medieval. Traditions in peasant society were changing particularly slowly. The story of *Martin Guerre,* 'invented', as it were, by life itself in keeping with fairy-tale or novel scripts and used on several occasions by poets, dramatists and screenwriters, has been most competently researched by Natalie Zemon Davis,[4] who has placed this episode into the real social context of the age. All I shall do here is to remind the reader of the main outline of the story.

The marriage between young Martin and Bertrande, daughter of a rich peasant in the Languedoc, was an unhappy one. First of all, the husband's long period of impotence meant that the marriage had initially been childless and then, after Bertrande had at last given birth to a son, Martin disappeared. He left home and was not seen for many a long year. When he finally came back, it turned out that his place had been taken by another. The fact was that, several years earlier, a young stalwart named Arnaud du Thil, who had pretended to be Martin Guerre, had been so successful that everyone – his relatives, neighbours and, most important of all, his wife – had accepted him as genuine.

Suspicions were aroused only when a quarrel regarding property flared up between an uncle and the impostor-nephew. The risk of perhaps losing land opened the uncle's eyes about the newcomer and a bitter legal battle ensued. Several dozen witnesses were questioned by the judges but they were unable to establish the truth, because some of them denied that

Bertrande's husband was the real Martin, while others were sure that the man with whom Bertrande had spent several happy years and who had given her a daughter was indeed her lawful husband. As for the defendant himself, he tenaciously overturned the accusations of deception so convincingly that the Toulouse parliament – the supreme court in the province – was about to acquit him. Yet, at that very moment when the judges were preparing to pronounce their verdict, who should enter the courtroom but Martin Guerre in person: he looked very different and had only one leg, but there was no doubt that this was the real man! Bertrande and all the others recognized him immediately. The fraud was exposed, condemned to death and hanged in front of the house of the man he had pretended for so long and so successfully to be.

There are several aspects of this episode that attract the attention of the historian. Natalie Davis focuses mainly on Bertrande: how had the wife been able to 'recognize' her husband in the impostor? Had she genuinely been deceived or, after giving up hope that Martin would ever return and knowing that she could not marry again until his death had been proven, had she been anxious to resume a normal family life (for even after the accusations had been levelled at Arnaud, she continued to insist that he was the true Martin almost until the end of the proceedings)? To concentrate attention like this on Bertrande is perfectly understandable but Arnaud du Thil, who had pretended to be Martin Guerre, is no less interesting. Davis aptly points out that we are confronted here, not with a case of common fraud or by an attempt on Arnaud's part simply to 'pass himself off as another person', but with a carefully elaborated strategy to 'take over another man's life'. This meant that the return of the real Martin signified that he was carrying out his intention of taking his life, his *persona*, back again.

Clearly, Arnaud du Thil must have encountered Martin Guerre during his wanderings and then realized that there was a physical resemblance between them (although by no means in all respects). He then found out a great deal about Martin's former life and the people with whom he had associated. He has to be credited with learning the part he was planning to play very thoroughly. It is not made absolutely clear how he achieved it but there is no denying the fact that Arnaud knew all the people in the village by their names and recognized them by their appearance: after he appeared in their midst, he 'recalled' incidents experienced with them and conversations from the past so well that, at first, no-one seriously doubted that he was indeed Martin Guerre. Comments were made about the differences between him and Martin really only after the quarrel had broken out between uncle and 'nephew'. Natalie Davis points out that, at that period, peasants had no clear-cut criteria for identifying the individual, as there were no documents for this purpose or examples of handwriting to use, and it was not customary to look hard at an individual's facial features – something which becomes a habit for people who use mirrors. It is possible that, in those conditions, people do not acquire sensitivity to details of physiognomy, and small differences between people do not attract attention. Here let us recall the comment by Fèvres concerning the 'visual backwardness' of people in the sixteenth century: they were used to relying more on their hearing than their sight.

All this helps us to answer the question as to why the people in the village, on seeing Arnaud du Thil pretending to be Martin Guerre, believed that it really was Martin Guerre standing before them. It would surely be only natural, however, to ask at this point how the impostor had imagined this situation to himself. It is, of course, impossible to obtain a clear answer. All we know is that Arnaud overturned all the objections raised against his authenticity with great conviction (although it must be said that there was little else he could do, having already taking his deception so far), and he was so convincing and consistent in his self-defence that dozens of neighbours testified in his favour during the trial: moreover, he even convinced the experienced and educated Judge de Coras from Toulouse, who left behind for posterity a detailed description of this 'astonishing and memorable' case. It was only after Arnaud had been condemned and a public denial was demanded from him before his death, that he finally acknowledged that he was a fraud and impostor as he prepared to meet his Supreme Judge.

It must be assumed here that a person who collected so carefully and for such a long time all possible information about the life of another, even down to the tiniest details of his dealings with his neighbours and relatives, as well as a great deal of information about the latter (the number of witnesses who gave evidence at the trial in the local court and who therefore had been interacting with pseudo-Martin until he was first summoned before the law, was almost 150 including Martin Guerre's blood relatives and relatives by marriage), could not fail in the end to start living the part. He had planned to wear the mask of Martin Guerre for the rest of his life and for several years succeeded totally. The mask must have started to fit the face, to become part of Arnaud. Could he help but start to imagine himself as Martin? Would not a psychological transformation of this sort serve to explain the conviction with which he defended his new identity and the persuasiveness that made such a powerful impression on the judge?

It would naturally be impossible, however, for the new Martin Guerre to have forgotten completely that he was Arnaud du Thil. He was acting and pretending. It was common knowledge, however, what price had to be paid by those who indulged in long-term make-believe. Yet I ask myself: when medieval writers identified themselves with certain models – Abelard with St Jerome, Guibert de Nogent with St Augustine, Sverrir with Magnus, son of Saint Olaf, Opicinus with Boethius – they must surely have known that they were Abelard not St Jerome and still less Christ, or Guibert not St Augustine and so on? This means of self-identification did not involve any total rejection of their own selves or complete absorption of the writer by the model, merely comparison of the one with the other. The impostor living with Bertrande and talking to her and Martin's neighbours and relatives was, at the same time, Martin Guerre and Arnaud du Thil. The medieval individual was primarily a member of a group and it was mainly within the group that he or she acquired an identity. Natalie Davis states with every justification that the adventurer and impostor Arnaud du Thil achieved his goal, when he succeeded in becoming part of the life of the Guerre family.[5]

In this book we have of necessity (because of the nature of

the available sources) been concerned mainly with the intellectuals of the Middle Ages. Their means of self-identification were through comparisons of themselves with models drawn from books and, at first glance, their technique has nothing in common with the case of Arnaud du Thil. Yet perhaps this difference should not be viewed as something absolute? Arnaud, who played the part of Martin Guerre so brilliantly, displayed no small degree of artistry. What we have before us is yet another outstanding individual. If he had not started quarrelling with Martin's relatives about a plot of land and if the real Martin Guerre had not returned, he could have continued just as successfully as before to live in the guise he had assumed. In this case, we encounter an individual of great flexibility, able to transform himself into someone else. It would appear that Arnaud du Thil experienced no insuperable problems in 'becoming' Martin Guerre.

Surely this would demonstrate that the individuality of men and women in the Middle Ages was not something clearly delineated or independent of their immediate surroundings? The urge to find a ready made model, to achieve fusion with a prototype and the ease with which the individual compared himself or herself with a model are all signs that this individuality was comparatively ill-defined and still had a long way to go. It is common knowledge that the Middle Ages were a time that brought forth an abundance of impostors. I would see the problem of the impostor as a psychological problem.

If, in conclusion, we consider the history of the individual and individuality in medieval Western Europe as a whole, then we are forced to admit that putting together any kind of general picture is extremely difficult. Our knowledge is fragmentary, the gaps are many, probably even more numerous than we imagine. The history of the individual in the Middle Ages is to a large extent concealed from the gaze of the scholar: it developed at a level that can only partly be traced in the available sources. This is why I was able only to point to certain aspects of the problem, to sketch in only scattered chapters of this history.

Are we entitled to speak of the 'discovery' of the individual and individuality in any specific period of the Middle Ages. It does indeed emerge that attention became more closely focused on this phenomenon in the twelfth and thirteenth centuries, although it is still possible that this conclusion forces itself upon the historian because of the state of the source material: the earlier period is not so rich in written sources and, from their scattered testimony, it is difficult to piece together a general picture. The change in the system of values that was beginning at that time, as the latter 'came down to earth' (Jacques Le Goff)[6] was undoubtedly bound up with the individual's growing self-awareness.

Yet fact is fact: the most profound penetration of the secret recesses of a person's own soul is that provided by the *Confessions* of St Augustine. The high point of the development of the individual is to be found at the very threshold of the Middle Ages not, as might well have been expected, at its end. In the course of a thousand years, there is no other revelation of a person's inner self that is so candid. Petrarch, St Augustine's disciple, drew lessons from him in what by then was a radically changed world: while St Augustine's personality is revealed as he draws nearer to God and seeks spiritual union with Him, Petrarch's attention, on the other hand, is concentrated on his own significant self, as he carefully and prudently moulds his own biography and personality.

The thousand years that divided these two figures had their fair share of talent, creativity and profound thinkers, but these geniuses and these creative artists did not have scope for full revelation of their individuality. It is possible that many of them did not feel the need to assert their individualities, or, to be more precise, found their own specific ways of asserting them. The system of values substantiated by medieval Christianity did not encourage men and women to proclaim and assert their unique individualities.

The inclusion in this study of works of Scandinavian literature could, I think, provide material for additional conclusions as well. Different aspects of the individual personality are recorded in these writings – the incorporation of the individual into the group, whose moral demands would be satisfied without question, and, at the same time, people's awareness of their own worth and a certain degree of separateness. Christian rigour, forcing individuals to hold themselves in check and submit to their Creator, so that their own identities might be lost in that of the Lord, had not yet taken hold of the inner world of the Germanic people of the north. This makes it possible for the writings that have come down to us from northern Europe to lift part of the curtain, which conceals the deeper layers of the individual's self-awareness, that must have existed further south as well, but that 'went underground' as Christianity spread.

The gradual emergence of the individual and individuality was by no means a smooth process: it moved by fits and starts, sometimes even backwards, and there was much marking time. There was no straightforward evolutionary progression from the individual of the Middle Ages to that of the New Age, because these individuals were different human types. The individual of the Middle Ages was our predecessor and, at the same time, **different** – not alien but simply different – and needs to be understood with all his or her inimitable qualities.

Notes

1 The Individual is Ineffable

1   Colin Morris, *The Discovery of the Individual. 1050–1200* (London, 1972).
2   Mourning the crisis and even the eradication of individualism in modern Western society is now quite a widespread activity. There is no space or indeed need to assess this phenomenon here. I should like merely to point out that other opinions, more sensible ones in my view, are also being expressed at the same time as ideas of this sort. In effect, such opinions suggest that, in the course of history, individualism has changed and continues to change its outward form and that at the present time it would be more appropriate to talk not of the decline of individualism but of changes in its content. See: *Reconstructing Individualism. Autonomy, Individuality, and the Self in Western Thought*, ed. T. C. Heller, M. Sosna and D.E Wellbery (Stanford, 1986).
3   Georg Misch, *Geschichte der Autobiographie*, 2nd edn (vols I-IV, Frankfurt am Main, 1949–62).
4   Colin Morris, op. cit., p. 158, note.
5   Caroline Walker Bynum, 'Did the Twentieth Century Discover the Individual?' *The Journal of Ecclesiastical History*, 31 (1980), pp.1-17 [C. W. Bynum, *Jesus as Mother: Studies in the Spirituality of the High Middle Ages* (Berkeley, Los Angeles, 1982), pp. 82-109].
6   C. W. Bynum, *Jesus as Mother*, pp. 95-97, 101.
7   *Ibidem*, p. 11. This quotation is taken from a work by Yves Congar, published in *Études de civilisation médiévale* (Poitiers,

1973), p. 159.

8   C. W. Bynum, op. cit., pp. 88-90, 104 ff. Morris responded to criticism standing by his thesis with regard to the 'discovery of the individual' in the twelfth century. Colin Morris, 'Individualism in Twelfth-Century Religion. Some Further Reflections', *Journal of Ecclesiastical History* 31, No. 2 (1980), pp. 195-206.

9   Jean-Claude Schmitt, 'La découverte de l'individu, une fiction historiographique?', *La fabrique, la figure et la feinte. Fictions et Statut des Fictions en Psychologie.* Edited by P. Mengal and F. Parot (Paris, 1989), pp. 213-236.

10 See: Marcel Mauss, 'Une catégorie de l'esprit humain, la notion de personne', *Sociologie et anthropologie* (Paris, 1968); I. Meyerson, *Problèmes de la personne. Exposés . . .* (Paris-La Haye, 1973).

11 Walter Ullmann [*The Individual and Society in the Middle Ages* (Baltimore, 1966)], whose research was focused on the political and legal aspects of the question of the relationship between the individual and society in the Middle Ages and who also analyses this question in the light of the evolution in the direction of the civic society of the Modern Age. The humane quality of the individual, according to Ullman, is gradually coming to occupy centre stage and the individual is beginning to take priority over society. The first seeds of these changes can, in his opinion, be traced back as far as the twelfth or thirteenth centuries. See: Georg Vogt, *Die Wiederbelebung des klassischen Altertums, oder das erste Jahrhundert des Humanismus (The Revival of the Classical Past, or the First Century of Humanism)* (Berlin, 1859), pp. 80 and following: Petrarch 'prophet of the New Age, forefather of the modern world'.

12 R. R. Bolgar (ed.), *Classical Influences on European Culture, 500–1500* (Cambridge, 1971), p. 188. Morris quotes these words with feeling. C. Morrris, op. cit., p. 7.

13 M.-D. Chenu, *L'éveil de la conscience dans la civilisation médiévale* (Montreal-Paris, 1869), pp. 14-15. Cf. M.-D.Chenu, *La théologie au douzième siècle* (Paris, 1957).

14 M.-D. Chenu, *L'éveil de la conscience*, pp. 31, 32.

15 See: Hans Bayer, 'Zur Soziologie des mittelalterlichen Individualisierungsprozeßes. Ein Beitrag zu einer wirklichkeitsbezogenen Geistesgeschichte', *Archiv für Kulturgeschichte*, 58, Book 1 (1976), pp. 115-153.

16 N. J. Smelser, W. T. Smelser, (eds) *Personality and Social Systems*, ed. by , New York, 1967.

17 *L'uomo medievale*, edited by Jacques Le Goff (Roma-Bari, 1987).

18 G. B. Ladner, '*Homo viator*: Mediaeval Ideas on Alienation and Order', *Speculum*, 42 (1967), pp. 235-259.

19 E. Castelnuovo, 'L'artista' in *L'uomo medievale*, p. 237-390.

21 *L'uomo medievale*, p.29.

22 *L'uomo medievale*, p.34.

23 Naturally, only a few works have been mentioned here: more specialized research works are discussed later in various sections of the book.

24 For the search by Italian humanists to define their own individuality see works by L. M. Batkin, *The Italian Humanists: their styles of life and thought* (*Ital'yanskiye gumanisty: stil' zhizni i stil' myshleniya*) (Moscow, 1978); *The Italian Renaissance in search of Individuality* (*Ital'yanskoye Vozrozhdeniye v poiskakh individual'nosti*) (Moscow, 1989); *Leonardo da Vinci and features of Renaissance creative thought* (*Leonardo da Vinchi i osobennosti renessanskogo tvorcheskogo myshleniya*) (Moscow, 1990).

25 B. A. Shkuratov, 'Do not Forget to Turn Back', *An Odyssey. Man in History – 1990* ('Ne pozabyt' vernut'sya nazad', *Odissei. Chelovek v istorii – 1990*) (Moscow, 1990), p. 35.

26 In the course of a discussion, that took place in 1988 during the Moscow Seminar on historical psychology, on the subject 'Individuality and Personality in History' (see: *An Odyssey. Man in History – 1990*, Odyssey, pp. 6-89) various interesting thoughts were propounded by some of the scholars attending who represented a variety of different fields. At the same time the extreme divergence in interpretations of personality and individuality came to the fore and also the degree to which these concepts still need to be made the subject of further, more logical investigation.

27 Peter Dronke, *Abelard and Héloïse in Medieval Testimonies*, Glasgow, 1976.

28 Virtually the only exception is the work by Georg Misch, *A History of Autobiography*: in it Misch devoted a whole chapter to the personality and work of the Icelandic skald Egill Skallagrimsson. Georg Misch, *Geschichte der Autobiographie*, 2nd edn (Vol. 2, Part I, 1st half), pp. 131-177.

29 Alfons Dopsch, *Beiträge zur Sozial- und Wirtschaftsgeschichte*.

Gesammelte Aufsätze (*Contributions to Social and Economic History. Collected Essays*), 2nd Series, Vienna, 1938. Dopsch's article 'Wirtschaftsgeist und Individualismus im Frühmittelalter' ('The Economic Spirit and Individualism in the Early Middle Ages') was first published in 1929.

30 G. Hatt, 'Prehistoric Fields in Jutland', *Acta archaeologica*, II, 1931; ibid., 'Oldtidsagre', *Det Kongelige Danske Videnskabernes Selskab, Arkaeologisk-kunsthistoriske skrifter*, 2, No. 2, (Copenhagen, 1949); H. Jahnkuhn, *Archäologie und Geschichte. Vorträge und Aufsätze* (Archaeology and History. Lectures and Essays), Vol.1 (Berlin, New York, 1976); W. Haarnagel, *Die Grabung Feddersen Wierde. Methode, Hausbau, Siedlungs- und Wirtschaftsformen sowie Sozialstruktur* (*The Excavation of Feddersen Wierde. Methods, House Construction, Types of Settlement and Economy and Social Structure*) (Wiesbaden, 1979).

31 A. Dopsch, op. cit., pp. 164 ff.

2 The Individual and the Epic Tradition

1 C. M. Bowra, *Heroic Poetry* (London, 1952), p. 71 ff.
2 O. Höfler, 'Deutsche Heldensage' in *Zur germanisch-deutschen Heldensage*, ed. by K. Hauck (Darmstadt,1965), pp. 67-69, 73-75.
3 Michail Steblin-Kamenskij, 'Valkyries and Heroes' in *Arkiv för nordisk filologi* 97 (1982), pp. 81-93.
4 A. Heusler, *Kleine Schriften* (Berlin, 1969), vol. 2, pp. 221-222.
5 Klaus von See points out that the narrator in *The Lesson of the High One* is not a man rooted in a family or clan group or in a political community but a separate, isolated individual contrasted with other, sometimes hostile, individuals, a man who does not sense he has the support of a mighty clan and who therefore has to develop within himself qualities appropriate to his situation, including a rather small-minded calculating utilitarianism. The figure which emerges in this poem contrasts strikingly with the figures of the heroes found in sagas, skaldic poetry and the heroic poems of the *Edda*. From this von See goes on to draw what to me is a rather unexpected conclusion to the effect that *The Lesson of the High One* should be approached as part of the scholarly tradition in association with the works of Seneca and biblical texts. K. von See, *Edda, Saga, Skaldendichtung. Aufsätze zur skandinavischen Literatur*

des Mittelalters (Heidelberg, 1981), pp. 39 ff.

6 *Die Bosa-saga in zwei Fassungen,* ed. by O. L. Jiriczek (Strasbourg,1893), Chapter 2, pp. 6-7.

7 A. Heusler, *Kleine Schriften,* p. 199.

8 M. I. Steblin-Kamenskij, *Controversial Issues in Philology* (*Spornoye v yazykoznanii*), (Leningrad, 1974), pp. 61-74.

9 Michail Steblin-Kamenskij, *The Saga Mind* (Odense, 1973).

10 Einar Ól. Svensson, *Njáls saga: A Literary Masterpiece* (Lincoln, Nebraska, 1971).

11 C. J. Clover, 'Skaldic Sensibility', *Arkiv för nordisk filologi,* 93 (1978), p. 80.

12 See: P. Zumthor, 'Le je du poète', *Langue, texte, énigme* (Paris, 1973), pp. 181-196.

13 See: G. Kreutzer, *Die Dichtungslehre der Skalden. Poetologische Terminologie und Autorenreklame als Grundlagen einer Gattungspoetik* 2nd edn (Meisenheim am Glan, 1977), pp. 172 ff., pp. 264 ff.

14 Berserk was the name given to warriors who stood out because of their extraordinary physical strength and ferocity: in battle, they threw off their clothes, howled, roared and were held to be invulnerable. The Berserks were protected by Odin.

15 In other sagas about the skalds reference is usually made to their strange appearance as well: it would seem that this was a sign of their special distinction and the danger that they could embody. See: M. S. Ross, 'The Art of Poetry and the Figure of the Poet in Egills Saga', in *Parergon* 22 (1978).

16 G. Misch, *Geschichte der Autobiographie.*

17 Here we are presented with a pun, for the Ancient Icelandic word *ekkja* means both 'heel' and 'widow'.

18 Other 'royal sagas' were devoted to the period that preceded the appearance of Sverrir on the historical arena. The events narrated in *Sverris saga* begin in 1177, while the events recounted in the other sagas end in that year. Snorri Sturluson, while working on his *Heimskringla,* was clearly already acquainted with the *Sverris saga* and referring to its content.

19 S. S. Nilsson, 'Kva slag mann var kong Sverre?', *Syn og segn* (1948), pp. 445-57; *ejusd.,* 'Kong Sverre og kong David', *Edda,* 1948, pp. 73-86; J. Schreiner, 'Kong David i Sverres saga og Kongespeilet', *Historisk tidsskrift* 37 (Oslo, 1954), pp. 22-24.

20 K. Lunden, *Norges historie* (Oslo, 1976), vol. 3, p. 122.

21 P. A. Munch, *Det norske Folks Historie* (Christiania, 1857), vol. III, pp. 390-1; A. Bugge, *Norges historie fremstillet for det*

norske folk (Kristiania, 1916), vol. II, part 2, pp. 48, 204.

22 Before the beginning of one of the decisive battles, Sverrir turned to his Birchlegs or *Birkebeiner* in an effort to boost their fighting spirit with the words: 'The time is come when you should receive more profit than has yet been in our reach from the toil and great danger you have undergone . . . now there is a prize to be won in the town of Nidaros, somewhat more valuable . . . I will now make known to you what is to be gained: whoever slays a baron (*lendr mann*) and can bring forward evidence of his deed, shall himself be a baron; and whatever title a man shall cause to be vacant, that title shall be his . . .' (*Sverris saga*, 35).

3 The 'Persona' in Search of the Individual

1 G. Le Bras, 'La personne dans le droit classique de l'église', *Problèmes de la personne* ed. by I. Meyerson (Paris-La Haye, 1973), p. 193.

2 Manfried Fuhrmann, 'Persona, römischer Rollenbegriff' in *Identität* ed. by O. Marquard and K. Stierle (Munich, 1979), pp. 83-106).

3 J.-P. Vernant, 'Aspects de la personne dans la religion grecque', *Problèmes de la personne* , pp. 23 ff.; *ejusd., Mythe et pensée chez les Grecs. Études de psychologie historique*, (Paris, 1971).

4 P. L. (*Patrologia latina*), vol. 36, column 268.

5 P. Courcelle, *Les 'Confessions' de Saint Augustin dans la tradition littéraire. Antécédents et postérité* (Paris, 1963).

6 The text of the confession: Walter Berschin, 'I Patricius . . . Die Autobiographie des Apostels der Iren', *Die Iren und Europa im früheren Mittelalter*, ed. by H. Lowe, vol. 1, pp. 9-25, (Stuttgart, 1982)

7 P. L., vol. 64, column 1343. Alanus ab Insulis favoured another definition of *persona*,which, once again, could be traced back to Boethius: '*Etiam apud illos qui tractant comoedias vel tragoedias persona dicitur histrio qui variis modis personando diversos status hominum repraesantat, et dicitur persona a personando*'. P. L., vol. 210, column 899A. ('Authors of comedies and tragedies give the name *persona* to the actor who, using different voices, portrays people of different status; thus the word *persona* comes from *personando* [to sound, to talk]'). See: Hans Rheinfelder, *Das Wort 'Persona'* (Halle, 1928), p. 19.

8   Thomas Aquinas, *Summa Theologiae I*, qu, 29, art. 3.
9   *Historisches Wörterbuch der Philosophie*, ed. by J. Rittert and
     K. Gründer, vol. 7, (Darmstadt, 1989), s.v. Person, pp. 276 ff.
10   See: V. P. Losskii, 'The Theological Concept of the Individual'
     ('Bogoslovskoye ponyatie lichnosti') in *Bogoslovkiye trudy*
     (*Theological Works*) (Moscow, 1970).
11   Nikolai Kuzanskii (Nikolaus von Cües), *Works* (*Trudy*)
     (Moscow, 1988), vol. 2, p. 497; vol. 1, p. 163.
12   See: H. Adolf, 'On Medieval Laughter', *Speculum* (1947) 22,
     No. 2, p. 251.
13   S. Ullmann, 'Le vocabulaire, moule et norme de la pensée' in
     Problèmes de la Personne, pp. 260-3.

4 Biography and Death

1   Philippe Ariès, *L'homme devant la mort* (*Man faced by Death*)
     (Paris, 1977), p. 13 ff.
2   Arno Borst, 'Zwei mittelalterliche Sterbefälle' ('Two Medieval
     Deaths'), *Merkur* 34m (1980), pp.1081-98.
3   D. d'Avray, 'Sermons on the Dead before 1350', *Studi medievali*
     (*Medieval Studies*)) XXXI–I (1990), 3rd Series, pp. 207-23. I
     was also able, thanks to Dr d'Avray, to acquaint myself with
     a manuscript of his on the same subject and for this I am
     extremely grateful.
4   Philippe Ariès, *L'homme devant la mort*, p. 287.
5   Beat Brenk, *Tradition und Neuerung in der christlichen Kunst
     des ersten Jahrtausends: Studien zur Geschichte des
     Weltgerichtsbildes* (*Tradition and Innovation in Christian Art
     of the First Millennium* AD: *Studies towards a History of
     Conceptions of the Day of Judgement*) (Vienna, 1966).

5 Autobiography: Confession or Apologia?

1   M. M. Bakhtin, *Aesthetics of Literary Creation* (*Estetika
     slovesnogo tvorchestva*) (Moscow, 1979), pp. 128-31.
2   Admittedly, as early as the second half of the seventh century,
     the Visigoth Valerius wrote the story of his life (P. L., 87, col.
     439-47), but it would be futile to look for the expression of his
     personality in this work composed according to hagiographical
     models or to search for information in it about his origins,
     education and how he developed.
3   A. Murray, *Reason and Society in the Middle Ages* (Oxford,

1985), p.162 ff.

4   See: B. Stock, *The Implications of Literacy. Written Language and Models of Interpretation in the Eleventh and Twelfth Centuries* (Princeton, New Jersey, 1983).

5   See: J. Leclerq, 'Modern Psychology and the Interpretation of Medieval Texts', *Speculum* XLVIII (1973), No. 3, pp. 476-90; M. de Gandillac, 'Abélard (et Héloïse)', *Individualisme et autobiographie en Occident (Individualism and Autobiography in the West)* (Brussels, 1983) pp. 85-99.

6   See: M. Carruthers, *A Study of Memory in Medieval Culture* (Cambridge, 1990), pp. 179-80, 182.

7   P.L., CLVI, col. 607-80 (Concerning tokens of the Saints).

8   See: K. Guth, *Guibert von Nogent und die hochmittelalterliche Kritik an der Reliquienverehrung (Guibert of Nogent and Criticism of Relic Worship in the High Middle Ages)* (Ottobeuren, 1970); C. Morris, 'A Critique of Popular Religion: Guibert of Nogent on The Relics of the Saints', *Popular Belief and Practice*, ed. G. J. Cuming and D. Baker (Cambridge, 1972), pp. 55-60.

9   J. E. Benton, 'The Personality of Guibert of Nogent', *Psychoanalytic Review* 57 (1970-1), No. 4, pp. 563-86; cf. J. B. Benton, *Self and Society in Medieval France: The Memoirs of Abbot Guibert of Nogent* (New York, 1970).

10   Guibert of Nogent, *Autobiographie* (Introduction) edited and translated by E.-R. Labande (Paris, 1981).

11   Scholars draw attention to the parallel between the 'confessions' of Guibert de Nogent and St Augustine: in both their lives, their mothers played important roles, in particular when it came to their 'conversions' to the true faith and to a righteous way of life, although the characters of Monique and Guibert's mother were quite different.

12   See: J.-C. Schmitt, 'Sognare nel XII secolo' ('Dreaming in the Twelfth Century')and 'L'autobiografia sognata' ('Autobiography via Dreams')in his book *Religione, folklore e societa nell'Occidente medievale (Religion, Folklore and Society in the Medieval West)* (Roma-Bari, 1988); See also: M. E. Wittmer-Butsch, *Zur Bedeutung von Schlaf und Traum im Mittelalter (On the Meaning of Sleep and Dreams in the Middle Ages)* (Krems, 1990).

13   See: F. Amory, 'The Confessional Superstructure of Guibert of Nogent's Vita', *Classsica et medievale*, XXV (1964).

14   P. Brown, 'Society and the Supernatural: A Medieval Change',

Daedalus Spring (1975), pp. 133-51; *idem, Society and the Holy in Late Antiquity* (London, 1982), p. 305 ff.

15 A. Borst, 'Findung und Spaltung der öffentlichen Persönlichkeit (6. bis 13. Jahrhundert)' [' and Splits in the Public Personality (sixth-thirteenth centuries)'], *Identität* ed. by O. Marquard and K. Stierle in the series *Poetik und Hermeneutik* VIII (Munich, 1970), p. 633 ff.

16 F. Wade, 'Abelard and Individuality', *Die Metaphysik im Mittelalter. Ihr Ursprung und ihre Bedeutung (Metaphysics in the Middle Ages)* ed. by P. Wilpert (Volume 2 of the series *Miscellanea mediaevalia*) (Berlin, 1963), pp. 165-71.

17 M.-D. Chenu, *L'éveil de la conscience dans la civilisation médiévale (The Awakening of Consciousness in Medieval Civilization)* p. 15.

18 G. P. Fedotov, *Abélard* (St Petersburg, 1924), pp. 9,10.

19 J. T. Muckle, 'Abélard's Letter of Consolation to a Friend' (*Historia Calamitatum*) in *Medieval Studies*, XII (1950), pp. 163-213.

20 It has been suggested that, like the correspondence between Abélard and Héloïse (the authenticity of this correspondence in particular is doubted by a number of scholars) *Historia calamitatum mearum* is a forgery composed after Abélard's death and perhaps even in the next century (the earliest extant manuscripts date from the thirteenth century). Arguments as to whether or not these works are authentic recur every now and then. We shall start out from the hypothesis that *Historia calamitatum mearum* was composed by Abélard, although it is possible that the text was subjected to editing after he wrote it.

21 'We are here like warriors, attempting by force to conquer the heavens and is not man's life on earth indeed similar to that of a soldier?' asked Bernard of Clairvaux. Immediately afterwards, however, he went on to add:' Yet while we, still possessed of earthly bodies, wage these battles, we remain far removed from the Lord . . .' G. Duby, *Saint Bernard. L'art cistercien (Saint Bernard. Cistercian Art)* (Paris, 1979), p. 80.

22 R. W. Southern, *Medieval Humanism and Other Studies* (Oxford, 1970), pp. 91-3; J. Verger, 'Abelard et les milieux sociaux de son temps' ('Abelard and the social milieux of his Time') in *Abelard en son temps (Abelard in his Time)*, International Colloquium (Paris, 1981), pp. 107-31. R. W. Hanning suggests, among other things, that one of the literary models, to which Abélard turned, was the Life of Saint Jerome

written by St Athanasius. Abélard refers to him in his account of one of the most tragic moments in his life – his condemnation at the provincial Council, when he was obliged to recite the Creed. R. W. Hanning, *The Individual in Twelfth-Century Romance* (New Haven and London, 1977), pp. 24 ff., 27.

23 See: R. W. Southern, *Medieval Humanism and other Studies*, pp. 93-4.

24 M. T. Clanchy, 'Abelard's Mockery of St. Anselm' in *Journal of Ecclesiastical History* 41 (1990), No. 1, pp. 1-23.

25 Abbot Suger, *On the Abbey Church of St. Denis and Its Art Treasures* ed. by E. Panofsky (Princeton, New Jersey, 1944), p. 17.

26 G. P. Fedotov, *Abelard*, pp. 83-5.

27 Admittedly, at the end of his life Abélard wrote a long edifying poem for his son; it consisted of various aphorisms relating to everyday life and maxims formulated by Abélard himself in a similar vein. These moral statements were extremely general in nature and not adapted to fit the personality of his son at all although Abélard, who was a concerned and loving father, was well acquainted with his character. He praises friendship, hospitality and generosity, stresses the need to live in fear of God, to read the Holy Scriptures frequently, to set little store by this world, not to commit the sin of pride, while at the same time guarding one's good reputation: along with all this, however, Abélard gives expression to his low opinion of the female sex. In this respect he does not differ at all from other medieval monks. As G. Misch points out, Abélard's rare good fortune to have a wife like Héloïse did not open his eyes to the true nature of the female sex. G. Misch, op. cit., p. 698. Strangely he finds it possible to refer here, in his exhortations to his son, to his intimate relations with Héloïse.

28 I shall not be touching upon the correspondence between Abélard and Héloïse, not only because the differences between scholars regarding its authenticity are unlikely to be resolved conclusively, but also because these missives do not appear to shed any new light on the character of Abélard. On the other hand, the letters from Héloïse, who entered a convent after disaster had befallen the lovers and later became its Mother Superior, cannot fail to strike us on account of the power of her love and boundless devotion to Abélard who, in his replies, tries to maintain a distance between them, remains coldly polite and eventually makes it impossible for Héloïse to pour

out her feelings any further. Unlike those of Abélard, Héloïse's letters reveal her as an individual. See: L. M. Batkin, 'Héloïse's Letters to Abelard. Personal Feelings and their Cultural Mediation' ('Pis'ma Eloizy k Abelyaru. Lichnoye chuvstvo i ego kul'turnoye oposredovanie')in *Man and Culture. Individuality in the History of Culture (Chelovek i kul'tura. Individual'nost' v istorii kul'tury)* (Moscow, 1990).

29 M. M. McLaughlin, 'Abelard as Autobiographer: The Motives and Meaning of his "Story of Calamities"', *Speculum* XLII (1967) No. 3, pp. 463-88.

30 L. M. Batkin, *Man and Culture . . .*, p. 151.

31 G. Misch, *Geschichte der Autobiographie (A History of Autobiography)* vol. III, part 2, first half, p. 529. See also: P. Dronke, *Abelard and Héloïse in Medieval Testimonies* (Glasgow, 1976), p. 51: '. . . *Cui soli patuit scibile quicquid erat*'.

32 See: J. Le Goff, 'Quelle conscience l'Université médiévale a-t-elle eue d'elle-même?' ('How did the Medieval University see itself?') in *Pour un autre Moyen Age. Temps, travail et culture en Occident: 18 essais (For a Different Middle Ages. Time, Work and Culture in the West)* (Paris, 1977), pp. 182-6.

33 G. Misch, *Geschichte der Autobiographie (A History of Autobiography)*, vol. II, part 1, first half, **pp. 21-3; vol. III, part 2, first half, p. 365.

34 E. Panofsky (ed.), Abbot Suger, *On the Abbey Church of St.-Denis and Its Art Treasures*, pp. 29 ff.

35 J. Leclerq, 'Modern Psychology and the Interpretation of Medieval Texts', *Speculum* XLVIII (1973) No. 3.

36 P.L., vol.146, columns 29-58.

37 P. Lehmann, 'Autobiographies of the Middle Ages', *Transactions of the Royal Historical Society*, vol. 3 (1953) 5th series, p. 46.

38 All examples quoted here can be found in the work by E. Castelnuovo entitled 'L'artista' ('The Artist') in *L'uomo medievale (The Medieval World)*, pp. 244-53.

39 E. R. Curtius, *Europäische Literatur und lateinisches Mittelalter (European Literature and the Latin Middle Ages)*, 8th edition (Bern and Munich, 1979), pp. 503-5.

40 See: G. Misch, *Geschichte der Autobiographie (A History of Autobiography)* vol. III, first half, p. 92.

41 Rudolf Teuffel, *Individuelle Persönlichkeitsschilderung in den deutschen Geschichtswerken des 10. und 11. Jahrhunderts*

(*Depiction of Individual Personalities in the German Historical Works of the Tenth and Eleventh Centuries*) (Leipzig-Berlin, 1914).

42 Etienne Gilson, *Héloïse et Abélard* (Paris, 1948).

6 The Parable of the Five Talents

1   I have already mentioned this sermon in some of my other works {A. Ja Gurevic, 'Il mercante', *L'uomo medievale* [published in English as *The Medieval World* (Collins and Brown, 1990)], pp. 288-90; A. Y. Gurevich, *The Medieval World* [*Srednevekovyi mir*], pp. 198-211; A. Gurevich, 'The "Sociology" and "Anthropology" of Berthold von Regensburg', *Journal of Historical Sociology* 4 [1991] No. 2, pp. 112-20.}

2   Willibald Sauerländer, 'Die Naumburger Stifterfiguren: Rückblick und Fragen' ('The Founder-figures in Naumburg'), *Die Zeit der Staufer: Geschichte, Kunst, Kultur* (Stuttgart, 1979) vol. 5, pp. 169-245.

3   Berthold von Regensburg, *Vollständige Ausgabe seiner Predigten*, ed. Fr Pfeiffer (Vienna, 1862-80) vols 1-2, No. 30.

4   Berthold von Regensburg, op. cit., No. 10.

5   Berthold von Regensburg, op. cit., No. 2.

6   See: D. Richter, *Die deutsche Uberlieferung der Predigten Bertholds von Regensburg. Untersuchungen zur geistlichen Literatur des Spätmittelalters* (*The German Version of the Sermons of Berthold von Regensburg. Research into the Religious Literature of the Late Middle Ages*) (Munich, 1969).

7   H. Stahleder, *Arbeit in der mittelatlerlichen Gesellschaft* (*Work in Medieval Society*) (*Miscellanea bavarica monacensia*: Book 42) (Munich, 1972); I. von der Lühe, W. Rücke, 'Ständekritische Predigt des Spätmittelalters am Beispiel Berthold von Regensburg' ('The Socially Critical Sermon of the Late Middle Ages taking Berthold von Regensburg as an example'), *Literatur im Feudalismus* (*Literaturwissenschaft und Sozialwissenschaften, 5*) (Stuttgart, 1975), pp. 41-82.

8   John F. Benton, 'Consciousness of Self and Perceptions of Individuality', *Renaissance and Renewal in the Twelfth Century* ed. by R. Benson and G. Constable (Cambridge, Mass., 1982), p. 284. Benton's is not a lone voice, his opinion is the generally accepted one.

9   G. Duby, *Les Trois ordres ou l'imaginaire du féodalisme* (Paris, 1978).

10 It is possible, if desired, to see in these words an allusion to the poem *Meier Helmbrecht* by Wernher der Gartenaere referred to earlier. In that poem the young Helmbrecht, who finds the peasant's lot oppressive, is anxious to become a member of the nobility and joins a band of robbers imagining that, in doing so, he will become a knight. He even adopts vocabulary that is alien to the common people. His attempt to break away from his own social estate, into which he had been born, leads to the sorry downfall of this upstart. The young Helmbrecht is opposed by his father Helmbrecht the Elder, wise on account of his experience and proud of belonging to the 'estate of the plough'. He disowns his offspring in this poetic parable about a Prodigal Son turned on its head. See: J. Le Goff, *L'imaginaire médiéval. Essais* (Paris, 1985), pp. 317-30; A. Y. Gurevich, *The Medieval World: the Culture of a Silent Majority (Srednevekovyi mir: kul'tura bezmolvstvuyushchego bol'shinstva)*, pp. 264-77.

11 Berthold von Regensburg, No. 19.

12 H. Stahleder, *Arbeit in der mittelalterlichen Gesellschaft*, pp. 118 ff, 186.

13 K. Bosl, *Die Grundlagen der modernen Gesellschaft im Mittelalter. Eine deutsche Gesellschaftsgeschichte des Mittelalters* (Stuttgart, 1972) vol. 2, pp. 212 ff., 354 ff.; I. von der Lühe, W. Röcke, *Ständekritische Predigt . . .*, p. 65.

14 Peter Brown, *The Body and Society. Men, Women and Sexual Renunciation in Early Christianity* (New York, 1988).

15 Berthold von Regensburg, op. cit., No. 23.

16 Ibid., No. 25.

7 Knights and Merchants

1 It would seem that Maria Ossowska crosses the dividing line that separates the world of the imagination from the real world of medieval knights with inordinate ease in her interesting study *Etos rycerski i jego odmiany* (*The Knightly Ethos and its Variations*) (Warsaw, 1973).

2 For more on this gulf at the end of the Middle Ages see: I. Kheizing, *The Autumn of the Middle Ages* (*Osen' Srednevekov'ya*) (Moscow, 1988), Chapters IV-VII.

3 J. Bumke, *Höfische Kultur. Literatur und Gesellschaft im hohen Mittelalter* (*Courtly Culture. Literature and Society in the High Middle Ages*) (Munich, 1987) vol. 1, pp. 26-9.

4   P. Zumthor, *Langue, texte, énigme* (*Language, Text, Enigma*) (Paris, 1973).

5   See: A. Y. Gurevich, *The Categories of Medieval Culture* (*Kategorii srednevekovoi kul'tury*) (Moscow, 1984), 2nd edn, p. 148 ff.

6   R. W. Hanning, *The Individual in Twelfth-Century Romance* (New Haven and London, 1977), Chapter 4.

7   See: M. Zink, *La subjectivité littéraire. Autour du siècle de Saint Louis* (*Literary Subjectivity. Around the time of Saint Louis*) (Paris, 1985).

8   See: G. Ladner, 'Homo Viator. Mediaeval Ideas on Alienation and Order', *Speculum* XLII (1967), No. 2.

9   R. W. Hanning, op. cit., pp. 234-42.

10   E. M. Meletinskii, *The Medieval Romance. Origins and Classic Forms* (*Srednevekovyi roman. Proiskhozhdenie i klassicheskiye formy*) (Moscow, 1983), pp. 3, 270.

11   *A Good Short Debate between Winner and Waster. An Alliterative Poem on Social and Economic Problems in England in the year 1352* ed. by I. Gollancz (Oxford, 1930).

12   Ibid., lines 253-6, 297-9.

13   Jacques Le Goff, *La bourse et la vie. Economie et religion au Moyen Age* (*The Purse and Life. Money-making and Religion in the Middle Ages*) (Paris, 1986); A. Y. Gurevich, *The Culture and Society of Medieval Europe through the Eyes of Contemporaries (Exempla of the Thirteenth Century)* [*Kul'tura i obshchestvo srednevekovoi Evropy glazami sovremennikov (Exempla XIII veka)*] (Moscow, 1989), p. 197 ff.

14   A. Y. Gurevich, *The Medieval World: the Culture of the Silent Majority* (*Srednevekovyi mir: kul'tura bezmolvstvuyushchego bol'shinstva*) (Moscow, 1990), pp. 222-4. The land which opened up beneath their feet swallowed up Dathan and Abiram, who had been in rebellion against Moses (Numbers, 16: 1-36).

15   Georges Espinas, *Les Origines du capitalisme* (*The Origins of Capitalism*) vol. 1: *Sire Jehan Boinebroke, patricien et drapier douaisien (?-c.1286)* [*Sire Jehan Boinebroke, patrician and draper from Douai (?-c.1286)*] (Lille, 1933).

16   Alexander Murray, *Reason and Society in the Middle Ages* (Oxford, 1985), p. 100.

17   A. Gourevitch, *Le Marchand* (*The Merchant*) in *L'homme mediéval* (published in England as *The Medieval World*), p. 302.

18   Quoted in Maria Ossovskaya, *Rytsar i burzhua. Issledovaniya*

po istorii morali (*The Knight and the Merchant. Studies in the History of Morality*) (Moscow, 1987), p. 392.

8 Brother Salimbene and Others

1   John F. Benton, 'Consciousness of Self and Perceptions of Individuality' in *Renaissance and Renewal in the Twelfth Century*, ed. by R. L. Benson and G. Constable (Cambridge, Mass., 1982), p. 268 ff.
2   H. Beumann, 'Topos und Gedankenfüge bei Einhard' ('Topos and Thought Patterns in the work of Einhard'), *Archiv für Kulturgeschichte* 33 (1951) Book 3.
3   L. Zoepf, *Das Heiligen-Leben im 10. Jahrhundert* (*Lives of the Saints in the Tenth Century*) (Leipzig and Berlin, 1908).
4   L. P. Karsavin, *The Foundations of Medieval Religiosity in the XII and XIII Centuries – with special emphasis on Italy* (*Osnovy srednevekovoi religioznosti v XII-XIII vekax, preimushchestvenno v Italii*) (Petrograd, 1915); P. M. Bitsilli, *Salimbene (Sketches of Italian Life XIII)* (Odessa,1916).
5   L. P. Karsavin, op. cit., p. 14.
6   P. M. Bitsilli, op. cit., pp. 8, 9,1 5.
7   P. M. Bitsilli, op. cit., p. 296. This author writes about the pessimism which coloured the mood of Italian society in the late thirteenth and early fourteenth centuries. J. Delumeau writes about the sense of fear and sinful guiltiness {J. Delumeau, *La Peur en Occident (XIVe-XVIIIe siècles). Une cité assiégée* [*Fear in the West (14th-18th Centuries). A City besieged*] (Paris, 1978)}; ejusdem. *Le péché et la peur. La culpabilité en Occident (XIIIe-XVIIIe siècles)* [*Sin and Fear. Culpability in the West (XIII-XVIII centuries)*] (Paris, 1983); A. F. Losev writes about the 'reverse side' of the Titanism of the Renaissance [A.F.Losev, *The Aesthetics of the Renaissance* (*Estetika Vozrozhdeniya*) (Moscow, 1978).]
8   Ibid, p. 86.
9   Ibid. Bitsilli bases these conclusions on the works of Bédier [J. Bédier, *Les légendes épiques* (*Epic Legends*) (Paris,1914)].
10 P. M. Bitsilli, op. cit., pp. 131, 137.
11 J. Bédier, *Les légendes épiques* (*Epic Legends*) vol.I (Paris, 1914), p. 57.
12 P. M. Bitsilli, op. cit., p. 143.
13 W. von den Steinen, *Der Kosmos des Mittelalters. Von Karl dem Grossen zu Bernard von Clairvaux* (*The Universe of the*

Middle Ages. From Charlemagne to Bernard of Clairvaux) (Bern-Munich, 1959), p. 372, note 104.

14 See: G. Duby, *Saint Bernard, l'art cistercien* (*Saint Bernard and Cistercian Art*) p. 78.

15 P. M. Bitsilli, op. cit., p. 146.

16 C. Morris, op. cit., Chapter 4.

17 P. Bitsilli, op. cit., p. 145.

18 Salimbene admits that church services are too long and that he gets tired of standing, especially in the summer when the fleas are biting. Ibid., p. 184.

19 'Chronica fr. Salimbene de Adam', ed. Holder-Egger in *Monumenta Germaniae Historica* XXXII, p. 643.

20 Quotation from Pseudo-Bernard, 'Meditationes' . . . P. L., t. 184, cols. 494-5 in the book: Etienne Gilson, *L'esprit de la philosophie médiévale* (*The Spirit of Medieval Philosophy*) (Paris, 1969), p. 223.

21 Quotation from P. M. Bitsilli, op. cit., p. 111.

22 Ibid., p. 114.

23 S. Gregorii ep. Turonensis (Saint Gregory, Bishop of Tours), *De Miraculis s. Martini* (*Concerning the Miracles of Saint Martin*), P. L., vol. 71, cols. 911-12.

24 V.S. Bibler, 'The Figure of the Simpleton and the Idea of the Individual in the Culture of the Middle Ages' ('Obraz Prostetsa i ideya lichnosti v kulture Srednikh vekov') in *Man and Culture. Individuality in the History of Culture* (*Chelovek i kul'tura. Individual'nost' v istorii kul'tury*) (Moscow, 1990), p. 104.

25 Ibid., p. 102.

26 See: J.-C.Schmitt, 'Les "superstitions"' in *Histoire de la France religieuse* (*Religious History of France*), vol. 1, *Des dieux de la Gaule à la papauté d'Avignon (des origines au XIVe siècle)* [*From the Gods of Gaul to the Avignon papacy (from the beginning to the 14th century)*] ed. J. Le Goff (Paris, 1988), pp. 417-551.

27 V. S. Bibler, op. cit., pp. 104-5.

28 V. S. Bibler, op. cit., p. 102.

9 In this Madness there be Method

1 Ernst Kris, *Psychoanalytic Explorations in Art* (New York, 1952), pp. 118-27.

2 Richard Salomon, 'Opicinus de Canistris, Weltbild und

Bekenntnisse eines avignonesischen Klerikers des 14 Jahrhunderts' ('Opicinus de Canistris. The World-View and Confessions of a Cleric from Avignon in the Fourteenth Century'), *Studies of the Warburg Institute* vol. 1A (London, 1936), p. 214.

3   Richard Salomon, 'A Newly Discovered Manuscript of Opicinus de Canistris', *Journal of the Warburg and Courtauld Institutes* vol. 16 (1953), p. 45.

4   Adelheid Heimann, 'Die Zeichnungen des Opicinus de Canistris' ('The Drawings of Opicinus de Canistris') in the book by R. Salomon, *Opicinus de Canistris*, Appendix I, pp. 295-321.

5   See: Karl Burdach, *Vom Mittelalter zur Reformation (From the Middle Ages to the Reformation)* vol. II (Berlin, 1913-28), part 1, p. 97.

6   R. Salomon, *Opicinus de Canistris*, p. 68.

7   R. Salomon, *Opicinus de Canistris*, p. 41.

8   Ibid., pp. 49, 275.

9   See: Hans Liebeschutz, *Das allegorische Weltbild der heiligen Hildegard von Bingen (The Allegorical World-View of Saint Hildegard von Bingen)* (Berlin, 1930), Plate III, Plate V.

10   Bertha Widmer, *Heilsordnung und Zeitgeschehen in der Mystik Hildegards von Bingen (The Ordering of Salvation and the Passing of Time in the Mysticism of Hildegard von Bingen)* (Basel and Stuttgart, 1955), pp. 4-5.

11   Ernst Cassirer, *Individuum und Kosmos in der Philosophie der Renaissance (The Individual and the Cosmos in the Philosophy of the Renaissance)*, pp. 4-5.

12   Jean Delumeau, *La Peur en Occident (XIVe-XVIIIe siècles). Une cité assiegée [Fear in the West (14th-18th Centuries). A City under Siege]* (Paris, 1978); ejusdem, *Le péché et la peur. La culpabilisation en Occident (XIIIe-XVIIIe siècles) [Sin and Fear. Culpability in the West (13th-18th centuries)]* (Paris,1983).

13   E. Kris, op. cit., pp. 126-7.

14   R. G. Salomon, 'A Newly Discovered Manuscript . . .', p. 49.

15   Ibid., p. 51.

16   Gerhart B. Ladner, '"Homo Viator". Mediaeval Ideas of Alienation and Order', *Speculum* XLII (1967) 2, pp. 233-59.

17   R. G. Salomon, 'A Newly Discovered Manuscript . . .', p. 57, Pl.15.

10 Dante and Petrarch

1   I. N. Golenishchev-Kutuzov, 'Life of Dante' in *Dante Alighieri: Minor Works (Dante Alighieri: Malye Proizvedeniya)*, Moscow, 1968, p. 424.

2   See: V. Branca, 'La "Vita Nuova"' in *Cultura e scuola*, Nos 13-14, 1965; ejusd., 'Poetica del rinovamento e tradizione agiografica nella "Vita Nuova"' ('Poetics of the Renaissance and the Hagiographic Tradition in *La Vita Nuova'), Studi in onore di Italo Siciliano*, Florence, 1966.

3   See: I. N. Golenishchev-Kutuzov, *The Work of Dante and World Culture (Tvorchestvo Dante i mirovaya kultura)*, Moscow, 1971, p. 183.

4   Thomas Aquinas, *Summa Theologica* 2a, 2ae, Q. CIX, Art. I: 'Public utterances about oneself are only admissible, when it is necessary to repudiate slander of evil intent (as in the case of Job for example) or when a writer intends to lead his audience to higher truth'.

5   *The Feast* (I, 2) contains a lengthy deliberation on the fact that it is not appropriate to talk about one's own persona. He who reproaches himself thereby testifies to the fact that he is aware of his shortcomings and thus acknowledges himself to be wretched and from this one should refrain. Only 'in the secluded cell of his thoughts should [he] reproach himself and lament his imperfections, not in the presence of others'.

> Praise rendered unto oneself should be avoided, like any relative wrongdoing, since it is impossible to praise, without praise degenerating into indignities . . . therefore he who praises himself shows that he does not believe good opinions about himself and this does not take place without malicious hypocrisy, which men manifest, when they praise themselves and by doing so censure themselves . . . There is no man, who might truthfully and fairly appraise himself, so misleading is our pride . . . Thus, when praising or censuring himself a man is lying either about what he is saying or about his own judgement, but both are false.

The only situation in which Dante sees it as justified for a man to talk about himself is when he seeks to avoid great disgrace

Notes to Chapter 10

270

or danger, as was the case with Boethius, or when 'talk of oneself is of supreme benefit to others as an exhortation' (*Confessions* of Saint Augustine). *Dante Alighieri: Minor Works*, pp. 114-5, cf. *La vita nuova*, XXVIII; ibid. p.40.

6   See: M. M. Bakhtin, op. cit., p. 131.
7   Nicholas Mann, *Petrarch*, (Oxford, 1987), p. 94.
8   Nicholas Mann, op. cit., p. 91.

11 The Historian in Search of the Individual

1   Henry James, 'The Private Life', Henry James, *The Figure in the Carpet and Other Stories*, (London, 1988) pp. 189-231.
2   Ibid., p. 212. James himself admits that he assumes, in the case of his famous friend Robert Browning (1812–89), there to have been a similar difference between the artist as he knew him and the same artist when he was on his own and engaged in creation. Ibid., p. 53.
3   Ibid., p.52.
4   Natalie Zemon Davis, *The Return of Martin Guerre*, (Cambridge, 1985).
5   Natalie Zemon Davis, 'Boundaries and the Sense of Self in Sixteenth-Century France', *Reconstructing Individualism. Autonomy, Individuality, and the Self in Western Thought* ed. by T. C. Heller, M. Sosna and D. E. Wellbery, (Stanford, 1986) p. 54.
6   Jacques Le Goff, 'From Heaven back to Earth (Changes in the System of Values in the Christian West in the Twelfth and Thirteenth Centuries)' ['*S nebes na zemlyu (Peremeny v sisteme tsennostnykh orientatsii na khristianskom Zapade XII-XIII vv.*'], *An Odyssey. Man in History – 1991 (Odissei. Chelovek v istorii - 1991)* (Moscow, 1991) pp. 25-47.

Bibliography

In accordance with the guidelines laid down for the series 'The Making of Europe', the number of bibliographical references had to be reduced to a minimum. This meant that the author was unable to refer to many scholarly works that he used. In particular, among writings of anthropologists, we need to single out the works of Louis Dumont and Alan Macfarlane.

Abelard en son temps, Actes du Colloque international, Paris, 1981.

Amory, F., 'The Confessional Superstructure of Guibert of Nogent's Vita', *Classica et mediaevalia*, XXV, (1964).

Ariès, Ph. *L'homme devant la Mort*, (Paris, 1977).

d'Avray, D., 'Sermons on the Dead before 1350', *Studi medievali* 3e serie, XXXI, 1, (1990).

Batkin, L. *Gli Umanisti italiani. Stile di vita et di pensiero*, (Rome-Bari, 1990).

Bayer, H., 'Zur Soziologie des mittelalterlichen Individualisierungsprozeßes. Ein Beitrag zu einer wirklichkeitsbezogenen Geistesgeschichte', *Archiv für Kulturgeschichte*, vol. 58, book 1, (1976).

Benton, J. E., *Self and Society in Medieval France: The Memoirs of Abbot Guibert de Nogent*, (New York, 1970).

'The Personality of Guibert of Nogent', in *Psychoanalytic Review*, vol. 57, No. 4, (1970–1).

'Consciousness of Self and Perceptions of Individuality', *Renaissance and Renewal in the Twelfth Century*, ed. by R. Benson and G. Constable, (Cambridge, Mass., 1982).

Bynum, C. W., *Jesus as Mother: Studies in the Spirituality of the High Middle Ages*, (Berkeley, Los Angeles, 1982).

Carruthers, M., *A Study of Memory in Medieval Culture*, (Cambridge, 1990).

Chenu, M.-D., *L'éveil de la conscience dans la civilisation médiévale*, (Montreal-Paris, 1969).

Courcelle, P., *'Confessions' de Saint Augustin dans la tradition littéraire. Antécédents et postérité*, (Paris, 1963).

Delumeau, J., *La Peur en Occident (XIVe-XVIIIe siècles). Une cité assiégée*, (Paris, 1978).
   La culpabilisation en Occident (XIIIe-XVIIIe siècles), (Paris, 1983).

Gronbech, W., *Kultur und Religion der Germanen*, vols. 1-2, (Darmstadt, 1961).

Gurevich, A., 'The "Sociology" and "Anthropology" of Berthold von Regensburg', *Journal of Historical Sociology*, vol. 4, No. 2, (1991).

Hanning, R. W., *The Individual in Twelfth-Century Romance*, (New Haven and London, 1977).

Identität, ed. by O. Marquard and K. Stierle, (Munich, 1979).

Ladner, G., *'Homo Viator*: Medieval Ideas on Alienation and Order', *Speculum*, vol. 42, (1967).

Leclerq, J., 'Modern Psychology and the Interpretation of Medieval Texts', *Speculum*, vol. XLVIII, No. 3, (1973).

Le Goff, J., *Pour un autre Moyen Age. Temps, travail et culture en Occident: 18 essais*, (Paris, 1977).
   L'imaginaire médiéval. Essais, (Paris, 1985).
   La bourse et la vie. Economie et religion au Moyen Age, (Paris, 1986).

Lehmann, P. 'Autobiographies of the Middle Ages', *Transactions of the Royal Historical Society*, 5th series, vol. 3, (1953).

McLaughlin, M. M., 'Abélard as Autobiographer: The Motives and Meaning of his "Story of Calamities"', *Speculum*, vol. XLII, No. 3, (1967).

Mann, N., *Petrarch*, (Oxford, 1987).

Mauss, M., *Sociologie et anthropologie*, (Paris, 1968).

Misch, G., *Geschichte der Autobiographie*, vols. I-IV, 2nd ed., (Frankfurt am Main, 1949–62).

Morris, C., *The Discovery of the Individual, 1050-1200*, (London, 1972).

Muckle, J. T., 'Abelard's Letter of Consolation to a Friend (*Historia Calamitatum*)', *Mediaeval Studies*, vol. XII, (1980).

Murray, A., *Reason and Society in the Middle Ages*, (Oxford, 1985).
Nilsson, S. S., 'Kva slag mann var kong Sverre?', *Syn og segn*, (1948).
'Kong Sverre og kong David', *Edda*, (1948).
Ossowska, M., *Etos rycerski i jego odmiany*, (Warsaw, 1973).
Problèmes de la personne, Exposés by I. Meyerson, (Paris-La Haye, 1973).
Rheinfelder, H., *Das Wort 'Persona'*, (Halle, 1928).
Ross, M. B., 'The Art of Poetry and the Figure of the Poet in Egils Saga', *Parergon*, No. 22.
Salomon, R., 'Opicinus de Canistris. Weltbild und Bekenntnisse eines avignonesischen Klerikers des 14. Jahrhunderts', *Studies of the Warburg Institute*, vol. IA, (London, 1936).
'A Newly Discovered Manuscript of Opicinus de Canistris', *Journal of the Warburg and Courtauld Institutes*, vol. 16, (1953).
Schmitt, J.-C., 'La découverte de l'individu, une fiction historiographique?', *La fabrique, la figure et la feinte. Fictions et Statut des Fictions en Psychologie*, under the general editorship of P. Mengal and F. Parot, (Paris, 1989).
Steblin-Kamenskij, M., *The Saga Mind*, (Odense, 1973).
'Valkyries and heroes', *Arkiv för nordisk filologi*, vol. 97, (1982).
Suger, Abbot, *On the Abbey Church of St. Denis and Its Art Treasures* ed. by E. Panofsky, (Princeton, N.J., 1944).
Ullmann, W., *The Individual and Society in the Middle Ages*, (Baltimore, 1966).
L'uomo medievale, under the general editorship of Jacques Le Goff, (Rome-Bari, 1987).
Zink, M., *La subjectivité littéraire. Autour du siècle de Saint Louis*, (Paris, 1985).
Zumthor, P., *Langue, texte, énigme*, (Paris, 1973).

Index